TURNING *the* WHEEL *of* TRUTH

TURNING *the* WHEEL *of* TRUTH

---

*Commentary on the
Buddha's First Teaching*

Ajahn Sucitto

SHAMBHALA
Boulder
2010

Shambhala Publications, Inc.
4720 Walnut Street
Boulder, Colorado 80301
www.shambhala.com

14 13 12 11 10 9 8 7 6

Designed by Daniel Urban-Brown

Printed in the United States of America

♾ This edition is printed on acid-free paper that meets the American National Standards Institute z39.48 Standard.
♻ Shambhala Publications makes every effort to print on recycled paper. For more information please visit www.shambhala.com.

Shambhala Publications is distributed worldwide by Penguin Random House, Inc., and its subsidiaries.

Library of Congress Cataloging-in-Publication Data
Sucitto, Ajahn, 1949–
Turning the wheel of truth: commentary on the Buddha's
first teaching/Ajahn Sucitto.—1st ed.
p. cm.
ISBN 978-1-59030-764-9 (pbk.: alk. paper) 1. Tipitaka. Suttapitaka.
Samyuttanikaya. Dhammacakkapavattana Sutta—Criticism,
interpretation, etc. I. Tipitaka. Suttapitaka.
Samyuttanikaya. Dhammacakkapavattana Sutta. English. II. Title.
BQ1339.5.D457S83 2010
294.3'823—dc22
2009051665

Dedicated to Phra Rajasumedhacariya (Ajahn Sumedho). Single gratitude.

CONTENTS

A NOTE ON THE TEXT, TRANSLATION, AND ABBREVIATIONS

The Discourse That Sets Turning the Wheel of Truth (Dhammacakkappavattana Sutta) is one of the many texts that appear in what is known as the Pāli Canon. This Canon is a collection of texts pertaining to the Buddha's teachings that were composed in the Pāli language. Most of these texts were assembled within the first hundred years after the Buddha's decease by dedicated groups of monks who collected all the teachings and stories that they could find and put them into a form that suited oral recitation. Neither the Buddha nor his disciples wrote anything down. As they listened to his teachings, people would remember passages, phrases, or the gist of what the Buddha had said and would practice recitation to commit them to memory. In addition to traditional teachings, there were also expositions, verses, stories, profound utterances, and decisions about monastic conduct that the disciples also committed to memory. In collecting this wide range of teachings given over forty-five-years, the early reciters decided to put them all into metaphorical "baskets" (*piṭaka* in Pāli), which are repositories much like computer folders. Eventually three baskets were created, while they wove the teachings into more coherent and fleshed-out forms in order to preserve the words of the Buddha and his chief disciples. The basket containing *suttas*, or formal discourses, was called Sutta Piṭaka. Another basket containing the decisions on conduct was called Vinaya Piṭaka (*vinaya* means "that which breaks up corruptions"). Finally, a third basket was created, called Abhidhamma Piṭaka, which contains a more scholarly classification of factors and aggregates and mind-states.

To weave this material into a cohesive form meant standardizing the Buddha's language and experiences without compromising his teachings.

The present suttas of the Sutta Piṭaka often have expositions, verses, and mythic material woven around a central "thread" of the teaching. A solid framework was also provided by locating the teachings in time and place. The framework was further stabilized by gathering the suttas in the Sutta Piṭaka into collections (or *Nikāya*), which the monks could learn by heart. The Sutta Piṭaka, as it now stands, is divided into many collections.

Two collections were compiled according to the length of the suttas—the Long Discourses (Dīgha Nikāya) and the Middle Length Discourses (Majjhima Nikāya). The Connected Discourses (Saṃyutta Nikāya) were arranged according to themes, so it contains suttas on groupings such as the aggregates or the factors of awakening. The Gradual Sayings (Aṅguttara Nikāya), is found in the collection according to the salient number in the sutta. So, for example, we have suttas on five hindrances in the Book of Fives. This collection is called such because it is ordered sequentially, extending its numerical factor one number at a time. Finally the Lesser Collection (Khuddaka Nikāya) contains a great range of what probably started out as short bunches of discourses, but kept growing as the catch-all collection of texts that had been left out of the other collections. This is now the largest collection and it contains very early material such as Sutta-Nipāta, very popular material such as Dhammapada, and also texts from much later times, including legends and fables.

The methodology of creating the three baskets and the Sutta Piṭaka's collections probably evolved over time, and they don't present the teachings in any step-by-step or chronological order. In fact, its lack of a single overriding order shows that its compilation was an effort made by many people. For example, an attempt at a chronological account of the early years of the Buddha's postenlightened life was placed in the Vinaya Piṭaka, whereas the narrative of the end of his life was put into the Sutta Piṭaka, in the middle of the Long Discourses.

The Buddha's first discourse, the Dhammacakkappavattana Sutta, appears twice in the Canon. It is tucked away in the Sutta Piṭaka where it was placed as one of a group of suttas that contain the topic of the noble truths. (Specifically, it is found under Connected Discourses 56: Truths 11.) However, being a landmark in the Buddha's life, it was also placed in the Vinaya Piṭaka, where it can be found in the chronologically-oriented first section of the Mahavagga. (Specifically, it's under Mahavagga 1: Discipline 3). These aren't the most readily accessible places in Pāli cannon—you might think, "Why not put the first sutta at the beginning of the Sutta Piṭaka?"—but the Canon wasn't composed as a literary document. Despite its placement, the Dhammacakkappavattana Sutta is, however, one of the most commonly recited suttas in Theravada monasteries throughout the world, particularly on the day that commemorates the occasion when the Blessed One gave his first teaching.

Translations and Key Terms

The suttas that we find in the Pāli Canon are represented as core texts in all the schools of Buddhism, although it's only the Theravāda school that refers to them in their Pāli form—the Mahāyāna and Vajrayāna schools use Sanskrit, Chinese, Tibetan, and other translations. The work of collecting the Pāli texts and publishing them in Roman script began in the late nineteenth century with the foundation of the Pāli Text Society. Subsequent to that, the Pāli Text Society has systematically translated into English the major texts from the Sutta Piṭaka as well as the Vinaya and Abhidhamma Piṭakas. Some of these translations are quite old now and further research, as well as a couple of generations of established Buddhist practice in the West, has deepened the understanding of the meaning of much of the terminology. Although the overall meaning of the discourses is clear, translators will often use different English words to capture the fullest meaning and nuance of the Pāli. *Āsava,* for example, has been translated as "canker," "taint," "corruption," "effluent," "outflow," and "inflow."

The language of the discourses is full of metaphors and analogies that dramatically heighten the effect of the teachings. This is done, no doubt, with the intention to make subtle or unconscious areas of the mind stand out, and also to give them strong nuances that illuminate the Buddha's message. For example, the happiness of the senses is likened to the momentary relief a leper might get from cauterizing his sores. The four levels of absorptive concentration are, on the other hand, likened to couches because of the ease that they bring to the mind. This effect carries through to individual English terms: we hear of *fetters* and *hindrances* on the one hand, and "the Blessed One" and "the Triple Gem" on the other. The language, much of which was spoken to men of the warrior caste, often alludes to aspects of martial struggle. Readers have to make use of this language without taking on the less encouraging nuances of moralizing or aggression that might get inferred. The words are a medicine—astringent at times—and are to be taken in doses as needed.

I have translated the Dhammacakkappavattana Sutta as well as most of the extracts from the Aṅguttara Nikāya. In my rendering, I have attempted to present both a translation that is broadly consistent with other versions and newly elucidating. So the four truths (*ariya sacca*) are generally called "noble" truths, although one might also translate *ariya* as "precious." *Dukkha* is often translated as "suffering," but I have presented a few other ways in which we can understand this term: "difficult," "painful," "hard," "hard to bear," "stress," "unsatisfactory," or "giving no real satisfaction." These various words may help to flesh out the many flavors of this term, which literally means something like "bad-made." After a while, hoping that the reader has gotten a feel for the word, I've placed the Pāli word into the English text.

Another key term is *sankhāra*. This derives from the root word meaning "to do" or "to make," with a prefix that indicates "together" or "conjoined." Part of the difficulty of finding a suitable English word is that *sankhāra* refers both to the activity of making or conjoining, and to the result—a made pattern or form. Venerable Bhikkhu Bodhi often translates this as "formations" or "volitional formations," both of which present the result as a mental tendency or pattern of activity. In a similar vein, other translators use the terms *fabrication, determination,* or *condition.* I often use *activities,* a term that places more emphasis on the creative aspect of sankhāra, and which is perhaps a more tangible word than the rather general *formations.* I also use *programs* to indicate how these activities are programmed, that they are conditioned energies and have the potential—like a computer program—to adjust, remove, or add further programs to the existing ones. The reader should bear in mind that these sankhāra are energies that form kamma; they are creative energies and are also patterned in our mind as results of previous kamma. It is the patterning of these sankhāra that generates the sense of a solid and continuing self. Through the very "personal" quality of these sankhāra, the sense "I am" keeps forming moment after moment.

Although this terminology can be difficult to grasp in abstract, it is revealingly relevant in meditation when we can more fully feel mental behavior and learn to unravel its compulsive knots. This is why and how the Buddha taught—not to establish a philosophy, but to place some landmarks and some equipment on the terrain of the mind. It is with like intent that this book is offered.

Abbreviations

I have abbreviated texts from the Pāli Canon as follows:

AN	Aṅguttara Nikāya (Numerical Discourses or Gradual Sayings)
DN	Dīgha Nikāya (Long Discourses)
MN	Majjhima Nikāya (Middle-Length Discourses)
SN	Saṃyutta Nikāya (Connected Discourses)
D	Dhammapada (from the Khuddaka Nikāya)
M	Mahavagga (from the Vinaya Piṭaka)
Su-N	Sutta-Nipāta (from the Khuddaka Nikāya)
U	Udāna and the Itivuttaka (from the Khuddaka Nikāya)

References to AN are to the book number and the sutta number.
References to DN and MN are to the sutta number followed by the section number.
References to SN are to the saṃyutta number, the theme, and the sutta number.

INTRODUCTION

The Teaching and Its Background

This book is about a great teaching, a teaching that brings light into the world. It presents the first discourse given by the Buddha, who lived in India around twenty-five hundred years ago but whose experiential wisdom is still guiding people throughout the world today. The Discourse That Sets Turning the Wheel of Truth is still relevant because it focuses on a common feature of human life—the experience of trouble and stress and the search to get free of it. When freedom is achieved, it's like somebody switched the light on. It's that kind of teaching—it's not philosophical or of passing interest. It can reach out and bring blessings to all of us.

However, since the teaching was given so long ago in a culture different from our own, its wording and allusions can cause us modern readers to stumble. For starters, it's written in the Pāli language, which is an amalgam of various ancient, vernacular Indian dialects. This language of the text is similar to Sanskrit, but is deliberately more colloquial. This is because the Buddha chose to teach in the spoken dialects of ordinary people in order to get his message across more readily—not that this helps the modern Westerner. Sanskrit was the literary language, reserved for the upper caste, so by using ordinary language, the Buddha was making the point that his teaching wasn't philosophical or only for the learned. Instead, it is supposed to reach ordinary people, be matter-of-fact, and accessible. So I'd like to support the Buddha's intention by presenting his discourse in English and commenting on it using what I hope is conversational language. I'll also refer to my understanding of Buddhist practice to illustrate the timeless relevance of the teaching it presents.

This discourse can be found in a series of texts that make up the bulk of what is called the Pāli Canon.* The Pāli Canon was assembled within the first hundred years after the Buddha's death by his disciples who had committed his teachings to memory and who wanted to put them into a form that would suit oral recitation. At that time, writing wasn't that usual, and wouldn't have been used for religious material. Instead, the mode of transmission was through human memory and voice. When a group decides to learn something by heart in this way, it's very effective: if someone makes a mistake, the others correct him or her and it's unlikely that everyone will have the same lapse in memory. There's no paper or papyrus to decompose or get eaten by termites, and when something is recited, it really sticks in the mind. However, while oral recitation can be an effective tool for memorization, it's helpful to recognize that what we have here is an account, perhaps with embellishments for dramatic effect; it is an account that frames a consistent thread, or *sutta,* which is one of the many that form the tapestry of the Pāli Canon.

What follows then is a commentary on one discourse that the Buddha gave among many throughout his teaching career of forty-five years. It was his first full discourse after his enlightenment (or awakening)—an experience of the ending of delusion, which set him free from all trouble and stress. And many would say that this was his most important discourse because it established the basis of the teaching that he added to throughout his life—the teaching of "suffering and the cessation of suffering," which he encapsulated in four great or "noble" truths.

---

* See the note on the text, translation, and abbreviations for more information.

The important thing to emphasize is that this teaching has to be put into practice, tested, and lived. It's a guide, a manual, not a treatise. It occurs within the dynamic of our own mind as we access where we're stuck or struggling or bruised—and decide to look into that experience rather than blame it on someone or cover it up. So when you take this teaching to heart, it sets you behind the steering wheel of an engine that's been driving your life: the urge to be happy, fulfilled, at peace; the urge to get clear of depression, guilt, anxiety, and all that the Buddha summed up as *dukkha,* which means "suffering," "trouble," and "general unsatisfactoriness." Although we all have this fundamental motivation for well-being, most of us don't get the right instructions on how to fulfill it. This lack of know-how is what the Buddha referred to as "unknowing" or "ignorance" and this is precisely what his teaching directly addresses. As long as we don't know our own mind and heart deeply, we can't steer them. Then instead of directing ourselves to what is most immediate and personal, we try to steer the world. But with wise instructions, you have a powerful resource to steer your life with. These instructions are called *Dhamma* (Skt.: *Dharma*) *Dhamma* has a number of meanings, some of which are exclusive to Buddhism and some are not. In the Indian culture that gave life to this concept, it most broadly means "the proper order of things." The Vedas, the ancient religious teachings that underlie that culture, teach that there is a unifying order in the cosmos, called Dharma. And within the society, rituals and sacrifices need to be performed in order to keep the human realm connected to that unifying order. This was the role of the priests, or brahmins. However, every person from king to slave, also had a duty to act in accordance with their status and responsibilities. That duty, that individual obligation, was also called dharma—the lowercase *d* is used by translators to distinguish a personal "proper order" from the "cosmic principle." If a person's duty was properly carried out, then harmony and prosperity would prevail. If not, the result would be chaos. Following this, a central theme in Indian culture is that it is people's duty to live in accordance with their "dharma"—a concept that encompasses the responsibilities and observances of caste, clan, and family, as well as their "religious" observances. The uppercase word *Dhamma* then means something wider than religion or even spirituality—it is the correct, balanced way of things. The most fitting representation of Dhamma is a many-spoked wheel (which sits in the center of India's present-day flag). As a wheel it carries the meaning of being complete, with an all-encompassing span. And as a wheel its still and central hub is supported by a range of duties and practices (mental, physical, and social), by which it is turned through the living cosmos thus bestowing its order and balance on the created world.

Based on this idea during the Buddha's time, every person had his or her dhamma, which was maintained by proper action. The priestly caste called brahmins performed the rituals and recited the correct mantras for every situation so that births, marriages, deaths, and so forth, would all be in accordance with Dhamma and would have a positive outcome. Meanwhile, religious seekers (or *samanas*) were all trying to find a way to directly experience Dhamma in themselves, often through yogic practices or asceticism. And when they met, they questioned each other by saying, "What is your Dhamma?" This means, "What's your experience of truth, or your way of realizing it?" So *Dhamma* can mean "cosmic law," "order," "truth," or "teachings."

In his teachings the Buddha generally referred to the values and meanings of the contemporary society, and tweaked them a little to suit his aims. In the Buddha's presentation, *Dhamma* means either the teachings or "way" of the Buddha, or "the true order that the teachings reveal to those who practice that way." The central principle of Buddha-Dhamma (the Buddha's teachings) is that it is directly visible (that is, factual and realizable), timeless, inviting one to enter into it (meaning it attracts interest), accessible, to be realized in oneself, and to be known through discernment (as opposed to belief). And the one text that forms the axis of the Buddha's "wheel" is the teaching in this Discourse That Sets Turning the Wheel of Truth, the teaching of the four noble truths: suffering, its origin, its ceasing, and the way that leads to its ceasing.

The Buddha's definition of Dhamma is dynamic: the four noble truths don't just tell you where things hurt, but what to do about the pain. They present a brief analysis of where and how we suffer, what is the underlying origin of that pain, what brings around its ending, and how to bring that experience of release into our own lives. Because it's going to a good place (and can take us with it), this Dhamma is the best wheel to ride. It rolls on down the bumpy road of life, to freedom, a freedom that isn't just a temporary break, but a truth, a realizable actuality that you can live by. From the time when it was first set rolling, people have begun or fulfilled the ending of suffering and stress following its guidance. The teaching works; it brings light where there was darkness. Thus for many of us, it has set something powerful in motion.

The Background

Because the discourse is set in a particular time and place with specific characters, I'll summarize what is known (or at least commonly agreed upon) in terms of history and geography, and also I'll add a dash of biography. There are all kinds of stories and legends that people have made up over the centuries, because neither the Buddha himself nor his early disciples thought his identity and early life was that important. To them, and to us, what really counts is the teaching. However, it does help to put his life and teaching in a temporal frame, just to emphasize that we're talking about a flesh-and-blood human here; moreover, an explanation of his cultural background may throw light on the concerns that the Buddha was addressing.

For starters *Buddha* is just a title, a way of addressing the man. It means "knowing," "awake," or "awakened." Actually he was more often called Bhagavā (One Who Is Full of Blessings), or Tathāgata (One Who Has Become Such, True, Thus-Gone, or Here-Come). These terms may seem strange; however, once he was enlightened, it was difficult to define this man—he was deeper and vaster than anyone could fathom—and yet, human. When was he born? Traditions vary, placing his birth date anywhere between 563 and 483 B.C.E. Modern research suggests 480 B.C.E. What is more commonly agreed upon is that he was born as the son and heir of Suddhodana, an elected chief of the Sakyan republic. This republic occupied a fragment of southern Nepal on the Indian border, and probably extended into what is now the Indian state of Uttar Pradesh. The boy was named Siddhattha Gotama (Skt.: Siddhartha Gotama). Although a lot is made in subsequent legends of his early life, the Buddha only referred to it a few times. The Sakyan republic was not a grand kingdom; it was a vassal state of another small kingdom occupying the northeast of Uttar Pradesh. So he was a nobleman in a small republic. In his teens he was bound into an arranged marriage for dynastic reasons. This marriage was anything but a love affair—it's unlikely that the couple had even laid eyes on each other before the wedding. However that's the way it was done in those days; the important thing was to bring forth a son as a guarantor for the future of the family. After thirteen years, the couple managed to do that, and so, after some protracted and painful negotiations, Siddhattha got permission from his family to take leave and pursue a spiritual quest as one "gone forth."* Siddhattha's departure meant that he gave up everything. He relinquished inheritance, statehood, livelihood, family network, friends, and caste—all the elements that in Indian society gave him a place in the cosmos—which included not only this world and life, but also a future birth. So with "going forth" he had put aside his ascribed place in the cosmic order to find a new one for himself. Relinquishment made life starkly simple—a "gone-forth" person had to survive on what he or she could glean, and put everything else aside to focus on developing his or her mind, soul, or spirit. Whatever you think of his domestic policy, you can't fault Siddhattha in terms of putting his life on the line. He wasn't entirely alone in this—there was a whole movement of samana seekers doing the same kind of thing—sometimes following a particular teacher and sometimes forming groups and adhering to an ethical code of harmlessness, celibacy, truthfulness, and renunciation. To be a true "gone-forth one," however, the essential factor was to wander free from the ties and comforts of home life. This was life with the veils and wrap-

---

* Many fables that present the life of the Buddha tell of his marriage and sudden nocturnal departure in a highly dramatic way that was designed to emphasize the great renunciation of the young seeker. Most of us these days would view nocturnal departures as anything but renunciation, so unfortunately this legend has caused the Buddha to be seen more as a jerk than one who negotiated his way out of the jam that his parents had put him in. However, according to many accounts, after realizing Dhamma, the Buddha headed back to his home-town to teach his family, and he brought some of them to complete awakening.

ping pulled off. It was life among wild animals, thieves, and outlaws— life lived on the hard earth at the roots of trees; seeking alms-food from villages; and looking for something to wear, often pulling the rags off the corpses whose jackal-chewed remains littered the charnel grounds. It was life held like a brief candle-flame in the vast stormy night of sickness, danger, and death. Only a few ventured into this way of life, some of dubious sanity, some quite saintly, but all were held in a mixture of fear and awe by the ordinary folk of town, clan, and family.

Among this ragged crew, there were a few teachers. We have records of some that the Buddha knew or knew of. The six that the Buddhist scriptures single out were Purāna Kassapa, Makkahali Gosāla, Ajita Kesakambalī, Pakudha Kaccāyana, Sañjaya Belatthaputta, and Nigantha Nātaputta. This last teacher was the leader of a sect now called Jains, and there are accounts in the Buddhist scriptures of various debates between the Buddha or his disciples and the followers of Nigantha, in which (surprise, surprise!) the Buddhists always come out on top. Actually Nigantha Nātaputta was the only one who advocated for living morally, but his views are presented as a rigid attribution of moral consequence to every action, intentional or unintentional. Scratching your body, for example, was considered to be a destructive action or *kamma* (Skt.: karma) that would have dire consequences and would keep your soul bound to a potentially endless series of rebirths. In his view, this kamma clung to the soul like a toxic creeper, and the best thing was to avoid any kind of action that would increase the infestation. This meant eating as little as possible, pulling out body hair to avoid having mites that one might then accidentally kill, and avoiding damaging creatures to the extent of sweeping the ground in front of you as you walked along.

How fairly the teachings of these six are represented isn't clear, but their teaching on kamma, on moral determinism, and on noncausality give some idea of what the samanas were looking at and thinking about. That is: "Why are we here? Is there such a thing as free will? Is there an eternal or deathless state? Why are we bound to aging, sickness, and death? Are we bound to these things because of our previous actions? Do we have a soul or self that has to endure all this, or can it be liberated from this scenario? Are we just organisms that live and die and have no soul and no purpose? In which case, why live ethically or in fact why do anything?" Accordingly some of these teachers lived in an animal or near-vegetable state of self-mortification and nonaction.

Other samanas responded to these questions and dilemmas about the nature of the soul, identity, and action in different ways. They generally chose to apply effort in one of two ways: to either transcend the body and earthly existence by going into states of formless mental absorption, or to suppress the sensory urges of the body by ascetic mortification. Through either one or both of these ways, the samanas aspired to liberate the soul, self, or atman from its bondage to a death-bound body. Siddhattha tried both of these methods, in a characteristically full and accomplished way.

First he took up the work of mental absorption. He had two teachers in succession: Āḷāra Kālāma taught the way to the attainment of "the sphere of nothingness," in which sensory phenomena and mental activity cease and the awareness that remains only perceives a vast empty nothing. Siddhattha excelled at this practice but remained dissatisfied with the attainment, considering that it was just a temporary release, like a hop into a netherworld, which was followed by a descent to the coarse realities of sickness, pain, and death. So he tried another teacher, Uddaka Rāmaputta, who took him a step further into an extremely attenuated form of awareness called the sphere of neither-perception-nor-nonperception. This essentially means you're barely here at all. Siddhattha perfected access to this just as he had to the sphere of nothingness, but again its temporary nature and strategy of diversion from earthly life left him dissatisfied.

So he went off without a teacher and kept companionship with five other wanderers—to whom this discourse was later addressed. There was that bond that arises among companions in the struggle, and struggle it was. Their little group's main practice seems to have been asceticism— which the Buddha subsequently dismissed as "unprofitable." But in keeping with his way of practice, Siddhattha gave it everything he had at the time. He was the leader in denying the body, and so he went off on his own to a place called Uruvela (subsequently named Bodhgaya in memory of his awakening, or *bodhi*) to get really serious. Reducing his food to a few beans a day, his body grew so lean that when he scratched his belly, he could feel his spine. He even reduced his breathing to almost nothing. So you get some idea of this man's resolve—he could have been spending time out there in the state of neither-perception-nor-nonperception, but instead he wanted to really understand the cosmos through understanding the peace that he could directly know—his body, senses, and mind.

It turns out that the approach of asceticism didn't work—it made his body weak, and at the same time offered no deep insights into the nature of his mind (which was the real source of the problem). In fact, asceticism merely locked his mind into a harsh attitude and behavior toward his body. He didn't have a practice that integrated body and mind; he only had ways of avoidance or suppression, neither of which took him to a free place. Fortunately for him and for us, he met a girl. Well, to put it another way, a local woman named Sujata saw this weird figure sitting under a tree and thought he couldn't be human, that he must be some kind of tree-spirit. Being of a pious nature, and hoping that a few offerings to the spirit would stand her in good stead with conceiving a child, she offered Siddhattha a bowl of sweet milk-rice at just the time when he was recognizing that the self-mortification practice was going nowhere.

This encounter marked the beginning of the "middle way" that the Buddha later laid out to his spiritual colleagues as "avoiding extremes of indulgence and self-mortification." So, having put aside the "get out of your senses" approach of otherworldly states, and the sensory suppression program of asceticism, Siddhattha found balance. Then remembering the sense of pure ease that he had experienced when sitting in the shade of a tree as a child, he tuned in to that "no-pressure" mode of being. And from there, grounded in the tremendous resolve that he had lived with for all these years, his mind unfolded, released its attachments and dark places . . . into awakening. This word may contain a variety of meanings for us, but for Siddhattha, a key part of his awakening was to realize the significance of action, or *kamma*.

He realized that *kamma* primarily meant action based on our choices and intentions—he saw that intentional actions produce results. So accidentally treading on an ant is not kamma, but deliberately fostering ill-will in the heart is. Even the action of asceticism and avoiding action is an action that we choose. So why not be up front about it and make deliberate choices that are based on human welfare? Why not choose a way and a practice that will lead us to a better life? But rather than a life committed to sensual happiness, Siddhattha realized that the good life is lived through sustaining an intention that is moral and compassionate to others as well as himself. And that such a way of life leads to acknowledging and relinquishing the biases, corruptions, and attachments that keep us from awakening. And without awakening, it's as if we are driving on and on without getting anywhere. The truth of the matter is that, rather than driving, we're being *driven*. And this drive goes through lifetimes.

It turns out that the driver of this whole traveling show (or samsāra) is the sense of being a permanent self or soul, of being someone who should be, or will be, or was *something*. But we only sense ourselves as being something through doing something such as thinking, feeling, acting, or suppressing. And doing can never arrive at simply, peacefully being. So who or what is behind all this kamma? After all the years of searching, Siddhattha realized that he couldn't find any lasting self. All he could find were psychophysical processes strung together around a need to be something solid. It was a need and a psychological hunger to be a separate self, either in control of experience or running away from it. On giving up that need and that compulsive doing, the entire cosmos of cause and effect ceased to hold him. Instead of a needy, dissatisfied self, there was clarity, truth, and peace. So this work, this action of penetrating the mind and clearing its sense of need, is the kamma that leads to the end of kamma.

However, as a practice-path aimed at clearing both harmful intentions and the need for intention, this understanding of skillful kamma lines up ethical living with the actions that give freedom from cause and effect, birth and death. It's quite an empowerment. We'll look at that more closely as we go through the text.

To continue the history—after spending weeks in the state of release, reviewing the way that consciousness operates, he was moved to share his realizations. The story is that at first he had doubts as to how to communicate what he'd seen, and whether, in fact, anyone would be interested. Luckily for us, a high divinity (a *brahma*) implored him to teach out of empathy for those "with but a little dust in their eyes." So who would that be? Immediately, he thought of his former teachers—good, sincere practitioners who had guided him and given him all they had. But the divine beings broke the news: both of his former teachers were dead. The Buddha considered again: "What about my five ascetic buddies? Unbalanced though they seem now, they had commitment. Yes," he thought, "I'll try to teach them."

So he left Bodhgaya and started walking to Isipatana near Vāranāsi. It was a trek of a couple of weeks in those days, journeying through thick forests, faring for alms-food in villages, and sleeping under trees at night. There was time to think of how he could present what he wanted to offer. And he found out what didn't work. Somewhere on the trail he met another wanderer, Upaka, who, in the manner of wanderers of those days, asked him who his teacher was and what his Dhamma was about. The Buddha gave him a brief statement, a kind of spiritual business card:

> I am an All-transcender, an All-knower
> unstained by theories, relinquishing all,
> liberated by terminating craving.
> Who should I give credit to?
>
> I have no teacher, and no-one like me
> exists in the world. . . .
> I'm going to Vāranāsi to set the wheel of the truth
> in motion. In a blindfold world
> I go to beat the Deathless Drum.
> (M 1)

True enough, but there was nothing in that statement for Upaka to get hold of—no wheel to ride. And recognizing this, Upaka just shook his head and said, "May it be so, friend," and departed.

Maybe the Buddha learned from that encounter. Liberation and its illumination are difficult things to talk about. And in the end, if the listener can't get on board with how to get there, then so what? At any rate, when the Buddha finally arrived at the Deer Park in Isipatana, where his five former colleagues were still mortifying themselves to their hearts' content, he had a few follow-up statements to his earlier declaration. The Group of Five wasn't very welcoming, feeling that he'd gone soft on the asceticism that was their standard. They even resolved not to greet him. But moved by his radiant presence, they found themselves offering him a place to sit, though they still didn't want to hear what he had to say. That all changed once the Buddha started speaking—he touched upon a theme that had immediate relevance to those seekers:

> Listen, bhikkhus, the Deathless has been attained. I shall instruct you, I teach you the law. By practicing as you are instructed, you will, by realizing it yourselves, here and now through direct knowledge, enter on and abide in the supreme goal of the Holy Life.
> (M 1)

Though still reluctant, the five were impressed by the clarity and confidence with which the Buddha spoke. So they listened and opened their hearts . . . and this is the point at which the Buddha's first discourse begins.

THE TURNING OF THE
WHEEL SUTTA

This is how I've heard it: Once, the Blessed One was living at Vāranāsi, at Isipatana in the Deer Park. There he addressed the Group of Five bhikkhus: "There are two extremes, bhikkhus, that are not to be followed by one who has Gone Forth. What two? Getting bound to and following sense-pleasure, which is cheap, coarse, worldly, unworthy, and doesn't take you anywhere useful. Then there's getting bound to self-mortification, which is painful, unworthy, and doesn't take you anywhere useful. Not going along with either of these extremes, a Tathāgata has awakened to the middle way; it conduces to seeing, insight, peace, deep knowledge, gnosis, and nibbāna.

"And what is this middle way that a Tathāgata has awakened to, that conduces to seeing, insight, peace, deep knowledge, gnosis, and nibbāna? It's the noble eightfold path, that is: right view, right intention, right speech, right action, right livelihood, right effort, right mindfulness, and right concentration. This is the middle way that a Tathāgata has awakened to.

"Bhikkhus, there is a noble truth with regard to suffering. Birth is difficult; aging is hard; dying is painful. Sorrow, grieving, pain, anguish, and despair are all painful. Being stuck with what you don't like is stressful; being separated from what you do like is stressful; not getting what you want is stressful. In brief the five aggregates that are affected by clinging bring no satisfaction.

"Bhikkhus, there is a noble truth concerning the arising of suffering: it arises with craving, a thirst for more that's bound up with relish and passion and is always running here and there. That is: thirst for sense-input, thirst to be something, thirst to not be something.

"Bhikkhus, there is a noble truth about the cessation of suffering. It is the complete fading away and cessation of this craving; its abandonment and relinquishment; getting free from and being independent of it.

"Bhikkhus, there is a noble truth of the way leading to the cessation of suffering. It is the noble eightfold path: namely, right view, right intention, right speech, right action, right livelihood, right effort, right mindfulness, and right concentration.

"There is this noble truth with regard to suffering: in this way, bhikkhus, vision, insight, wisdom, knowing, and light arose in me about things not heard before. This noble truth with regard to suffering is to be thoroughly understood: in this way, bhikkhus, vision, insight, wisdom, knowing, and light arose in me about things not heard before. This noble truth with regard to suffering has been thoroughly understood: in this way, bhikkhus, vision, insight, wisdom, knowing, and light arose in me about things not heard before.

"There is this noble truth concerning the arising of suffering: in this way, bhikkhus, vision, insight, wisdom, knowing, and light arose in me about things not heard before. This noble truth of the arising of suffering is that it is to be abandoned. . . . This noble truth of the arising of suffering is that it has been abandoned: such was the vision, insight, wisdom, knowing, and light that arose in me about things not heard before.

"There is this noble truth about the cessation of suffering: in this way, bhikkhus, vision, insight, wisdom, knowing, and light arose in me about things not heard before. This noble truth about the cessation of suffering is to be realized. . . . This noble truth about the cessation of suffering has been realized: such was the vision, insight, wisdom, knowing, and light that arose in me about things not heard before.

"There is this noble truth of the path leading to the cessation of suffering.... This noble truth of the path is to be cultivated.... This noble truth of the path has been cultivated: such was the vision, insight, wisdom, knowing, and light that arose in me about things not heard before.

"As long, bhikkhus, as these four noble truths in their twelve aspects were not seen by me; not seen with the purest insight as they are, then I didn't teach the world—with its devas, māras, and brahmas, its samanas and brahmins, its monarchs and ordinary folk—that I had fully realized complete awakening.

"But, bhikkhus, as soon as these four noble truths in their twelve aspects were seen by me; seen with the purest insight as they are, then I taught the world—with its devas, māras, and brahmas, its samanas and brahmins, its monarchs and ordinary folk—that I had fully realized complete awakening. The knowledge and the vision arose in me: 'My release is assured. This is the last birth. There is no further becoming.'"

This is what the Blessed One said—and the Group of Five bhikkhus were gladdened and approved of his words. And while this exposition was being delivered, the untarnished and clear vision of Dhamma arose in the Venerable Kondañña: "Whatever has the characteristic to arise, all that ceases."

When the wheel of Dhamma had been set rolling by the Blessed One, the devas of the earth raised the cry: "At Vāranāsi, in the Deer Park at Isipatana, the incomparable wheel of Dhamma has been set rolling by the Blessed One—and it can't be stopped by any samana, or brahmin, or deva, or māra, or brahma, or anyone whomsoever in the world."

When they heard what the earth devas had said, the devas of the realm of the Four Great Kings cried out with one voice: "At Vāranāsi" And when they heard the cry of the devas of the realm of the Four Great Kings, then the devas of the realm of the Thirty-Three cried out with one voice.... When they heard the cry of the Thirty-Three devas, the Yāma devas cried out with one voice.... When they heard the cry of the Yāma devas, the Tusitā devas cried out with one voice.... When they heard the cry of the Tusitā devas... the Nimmānaratī devas cried out with one voice.... When they heard the cry of the Nimmānaratī devas, the Paranimmitavasavattī devas cried out with one voice. . . . When they heard the cry of the Paranimmitavasavattī devas . . . the devas of the retinue of the Brahma deities took up the cry: "At Vāranāsi, in the Deer Park at Isipatana, the incomparable wheel of Dhamma has been set rolling by the Blessed One—and it can't be stopped by any samana or brahmin or deva or māra or brahma or anyone whomsoever in the world."

So in that instant, at that very moment, the word traveled up to the realm of the high divinities. This ten-thousandfold world system trembled and shook and resounded, and a great measureless radiance, surpassing the shining glory of the devas, was made manifest in the world. Then the Blessed One uttered the pronouncement: "It is Kondañña who has seen deeply! Kondañña who has seen deeply." And so it was that the name of Venerable Kondañña became "Kondañña the deep seer."

1

A PATH THROUGH THE JUNGLE

This is how I've heard it: Once, the Blessed One was living at Vāranāsi, at Isipatana in the Deer Park. There he addressed the Group of Five bhikkhus: "There are two extremes, bhikkhus, that are not to be followed by one who has Gone Forth. What two? Getting bound to and following sense-pleasure, which is cheap, coarse, worldly, unworthy, and doesn't take you anywhere useful. Then there's getting bound to self-mortification, which is painful, unworthy, and doesn't take you anywhere useful. Not going along with either of these extremes, a Tathāgata has awakened to the middle way; it conduces to seeing, insight, peace, deep knowledge, gnosis, and nibbāna."

Most of the suttas begin with a brief description of the place where the sermon was delivered. The setting here is the Deer Park at Isipatana, known in modern times as Sarnath, India. Widely regarded as the place where the

Buddha gave the First Sermon, Deer Park has been a Buddhist pilgrimage site for many years and is situated a few miles north of the ancient holy city of Varānāsi. It was the custom for kings to set aside groves and parks just outside major towns where seekers, ascetics, and sages could gather—and this was the place where Siddhattha Gotama (the Buddha's name before he became awakened) and his ascetic companions had been dwelling until he decided to withdraw from the others in order to practice in solitude. So naturally enough, it was here that Siddhattha Gotama returned as the Awakened One to begin teaching.

The Buddha addresses the discourse to his five former companions. They were ascetics but the Buddha addresses them as *bhikkhus,* which means "alms-mendicants," those who live on the free-will offerings of others. Nowadays, *bhikkhu* just means a Buddhist monk but *monk* is a Christian word that doesn't quite fit. Rather than confined to a monastery, these bhikkhus were wanderers living on what turned up.

The five bhikkhus at Deer Park were named Kondañña, Vappa, Bhaddiya, Mahanāma, and Assaji. Kondañña was the eldest. Many years previously, as a novice brahmin, he had been invited to the palace of the raja Suddhodana along with seven of his peers to see the baby Siddhattha Gotama and give predictions as to his destiny. They all agreed that this baby would be either a great emperor or a Buddha; perhaps this was why he was named *Siddhattha,* which means "Accomplishes the Goal." Interestingly, it was Kondañña alone who reckoned that Siddhattha was destined for Buddhahood. Four of the brahmins who had been present at the palace later told their sons to keep their eyes on Siddhattha, as he was destined for greatness. These sons grew up to become the other four of the Group of Five.

The Buddha here is addressed as *Bhagavā,* which means "one who has great fortune" or "Blessed One," sometimes translated as "Lord." This term was generally used by the Buddha's disciples, and it implies someone who has both a great deal of spiritual power to offer and the capacity to make it accessible to many. It is an inspirational and devotional honorific, a way of conceiving and focusing on someone who isn't conceivable in ordinary terms, and whose teachings ask you to focus on what's happening for you. Keeping in mind the Buddha's blessed quality is helpful: it encourages us to maintain a compassionate inner focus by reminding us that our own witnessing, our "Buddha-potential," should be benevolent rather than judgmental. It's vital to refer to that compassionate and peaceful witness rather than to the inner faultfinder when we meditate. That which continually criticizes you is a judge, not a witness!

Most people find an external reference, such as the example and image of the Buddha to be supportive. Visual images stick in our mind more readily than a thought or an idea (particularly when we are dealing with abstract ideas like enlightenment) and for this reason, images of the Awakened One have been common for centuries. However, in the early centuries of Buddhism, the images most often used were a tree with an empty space under it, a throne with no one sitting on it, a parasol with no one under it . . . get the point? Later the imagery firmed up around giant stylized footprints, a stupa (a memorial containing funeral ashes or relics), or a Dhamma-wheel. Finally in approximately the first century C.E., the "Buddha" appears as an image, often stylized as a contemporary nobleman. (Hence the long earlobes—those noblemen wore heavy earrings.) Such images can help us connect with Buddhism: certainly in my teenage years, the initial arousing of interest in Buddhism came from seeing a picture of a Buddha with calm dignity and his evocative, gentle smile. That image reminded me of how one could be a balanced and free human being. And that there was a path that led out of the jungle, even at the age of sixteen, I could sense thickening around me.

I didn't live in a jungle of dense vegetation and dangerous animals, but it was still a gloomy and tangled place. Personal uncertainty lurked in the shadows of the Cold War and the threat of a nuclear holocaust. Even at its best, the way of the world as I could sense it, was to push and struggle through an ongoing series of difficulties—the need to make a living, rather than enjoy being alive, seemed to be a life perspective that offered nothing more than material well-being. And advantageous though such a life might be, it was still marked by death, separation, grief, and pain. In this jungle, I didn't know what track to follow—not that any of the religious or political or even dropout tracks offered a convincing or satisfying arrival. But the Buddha as

I encountered him in images, and later in words, seemed to have already arrived. He exemplified a way that steered to peace in the present moment.

The Buddha's Teaching Method

Although there is a path to that peace, the main track that the Buddha lays out in this first discourse is what the Buddhist path (or way) is *not*. In a way, that "negative" approach is the most direct. In life, we're always on one track or another. If we stop running down the wrong tracks, we'll then be on the right track—and this track, or path, can be lived here and now. This approach is indicative of the Buddha's realization of *Dhamma* (or truth of the way things are) as being directly knowable, not delayed in time, inviting one to investigate, and leading inward. It is also to be realized by the wise within their own experience—as indicated by the Buddha, who attempts to make his teaching relevant to the experience of the people he was addressing.

Sometimes the Buddha would respond with silence to people who were just tangled up in confused ways of thinking—it was a way of indicating that truth went beyond speculation. Sometimes he would answer a question with a counter-question to encourage the person to examine his or her own views and beliefs. Sometimes he would highlight an incident that had just occurred or a particular experience that a person was going through. He always tried to reach into where a person's wisdom was established. In this sutta, addressed to a group who must have heard a whole range of ideas about the nature of existence and truth, but who manifested a strong commitment to seeing it for themselves, the Buddha concerned himself with talking about the means of their practice. He understood that how we apply ourselves determines where we arrive. So there was not much point in defining the place of arrival—that place is realized as a result of the way we travel.

In this way, his approach differed from that of the other samana teachers, who seem to have made proclamations and taught in metaphysical terms: that the self and the cosmos are the same, that they are different, or that the world is an illusion in which nothing has any reality. In this sutta, the Buddha focuses on the *experience* of the way rather than its notional goal. Liberation and salvation after death are only ideas and views in our mind; what can be directly known is how things are right now, at this time and place. Focusing on the means, the here and now of how our mind is set, its aims, its ethical mood, and its energies, brings us into the present moment and into a witnessing in which there is no view to defend or uphold. Then, direct seeing and knowing has the possibility to operate. This is the kind of process that the Buddha stimulated with his teaching.

For example, one time the villagers of Kesaputta asked the Buddha what they should believe in because so many people were giving them different ideas. His response was first to affirm their right to have doubts when given conflicting views. Then he appealed to their own understanding, in a dialogue that went something like this:

> "If you act in ways that are cruel or mean, does that seem good to you or not?"
>
> "No," they replied, "we don't think that's a very good thing to do."
>
> "Then it's best not to do that, isn't it?" commented the Buddha. "And what about being calm and kind, is that valued by you or not?"
>
> And they replied, "Well, we think it's very good."
> (see AN 3:53)

In this way, the Buddha helped these villagers realize the value of concentrating on means rather than doctrines. Otherwise people are liable to get caught in the tangle of views; they stay in that jungle and come no nearer to truth. The Buddha's teaching asks us to reflect on what we already know or on our principles, then to verify them with people whom we respect and value, and to proceed from that intuitive sense of certainty.

But in the case of the Group of Five, the Buddha was addressing "those who had gone forth." They were *samanas,* "strivers": they needed no recommendation that truth was worth seeking or that they had to apply themselves to it. They just needed to have the means clarified. So here the

Buddha addresses them with some advice on the cultivation of right means as an expression and experience of enlightenment itself. And he begins with affirming the view that the ascetics would already have adopted—that chasing after and getting hooked on sense-pleasure is unworthy and useless. He starts where they already are—where every path should start. Then he balances that out by negating the ascetic view: saying that getting caught up with self-mortification was also useless. He thereby cuts away the ground and leaves them dangling in the middle, saying that it is in this "no position" that peace is to be found.

Avoiding the Extremes

The Buddha's approach of "no position" is a way out of the jungle of views and dogmas. These two extremes of trying to get or get rid of represent the tracks that seekers might take if they are following the advice of a teacher who instructs in terms of a goal rather than a way. Their message is to have or get rid of something, and how to go about achieving that goal isn't important. At first glance, it seems obvious that anyone with a serious spiritual commitment would avoid such a position. However, avoiding this isn't as common as you might think. The very notion of a goal beyond conventional reality can encourage people to discard, sometimes with great vigor, all conventional restraints. This applies just as much to twenty-first-century seekers as to ancient ones—as anyone familiar with a spiritual network will know.

On one extreme, you have the pleasure seekers. Using sexual behavior or drugs and liquor can be viewed as a way to release ego-bound conditioning. But this is a risky approach, one prone to abuse at the best of times. What compounds this abuse is the fact that, in an intensely structured society, there is a lot of confused conditioning in terms of guilt and shame and "freedom." When a sense of shame is appended to sexuality at the same time as it is being presented as blissful, exciting, and sophisticated, the heart gets twisted and divided in its impulses. You might be thinking, "Why hold back from what is most desirable? Won't achieving that bring happiness?" Well, after a while, people who follow that line of thought get to recognize that indulgence leads to addiction and abuse rather than release and happiness. The clearer way of release is to let go of both the guilt and shame, *and* the myth that the sensory world can provide true and lasting happiness. In other words: to see, with insight, sense-pleasure as it really is—a brief exciting hit, a sense of fading, and then hunger for more. Do you want to keep this runaround going?

The other extreme of self-denial, or self-mortification, is rarer nowadays. Although asceticism does have a certain appeal to the modern seeker, it is usually in the religious life of traditional monastic orders that some degree of self-mortification, deprivation, or asceticism is practiced. Rigorous discipline and asceticism (including self-flagellation in a few Christian monastic orders) is not unusual, and members of some Buddhist sects today will still burn off a finger or strap burning incense to their arms out of a sense of offering themselves completely to the Dhamma. Certainly, in the continuing tradition of swamis and sadhus in India, long periods of fasting and other kinds of physical mortification are observed with the aim of transcending worldly life and reaching higher states of consciousness. There are still ascetics who practice standing on one leg for fifteen years or piercing their bodies with skewers. The ascetic tradition has had a longer duration than the Buddhist Sangha, and it still attracts aspirants today.

The relevance of reflecting on self-denial to an average Westerner who is not interested in hair shirts, may seem slight. But in purely mental terms, the extremes may be more subtle—and much more common. Often they're experienced as an oscillation of the mind between two positions. If we overindulge in food and drink, for example, the natural reaction (unless we're told that this extreme is good for us) is to feel a sense of regret and then to veer toward complete abstinence. We feel annoyed with our "weakness" and decide to be firm and cut it out. However, abstinence without wise reflection and insight doesn't solve the syndrome of need that made us indulge in the first place, so after a period of abstinence we either feel rather wretched, or we feel that there's no problem and decide to have just a *little* drink . . . which leads to another. . . . We stumble through our jungle of craving, either suppressing a habit or replacing it with another in order to cope with our addictive tendencies. It takes encouragement and skill to look into the very nature of need and craving—to see how we fill our hunger with something to eat, drink, read, or talk about. This is the penetrative inquiry that is the way out of our inner jungle.

In meditation, we can observe our mind following similar oscillating tendencies: periods of hard concentration, followed by periods of day-dreaming and laxity. Or moments of really applying ourselves—back straight, jaw tight, and fierce one-pointedness on the meditation object. Then, strained from the effort, or feeling that we have achieved something from that, we think that it's now time to relax and integrate into "normal life." Maybe we should get a few beers or just go to the movies. On a meditation retreat, we can adopt the view that we should not even think or talk. Then, at the end of the retreat, we return to the world of daily life having gained little or no understanding about our relationship to the peopled and relational world. By itself, refraining from activities or habits doesn't lead to a full Liberation—one not bound to time and dependent on a peaceful environment. For that, we have to get beyond being bound to these extremes—because such views block a careful investigation of our experience as it's happening now. It is from this very situation, of having seen the ultimate pointlessness of indulgence and of suppression, that we should be "going forth." It's a new direction. And it's signaled by the Buddha saying he has "awakened" to it.

2

THE BUDDHA'S
MIDDLE WAY

"And what is this middle way that a Tathāgata has awakened to, that conduces to seeing, insight, peace, deep knowledge, gnosis, and nibbāna? It's the noble eightfold path, that is: right view, right intention, right speech, right action, right livelihood, right effort, right mindfulness, and right concentration. This is the middle way that a Tathāgata has awakened to."

The Buddha awakened to and discovered the way. That is, he opened to it, rather than created it through getting things or rejecting them. In this respect, as awakened, the Buddha refers to himself as a *Tathāgata*. The word *Tathāgata* can be derived from *Tathā-gata* meaning, "Thus Gone"—from which we would understand that he has gone beyond birth and death, beyond suffering. It can also be derived from *Tathā-agata* meaning, "Thus Come" or "Truly Here," which emphasizes his presence, his here-and-now centeredness. Perhaps the dual meaning is intentional. Buddhas just aren't locatable in any fixed place. (Actually, the Buddha didn't encourage us to speculate about him at all—he said it would drive us crazy.)

Another implication of *Tathāgata* is explained by the Buddha in a subsequent discourse:

> Bhikkhus, as a Tathāgata speaks, so he acts; as he acts, so he speaks. Therefore he is called a Tathāgata.
> (AN 4:23)

So Tathāgatas are those who say what is known through direct experience, and live it out without doubt, fear, or favor. Their teaching is an explanation of the way they live, in accordance with vision, insight, knowledge, and leading to peace, profound understanding, full realization, and nibbāna. All the actions and words of a Tathāgata are then a "bringing here" of the "thus gone" qualities of liberation.

The "middleness" of the way a Buddha teaches and exemplifies points then to a balance of presence and nonattachment. Through this we are encouraged to see clearly and insightfully what is happening now rather than reject or adhere to experience. And the results? They are peacefulness and true understanding, nibbāna—the cooling of the fire, the calming of the wind, the settled quality, and the sensitivity of still water.

The middle way approaches human life broadly. Here, the Buddha is not formulating a particular set of beliefs or assumptions that you have to take on board before you can understand the teachings.

The Eightfold Path

The different aspects of the path are all characterized as *sammā*, meaning "right," "perfect," or "consummate." The Buddha is talking about following the principles of being "noble" or "worthy" in various aspects of life. There are eight qualities in this grouping, traditionally known as "the eightfold path." (See chapter 7 for more information about this topic.)

The first quality or factor, right view, is concerned with having a proper perspective on life. It encourages us to see things in terms of cause and effect.

We are in, and seem to be, a process of having been caused or born. We arise out of that process and at the same time we are creating it by our actions, which generate good and bad effects, or results. How we act determines what friends we have, what consequences come back to us, and so on. Results like these affect our thoughts and actions—we learn and adapt as best we can, and then act on the basis of what we've learned. This action then causes further effects—but unfortunately we're not always that astute in our learning. Actions that give short-term benefits like happiness or convenience often are more attractive to us than actions that produce further reaching long-term benefits, such as wisdom, calm, or compassion. This principle of the cause and the results of action—even mental action—is what is meant by "the law of kamma." The point of right view is to start learning very directly and thoroughly about cause and effect on an experiential, rather than abstract or theoretical, foundation. And we deepen our ability to learn by applying the other seven path-factors. So one aspect of right view is understanding that to get out of the jungle we need a path. The first step, then, is to establish that path, and in Buddhism the foundation for that is the understanding that we can learn from contemplating and considering our direct experience. Right view, then, focuses on cause and effect. Through noticing the results of our thoughts, attitudes, and actions, we learn what gives the best results—hence a path gets established beneath our own feet.

Such right view is the basis for the second path-factor, right intention (or right thought). That is, when you focus on cause and effect, you want to be more careful about what you cause. And what you cause depends on how you direct your mind. Accordingly the three root-intentions that the Buddha encouraged are harmlessness, compassion, and renunciation (simplifying needs). This is where wisdom and clarity start to move into action.

The list continues with "rightness" in action, beginning with right speech (the third factor), then extending to right bodily action (the fourth factor). It also includes right livelihood (the fifth factor). All this can be called ethics or virtue.

The last three factors relate to the direct practice of mind cultivation: right effort, right mindfulness, and right concentration. These are most often developed through formal meditation exercises.

These eight factors can be summed up into three qualities of wisdom, virtue, and meditation, which are reference points for anyone on the spiritual path. Together they present a complete and integrated approach. Various religions or different ways of cultivating the mind may emphasize one aspect or another. And sometimes, one aspect can be taken to the extreme. For example, some religions place a great emphasis on virtue, or morality and conventions, with promises of heavenly rewards for those who obey and punishment for those who don't. Such attitudes often omit and may even reject the possibility for personal reflection. Unguided by wisdom, moral commandments lead to fundamentalism with the intolerance, repression, and blinkered conceit that it brings about.

A subtler attachment to virtue is the belief that if you just keep performing good actions, such as ritual offerings to gods, then this in itself will get you somewhere without any further work on your mind. This misconception affects Buddhism too. In Buddhist countries, there's a very strong feeling about accumulating "merit" by making offerings to monks or temples. This view has a certain truth in it; as the Buddha acknowledged, generosity is a sign of a selfless heart—a great blessing to the world. Unfortunately, the idea of "gaining merit" can substitute for true selflessness and can make people feel that no further cultivation is necessary. So the Buddha said that giving alms is the purest form of generosity and has the best result when it is given with no interest in a payback of any kind: this clears the mind both of stinginess and manipulation. And he further pointed out that the highest kind of merit, even greater than giving alms to a Buddha, was to cultivate meditation properly:

> Even though generosity bears fruit, still to go in faith for refuge to the Buddha, the Dhamma, and the Sangha and determine the five moral precepts bears a greater fruit. Even though that bears fruit, to maintain kindness for the period of time that it takes to milk a cow bears a greater fruit. Even though that bears fruit, it is fruitful to maintain awareness of impermanence for only as long as a finger-snap bears a greater fruit.
> (AN 9:20)

In contrast to those who get attached to morality and gaining heavenly rewards are those who don't bother with any morality or conventions, and think that they can become enlightened just through sitting in meditation. This is more common in the West. People can get really obsessive about having the right conditions to *sit* in, and yet pay scant attention to selfless actions, kindness, or sense-restraint. It is always salutary to remember that the Buddha and many other great teachers didn't have a context that provided air-conditioning, central heating, a perfectly balanced diet, cushions, knee supports, and undisturbed silence. What they did have was great resolve, commitment, and patience. These are the prerequisites for letting go and awakening. When meditation becomes motivated by the need for self-affirmation, or by an impatient drive to get concentrated, experience bliss, or remodel oneself, that meditation-craving hinders and agitates the mind. The Buddha himself always related meditation not to ecstatic trances or complex abstractions, but rather to good sense and steady application of effort. These should manifest in terms of everything we do. Life is Dhamma practice.

Wisdom, too, can be taken to an extreme. It can be intellectually developed to the point where it loses contact with reality, as in the case of metaphysics. Philosophy and theology rely heavily upon intellectual understanding, yet fall short in the development of the wisdom that comes through attention to actual experience. So having a mind full of ideas does not necessarily grant us any clearer perspective on how to live our life. Even with proper wisdom and virtue, without the assiduous practice of inner contemplation that meditation exercises make possible, we are sowing good seeds but not tasting the fruit. With meditation however, we can feel the benefits; careful practice blends clarity and good will into a palpable energy that settles and nourishes the entire nervous system. Thus, clarity, virtue, and peace unite as a single integrated practice.

The results of meditation are that we feel spacious and peaceful, and therefore more easily let go of sense-desire, fixed views, and attainments. It is a pragmatic approach to the abandonment of what ties us up; provided that it's integrated with virtue and wisdom, and not hung on to as a thing in itself. As the Buddha points out:

I do not say that one attains purification by view, tradition, knowledge, virtue, or ritual, nor is it attained without [these]. It is only by taking these factors as the means and not grasping them as ends in themselves that one so attains and consequently does not crave for rebecoming.

(Su-N 839)

The middle way, that is, the eightfold path, is a summary of that integration. It guides us into a life based on Dhamma. And with this, the Buddha emphasizes that adopting a "whole life" approach is the way, rather than following one particular technique or belief. He summarizes the ways in which people cultivate a spiritual path and then qualifies that with the reminder that the path is to be cultivated in ways that are "right." Consider that prefix "right" (*sammā*) as meaning something like "whole" or "complete." It means ways that are not partial, biased, or self-oriented but rather ways that are properly guided and are of benefit to others as well as to ourselves. The word *sammā* conveys wholeness, balance. This is the "rightness" that is noble rather than perfectionist.

If we practice meditation with "wrong view," we will always remain obsessed with ourselves. We will constantly try to see ourselves as perfect—in which case we get caught up with trying to fix every less-than-ideal facet of our mental behavior, rather than acknowledging a nasty thought, not following it, and letting it pass. I've known people who have anguished over a particular problem, vice, or virtue for years; the need to see the face of their mind as fault free, prevents them from going any deeper into what's under their skin. Their intention isn't right, and so they get stuck. Instead, the most fruitful and immediate benefits come from stepping back from the activity of our mind. Step back, let go, and slip through—that's what we learn about when getting out of the jungle; we don't have to cut down every creeper. This may sound easy, but it means letting go of an apparent self, a sticky and tangling thing that gathers vines around it. In order to get out of the jungle, just following a meditation technique is not an adequate answer; we need an integrated approach and wise guidance to ward off the obsessiveness that can accumulate when we aim for a goal, rather than for developing skillful means. But to abandon self-conscious drives and ambitions without abandoning morality and responsibility requires skill. How can we, stuck in the jungle with a head full of noise, acquire that skill? An integrated way of doing just this is explained in the Buddha's subsequent teaching—a teaching that the Buddha said was peculiar to fully enlightened beings. Yet that teaching is based on something that *everybody* knows about.

3

THE FIRST NOBLE TRUTH

Having to Hold On Is Suffering

"Bhikkhus, there is a noble truth with regard to suffering. Birth is difficult; aging is hard; dying is painful. Sorrow, grieving, pain, anguish, and despair are all painful. Being stuck with what you don't like is stressful; being separated from what you do like is stressful; not getting what you want is stressful. In brief the five aggregates that are affected by clinging bring no satisfaction."

The Buddha then goes on to talk about suffering, stress, difficulty, dissatisfaction, trouble, and the rest of it—the very reason why these bhikkhus had taken on a spiritual path. This very direct prompting to return to the source of their motivation is how he begins to expound the four noble truths, the centerpiece of his teaching. The four noble truths are about "suffering," how it arises, how it ceases, and a way to bring around that ceasing. These occupy the center of the Buddha's teaching, because they already are central to human experience. Everyone knows the feeling of lack or loss or conflict in their lives: this is what the Buddha called dukkha, often translated as "suffering," but covering a whole range of meanings and nuances. At times, we feel it as a sense of need, or a dissatisfaction that can vary from mild weariness to utter despair. This feeling can be triggered either by physical experience or by mental impressions concerning ourselves or other beings. It is a feeling characterized by a sense that things are "out of balance." Even if we are physically well and mentally skilled, we can feel disappointed that life isn't offering us enough, or that we're not making enough of it or doing enough, or that there's not enough time, space, freedom. We can feel anxiety over the state of the planet and the environment; our perceptions of the present and the future are not secure and problem free. So that pulls on us emotionally. Then there's the sense of "too much"—feeling overwhelmed, not having enough space, time, and ease. In both cases there's a continual sense of subtle or gross stress. Just reflect upon your activities and pursuits: notice that they involve a constant effort to change or cope with what is disagreeable, or to stimulate well-being. This striving is universal.

It is worthwhile considering that, however altruistic our actions are, the *feeling* of unsatisfactoriness is the same. This feeling is what the Buddha pointed out as the dukkha that we can resolve. Dukkha is a characteristic of objective physical reality, with its disease and death. However, as a noble truth, the term points to something different. It means the subjective sense of stress that isn't bound to physical reality. Sometimes having little is fine or even peaceful in its simplicity; at other times, we can feel devastated that there's a stain on the dining room tablecloth. We can suffer in comfortable, affluent countries due to a lack of worth or meaning. This can drive people to suicide even though physically things seem OK. So this is the dukkha that is subjectively oriented, that can and should be removed.

Just to get in touch with that feeling is an introduction to how our mind works because it provides a reference point to where and how the experiences of life are affecting us in a very basic way. We may assume that we are beings guided by rational principles and a thinking mind, but we only choose to be rational when that cool and objective mode suits us. Why a specific mode or mental stance—playful, efficient, or detached—feels suitable, pleasing, inspiring, worthwhile, or the reverse is calibrated in a different zone of our mind. To get in touch with that feeling and reflex zone of the mind, or heart, is essential if we want to know where the triggers of action are located. This heart that experiences dukkha is the home of impulse, desire, love, and fear—and is the place for awakening. This is where we can find balance, truth, Dhamma.

By pointing at dukkha, the Buddha highlights a fundamental truth that we may have only glimpsed or seen as related to a particular set of circumstances. He is not implying that life is miserable; most things have a mixture of pleasure and pain and neutrality in them. It's just that human experience is characterized by a constant restless quality of disquiet. It's like a shadow. When we experience happiness, we also feel an undertone of wanting more of it, wanting to hold on to it or even continue to stimulate it; because by itself, happiness changes. And when the source of happiness passes, we begin to feel bored or dissatisfied, and we want to seek out something else. If we don't find that "something else," we feel worse yet.

Life does have its dark side, and it can be painful at times; but we often make it even more painful for ourselves, psychologically and emotionally, by wanting the happiness to last or the painful aspects never to manifest. In fact, psychological pain and fear can be borne. You can also practice with physical pain; you can work with it; you can become serene through it. What *is* really painful is the mental perception that you can't bear it for another moment. It's possible to understand this without having acute pain. Just with life being the way it is, things go wrong and your mind will think, "Why should this happen to me?" When you feel sick, thoughts may arise like, "Why should I have to put up with this? I wanted to do something, and this has spoiled it all." Or, "The weather's not very good, and it's ruined my day." Or, "Why do you have to say things like that? You know how that hurts me!" This kind of suffering goes on and on. We never seem to be able to get rid of it in normal activities, regardless of where we go and no matter what we do. Trying to avoid being blamed, avoid losing our job, or avoid disappointing others can lead people to states of extreme stress and nervous breakdown. Then, even if our personal situation is not causing us any anxiety, we are still aware of the suffering of others.

For many of us, the urge to take on spiritual practice arises through recognizing that whatever we do, wherever we go, this shadow of dukkha prevails; and it even follows us into Dhamma practice! I've seen this myself: being in a quiet place and living as a meditating monk not having to worry about anything, I could feel irritated at a frog croaking: "Why do there have to be frogs croaking? Why don't they shut up—and stop disturbing me!" It's not a deliberate, intended response—it's an instinctive reaction. So because it's instinctive, we feel that that's the way we are, and the possibility for change, even if we wish to change, seems remote. Habits and instincts define our identity, and that's where dukkha gnaws more deeply into our heart.

It's important, therefore, to understand that the Buddha's teaching separates (1) the dukkha that we experience because of the way life apparently is, from (2) the dukkha that is created emotionally from not wanting things to be that way, or (3) the dukkha from assuming that we're unalterably bound to a life of suffering. As the Buddha points out in his many discourses, things change, and change can be effected without the naïveté that assumes that solutions are going to be permanently satisfactory and without the pessimism that assumes that it's all hopeless. The Buddha taught dukkha, but also the cessation of dukkha. The particulars of unpleasant circumstances can come to an end or be brought to an end, even if problems then surface in other areas. And the way of meeting conflict and problems can be compassionate, calm, and peaceful in itself. So accepting that life has its dark, problematic side needn't be depressing. Most fruitfully, the kind of suffering that is the mental reaction to a situation, even on an instinctive plane, can be completely abolished. With the ending of that kind of suffering, the mind is clearer and wiser and more capable of effecting positive change in the world of ever-changing circumstances.

The Buddha talked about dukkha in a succession of examples, which begin with the way life appears and then take us into the heart of the matter—first with how we respond, and then, more profoundly, with what we take ourselves to be.

Birth, Aging, and Death

How is birth difficult, or how does it involve suffering? Well, giving birth is physically painful; and also birth is appearance into an uncertain realm. Notice how babies suffer: coming into the world must be a desperate and frightening experience. For the majority of beings, including people in the world today, it means the end of guaranteed nourishment and the beginning of the struggle to survive. Even for the small percentage of privileged humans who live in affluent societies, with birth begins a life in which some physical discomfort is guaranteed, along with the need to sustain or defend the comfort, the property, and the health that they do have. In every case, the obvious long- or short-term consequence of birth is death— the ultimate trajectory is an unavoidable decline. So whatever the joy that comes as a result of birth, birth includes an element of suffering or stress that will arise sooner or later. Birth can also be viewed as "the unfulfilled," which seeks fulfillment. That is, birth is the beginning of need, a shadow-mood that accompanies anything that arises.

When something new arises in your life, if it's pleasant and wished for, there is happiness—and then comes the need to sustain that happiness or the wish not to be parted from it. When something beautiful to behold arises, how long can you continue to be thrilled by it? A few minutes? Can you make it through an hour before it starts to pall? How about a day, let alone a year? Of course, we live with many options. If we get bored with looking at a painting, we read something; when that becomes boring, we go for a walk, perhaps visit a friend and go out for dinner together, then watch a movie. If this routine gets tedious, we might attempt to regress into our past life, pursue astral travel, then write a book about it . . . and so on. The pattern is that each new arising, or "birth" if you like, is experienced as unfulfilling. In this process of ongoing need, we keep moving from this to that without ever getting to the root of the process.

Another aspect of this need is the need to fix things, or to fix ourselves—

to make conflict or pain go away. By this I mean an instinctive response rather than a measured approach of understanding what is possible to fix and what dukkha has to be accommodated right now. Then there's the need to know, to have it all figured out. That gets us moving too.

This continued movement is an unenlightened being's response to dukkha. That movement is what is meant by *samsāra,* the wandering on. According to the Buddha, this process doesn't even stop with death—it's like the habit transfers almost genetically to a new consciousness and body. But even within this life, we can see all these "births," or as the Buddha put it, *birth*—the same habit taking different forms. And each new birth is unsatisfactory too, because sooner or later we meet with another obstacle, another disappointment, another option in the ongoing merry-go-round. High-option cultures just give you a few more spins on the wheel.

The sheer momentum of birth after birth has its disquieting aspects too: you can only be born into one thing at a time—are you sure you're doing the right thing? Maybe you're missing out on a really great opportunity somewhere else. Then these multiple options become a strain. Can you develop T'ai Ch'i; play classical guitar; study ecology and cybernetics; have a successful and fulfilling relationship with your partner, your parents, your children, your other relatives; come to a mature understanding of the political arena; grow your own organic food; and hold down a suitable job working with the right kinds of people for the right ends, all at the same time? It's a lot to keep going, isn't it? But if any of these go wrong, or if you miss out on a really fulfilling experience, you're likely to feel disappointed or personally to blame, so cram it in and hold on tight!

Jarā, the Pāli word for the aging process, means maturing—not only just getting old. Growing up is unsatisfactory because you start to get affected by all the stuff of a confused world. There's a lot said nowadays about having been emotionally (let alone physically) damaged as a child. Is there anybody who hasn't been damaged—by their parents, their uncle, their school, or their dog? Then what about falling under the influence of social prejudice, competitive behavior patterning, sexism, racism . . . whatever happened to our childhood innocence? It's scarred and stained by something sooner or later, isn't it? Psychologically we start to develop instincts and habits, and even good habits that provide comfort and security blunt the joyful wonder of childhood consciousness.

Our habits prescribe the way we relate to others, and of course they model our own future. This habitual activity is kamma. Its key feature is that its effects don't die away when the action is completed; it actually changes how we will perceive things and act—it molds our identity. That is, through habitually following tendencies, our mind gets into and deepens its ruts, and that affects how it works and how it intends. If we develop and foster thieving intentions, covetous "mental actions," then we see life and people in terms of what we can get out of them. You know the saying, "A thief notices a saint's pockets." On the other hand, if we foster harmlessness and compassion, we see the world very differently. Creating or developing an intention, a mental state, or train of thought is mental action, mental kamma. Through the workings of kamma, our own good and bad actions of body, speech, and mind affect ourselves and others. Life offers many opportunities to create good kamma, through actions of kindness for example. However, even taking good kamma to be what *I am* creates an identity that can become moralizing or can constantly need to do something because it hasn't come to terms with the afflicted aspects of our heart. Attachment to good kamma buys into the need to keep fixing, keep ironing out the waves of the sea. And good kamma alone doesn't transcend our experience of pain, separation from what we love, and death.

We are born into a kammic predicament in which everything affects everything else. We tend to see our world through the lens of our own attitudes, traumas, and problems, and project all that onto others. I want you to be the way I see you. (But how can that ever happen?) On the other hand, as we recognize what effect others may have on us, our relationships become guarded or take on the form of manipulating, or being manipulated by, fellow humans. So although most people would cherish having a totally trustworthy, harmonious relationship with someone else, that's not possible until each individual finds harmony within—through clearing their biases. Until we are clear, we feel unsteady and like to hold on to a few safeguards and have a few alternatives in mind in case our current set-up or relationship doesn't work out. And that leads to a wavering and lack of wholeheartedness. But having to live with feelings of insecurity, and an inability to commit oneself, is also far from blissful. Because of this, maybe you decide to go into counseling—which can be a pretty grueling experience and hard on the pocketbook. And meanwhile, as you grow up, you are saturated with the woes and horrors of the media, disillusioned by humanity, depressed by global warming. No one can take too much despair, so you seek out some place or some person or some habit to become absorbed into, just to limit the amount of stuff you have to be sensitive to. It's a shame that, even then, the body, with its needs and illnesses, doesn't leave you alone . . . now there are the medical bills . . . so you bluff your way into a meaningless job and get some insurance (if you are in a society where such things exist). Anyway, hold on—because here comes *māraṇam,* death.

Death and dying generally involve a certain amount of pain and degradation, as well as grieving. We imagine that death only happens to older people, but that's not true—human beings are always surrounded by forces of destruction that can terminate their lives at any moment. Life involves a lot of stressful holding on, even for ducks and squirrels, let alone for human beings who have surrounded themselves with, or invented, fire, electricity, cars, and lots of weapons. These are all created to make our life more secure, yet they are all very common sources of wounding and death. The fear of discomfort or of loss of security fills our life with potentially deadly things.

As the Buddha explained it, death may also refer to the disappearance of any mental or physical experience. When something pleasant ends, we can feel sad, or, if it wasn't too important, we can remember it and form some kind of view or opinion about it. When it's something you've created, perhaps a painting, for instance, you might feel critical of your work; or, maybe if you have no self-criticisms in the present moment, that feeling of success might set up a pattern of expectation for your next painting, or for someone else's painting. This can happen with anything that you've done; you think back on it and see its flaws. Alternatively, if it was something you enjoyed doing and now it is finished—that also brings an unhappy feeling, a feeling of longing or nostalgia. Death is the ending of the known and the familiar. So when we come to the end of something, we reach out for something new to hold on to. For example, after a meal, we can go for a walk, or maybe have a rest, or there's conversation in which we can bring back the pleasant past, or plan for a pleasant future, or create and sustain a pleasant present. All of that is the movement toward birth. And birth is the opportunity to go through this whole dukkha one more time....

Each birth is aimed at getting what is pleasing, getting away from what we don't like, and finding fulfillment. Birth, therefore, involves a lot of stressful reaching out, holding on, jealousy, possessiveness, and defensiveness. And those same old instincts crop up again in different scenarios. Birth is pretty deluding: it always looks like a fresh thing until we've learned to look at that shadowy feeling in our heart—the same old compulsive drives, needs, holding on . . . suffering. And in the blur of these drives and needs, the mind that goes through birth, aging, and death assumes "that is what I am." And so it tries to create a self to get out of there or to not be there. But all these creations are more "births," and more unsatisfactoriness. Frustrating, isn't it?

The Five Aggregates

A few important words finish this section of the sutta: "In brief the five aggregates that are affected by clinging bring no satisfaction." This sums up what has been said before about dukkha, but it does so in a significant way. The five aggregates (*khandha*) that are referred to represent the classifications by which the Buddha, perhaps following the terminology of the time, analyzed the experience of life. The word *khandha* is translated as "aggregate" (meaning a "composite of particles" or "heap") because the khandha are categories or groups of phenomena heaped together for the sake of reference. It should be remembered that they are a classification, a useful one, but are not fixed things themselves. The aggregates are: form (*rūpa*), feeling (*vedanā*), perception (*saññā*), mental activities (*sankhāra*), and sense consciousness (*viññāna*). I'll explain those terms in more detail in due course, but what the list implies is—everything.

The principle at work here is holistic. In this respect it differs from physical science. Rational science has dominated Western ways of perception and activity and, despite its technical brilliance, has created a gap between the observer and a universe from which he or she feels separate. A sense of connection with, and responsibility for, the world in which we live is thereby lost. This has led to all kinds of social, cultural, and personal disorders, whereby people tend to develop and live in their own controlled bubble. And that kind of life has disastrous social and relational consequences. The analysis of the five aggregates begins with the understanding that we are only observing our experience of the universe (science after Einstein shares this understanding). And our experience of the universe, or consciousness, is part of that universe. "No observation, only participation" is the quantum slogan. There is no separation; our perceptions and state of consciousness are aspects of the raw material of the experiential whole. This is what is meant by "world" in the Buddhist sense: it is the holistic entirety of psychophysical experience, not trees, rocks, planets, and stars.

We experience things in terms of their form (*rūpa*)—this aggregate is made up of four ways in which matter "behaves." Matter is experienced in terms of its ability to extend and have size (symbolized as earth), to stick together and have shape (symbolized as water), to have the possibility of movement (symbolized as air), and to be measured in terms of radiant energy such as heat or light (symbolized as fire). What things fundamentally "are," we don't know: thousands of years of more refined and complex definitions in terms of elements, atoms, particles, subatomic particles, and quarks has created a richer classification, but it is no nearer to absolute truth. And for most people, these scientific definitions are mind-boggling; they are not accessible in terms of direct experience. Earth, water, air, and fire are, however, a simple, accessible way of classifying the experience of form. And for the sake of proper relationships in the world, they are adequate. As always, the Buddha used systems and conceptual truth only for the purpose of directing the mind toward truth—the experience of nibbāna, enlightenment. And in terms of the practice of liberation, the work we need to do is on calming and seeing through the forces that blind and create a bound-up "self." For this purpose, coming to some manageable definitions of the experienced world is all that is necessary.

We experience things in terms of mental or physical feeling, *vedanā,* which may be painful, pleasant, or neutral based on physical or mental experience. *Vedanā* is no more specific than this. As with form, there are many further ways in which I can describe feeling, but this classification gives a simple way of understanding how things affect us. In the process of cognition, first of all there is a feeling, which attracts attention, and then a perception arises.

Perception, *saññā,* means the way in which we recognize something: as dark, light, hostile, familiar, human, inanimate . . . whatever. The Buddha's analysis points out that things are *interpreted* swiftly, and it is on this interpretation that mental impulses, attitudes, and activities (*sankhāra*) are founded.

Sankhāra are the "action-stations"; they are programs that we develop as we learn to interpret what things mean to us. They are therefore headed by volition—the push that jumps into our mind. Fashion, cosmetics, advertisements, and propaganda are notable examples of how perceptions are created and how effectively they trigger our mental activities. Here are some examples of how perception triggers mental activity: we mistrust some people because of the way they move; we detest "creepy" spiders; we adore "cuddly," furry cats; we buy a soft drink because of the shape of the bottle or because we saw a commercial with some good-looking people drinking it on a beach. The mental activity of detesting etc. may then turn into physical action—we go and pet the cat, buy the drink, or uh-oh . . . good-bye spider.

Consciousness, or *viññāna,* is that which makes phenomena present for us. It is sixfold—it comprises eye consciousness, ear consciousness, olfactory, taste, touch, and mind consciousnesses. The phenomena that arise that are dependent on mind consciousness (that is, thoughts, emotions, perceptions). It's why we call mental consciousness, the "inner" world, and call things arising because of the other five "physical" aspects of sense consciousness the "external" world. However, in the Buddha's analysis, this division is not so absolute. In fact, in his teaching, he often makes a point of overriding this apparent division by referring to "any feeling, mental or physical" or "contemplating things internally and externally." This is because his teaching does not discriminate between what appears as mind and what appears as matter; it comes from understanding the experience of all things—and that understanding occurs within the matrix of the six-fold sense-consciousness and its designations:

> That in the world by which one is a perceiver of the world, a conceiver of the world—that is called "world" in the Noble One's discipline. And what, friends, is that in the world by which one is a perceiver of the world, a conceiver of the world? The eye . . . ear . . . nose . . . tongue . . . body . . . mind.
> (SN 35: Sense Bases 116)

How the Aggregates Are Affected by Clinging

These five aggregates are described as "aggregates affected by clinging." They are categories, which when grasped at, when held as "me and my world," are suffering (dukkha). They are also seen as equivalent to birth, aging, and death—and yet they are taken on as the fundamental reality of our life. This "taking on" is called grasping or clinging—it's a strong blind reflex. Clinging is a vivid metaphor for what we otherwise term "attachment"; it means that something is held as permanent or absolute that is actually not that way. When you're attached to cigarettes, for example, cigarettes become an absolute necessity in life. You always have to have a pack with you. However, in reality, cigarettes are not necessary. So in the case of the aggregates, why or how is there the attachment that makes them unsatisfactory?

For a lifetime, at least, we are endowed with aspects of sense consciousness, perceptions, and mental formations. They certainly appear to be a real foundation for what we are. Is the Buddha implying that we shouldn't experience these, that as long as these aggregates are manifesting, we will suffer? Well, no. The Buddha points out that *holding on* to these is suffering. In other words, grasping, believing in, and being activated by thoughts and perceptions that arise in our mind—or clinging to, believing, and acting on the assumption that the sensory appearance of the world is lasting and solid—will always take us to dissatisfaction, and even to despair. Thoughts and perceptions are notoriously unreliable. People can believe in the craziest ideas and assumptions about the nature of the world, life after death, men, women, and God—not to mention their continually biased perceptions about ordinary daily life.

Moreover even the most innocuous thoughts and perceptions, when attached to, give rise to the experience of being separate from the world; an "inner being" is inferred who thinks and feels and perceives. Our opinions and attitudes give us a way of relating to an experience that they also separate us from. Based on that curious relationship, "self" arises. However, can your thoughts and perceptions be separate from the world that stimulates them? And don't they require the hardwiring of a physical nervous system to carry them? So our sense of self is neither autonomous from, nor commensurate with, the experience it depends on. It's bound in the world, and yet feels like it's hanging out and looking at the world. In this half-in, half-out state of not being able to really find a fitting place, nor being completely separate, our apparent self is rather like a hernia in the cosmos. No wonder it feels uncomfortable. No wonder it grumbles so much.

Yet is that almost incessant babble of thoughts, or the ups and downs of the emotions your true nature? We worry about them, defend them, and will motivate our lives around them. Why? Well, until we realize the deathless—an enigmatic yet repeated reference that the Buddha made to a Beyond or "Further Shore"—there's no other option. Our whole sense of personal existence is based upon clinging to these five aggregates as the home base, our inner being, our self. Although this "being" can never be located, and it is really just a shadow mood created by attachment to the khandha, or aggregates, it is held to be the author of thoughts and feelings, the owner and senior incumbent within the body, the director and controller of the senses. Once an identity gets created around the aggregates, we expect fulfillment from them. We instinctively assume that we will find fulfillment in our own body; or in feelings that are pleasing, stimulating, or soothing; or in great views and ideas; or out of some combination of all these as they manifest in sense consciousness. And although we always fail to find this fulfillment, we feel that this is just a temporary snag in the system, just an unlucky break—or that it is our fault. We feel there is something wrong with us if we are not fulfilled in the sensory world because we believe that we should be. At the same time, we're neither completely in that world, nor apart from it: how can that be satisfying? As long as we don't comprehend dukkha, the "wrongness" is the track we're on. Now when the social pressure is that I need to succeed, I need to get it right, dukkha is commonly grasped as "there's something wrong with me. I failed." In the West, this sense of social shame (I didn't *do* as well as I should have) gets transferred into generalized guilt (I *am* not good). So this need to be perfect conditions a need to fix the natural dukkha, forms judgments about not *doing* good enough and therefore about not *being* good enough. This assessment structures how I sense I am. This self-structuring, which is dependent on clinging, is called becoming. Becoming makes this inadequate self-view the governor of our life.

Thereby, we can fall into the two extremes of, on the one hand, naive optimism (I'll get a lucky break in the end) or, on the other, despairing pessimism (I'm a born loser). In either of those cases, we lose access to good kamma, which is based on the understanding that regardless of whoever and wherever we sense ourselves as being, we can do something good in this moment. If we lose touch with action—and mental action is the most important—we drift between blaming others and asserting ourselves, blaming the society and defending ourselves, or blaming ourselves and worshipping others. We may feel that somehow we have to get ourselves out of this predicament, but when we are the predicament, how do we get out? This endless going-on, this saṃsāra, is holding the five aggregates as self. This self-view is suffering; check it out for yourself.

Then consider when you see a newborn baby, who is born? Is it a man, a woman, a kind, sensitive soul, a burden on the earth's resources, an element of the divine, another mouth to feed, or what? And when someone dies? Who is that? And in between that, is it your friend, your peer, someone you yearn for, someone who disgusts you, or nobody special? Something is there, but all that we designate as the being (whether it is ourselves or someone else) is the arising and ceasing of these five aggregates, affected by birth, aging, and death. And it's also affected by the attitudes of the society (which hasn't gotten past suffering and clinging, either).

Think of the twin experiences of suffering and clinging as affecting both our outlook and our actions of body, speech, and mind. What if we didn't hold on to all that? This is not to reject the experience of the aggregates, but to respond to them, to calm, steady, and heal them rather than hang a self onto how they're manifesting at any given time. This "nonclinging" is possible. This is what the Buddha realized and tried to exemplify and explain when he taught about the five aggregates. He taught us to see the aggregates as they are, as dynamic processes, rather than to see self in the processes of birth, aging, and death. And with that clarity there is the end of all sorrow and a realization beyond clinging to ideas and dogmas. Whoever understands where and what dukkha really is, is on the path to that realization.

4

THE SECOND NOBLE
TRUTH

Craving

"Bhikkhus, there is a noble truth concerning the arising of suffering: it arises with craving, a thirst for more that's bound up with relish and passion and is always running here and there. That is: thirst for sense-input, thirst to be something, thirst to not be something."

Do you ever witness how you suffer? Generally there's someone or something you can blame, but put that aside, and just consider that blur and sense of sliding into, or being dumped into, a place where you feel unstable, attacked, rejected, or inadequate. Regardless of what triggered dukkha, try to recall and focus on the process of launching into suffering. There's a propellant, isn't there? And without that, would the insult, the pain, the being let down, and so forth, take you into full-blown dukkha? Being here in this world, it's not possible to be free from abuse, disease, and mishaps, but that trigger, that launch program that engages us in it, is the piece that we can address. And this is the piece that the Buddha calls the origin or the rising up of dukkha. It's the second noble truth, the launchpad of suffering.

Whatever the trigger, being launched, being propelled, is due to a mechanism in our own consciousness. It's called volition or intention (*cetana*), the "action-stations" program in our mind. Regardless of whether or not we are aware of it, everything we do is headed by volition. Quite a lot of volition is reactive or not clearly and consciously motivated. And the volition that launches us into suffering isn't clearly seen at all, obviously. Who would choose to suffer? Something has grabbed the wheel of our vehicle, something that we don't see clearly. It's another force in the shadows of our mind. It's how come we get captured by addictions that we know don't do us any good—our clarity isn't always in the driver's seat. Instead there's another volitional force. The Buddha called it craving.

So let's explore this second noble truth, the truth about the rising up of dukkha, by discussing craving or thirst, *taṇhā*. Sometimes *taṇhā* is translated as "desire," but that gives rise to some crucial misinterpretations with reference to the way of Liberation. As we shall see, some form of desire is essential in order to aspire to, and persist in, cultivating the path out of dukkha. Desire as an eagerness to offer, to commit, to apply oneself to meditation, is called *chanda*. It's a psychological "yes," a choice, not a pathology. In fact, you could summarize Dhamma training as the transformation of taṇhā into chanda. It's a process whereby we guide volition, grab and hold on to the steering wheel, and travel with clarity toward our deeper well-being. So we're not trying to get rid of desire (which would take another kind of desire, wouldn't it). Instead, we are trying to transmute it, take it out of the shadow of gratification and need, and use its aspiration and vigor to bring us into light and clarity.

However, *taṇhā,* meaning "thirst," is not a chosen kind of desire, it's a reflex. It's the desire to pull something in and feed on it, the desire that's never satisfied because it just shifts from one sense base to another, from one emotional need to the next, from one sense of achievement to another goal. It's the desire that comes from a black hole of need, however small and manageable that need is. The Buddha said that regardless of its specific topics, this thirst relates to three channels: sense-craving (*kāmataṇhā*); craving to be something, to unite with an experience (*bhavataṇhā*); and craving to be nothing, or to dissociate from an experience (*vibhavataṇhā*).

Sense-Craving

The first channel, though difficult to shift, is easy enough to understand. The Buddha defined sense-craving as:

> Craving for forms, craving for sounds, . . . odours, . . . tastes, . . . tactile objects, . . . mental phenomena. This is called craving.
> (SN 12: Causation 2)

If you abstain from any specific sense-input for a few hours, you'll probably experience the itch and hankering of this "thirst." It's a part of what motivates our day, isn't it? But when you look at it, this form of desire puts us in a pretty dependent and needy position because all those sensory things pass and are subject to a supply that we can't always rely on. And because the fulfillment that sensory input provides doesn't last, it's a supply that gets exceeded by demand. In fact the more you get used to sense-gratification, the more you depend on it, and the more you want it—it's addictive. But does the pursuit of happiness have to go down that track? With skillful management of desire and volition, we can generate other forms of happiness—the most obvious being kindness and compassion, but also including the happiness of calm in meditation. In the latter case, the reminder is—don't let your aspiration turn into thirst! Hankering after blissful mind-states is a sure way to get suffering rather than calm.

The other forms of craving (*bhava-* and *vibhava-*) deal more with the structure of our reality, our sense of self and its relationship with the world around it. This is the reality that our life seems to be embedded in, a reality that the first noble truth says is inherently unsatisfactory. And yes, life experienced in this way is bound up with difficulties, pain, sickness, and death. However, the Buddha's insight was that *this very reality itself is the result of craving*. It's not an enduring ultimate truth, it's a relative experience that we're subject to as long as we don't cast off the unconscious reflex-craving that establishes it. Now this may seem hard to accept, so we'll look at particular pieces of that unconscious structure. And we'll enter the shadow through the door that the Buddha points to in this second truth: that craving has an origin; it rises up.

Craving to Be

Craving to be something is not a decision, it's a reflex. Every sane person wants to be happy rather than unhappy; to be loved and liked rather than disliked and rejected. There's a natural enough inclination to be always happy, be seen in a positive light, and live in a balanced and cooperative world. However as "the world" in terms of the sociopolitical and economic spheres isn't balanced or co-operative—there's dissonance. As long as we attach to that world, the dissonance is felt and experienced as "things are going wrong" and that sense internalizes dukkha as suffering. Yet life is always "going wrong"—it always has been, and so we can surmise that it probably always will be. (Not that we shouldn't do anything about this situation.) But right now let's again refer to the launchpad that throws us into frustration, despair, rage, cynicism, and suffering. Isn't that dependent on the blind expectation for things to be another way? That unconscious craving brings up frustration, demands, and even violence. And those negative responses glue us to the things that disappoint us, and become part of our holistic world. Our reality is then based on the felt experiences of need, expectation, and disappointment and on the strategies we create around them.

People can spend half their life still belonging to the past, unable to free themselves from grudges and sorrows. Those moods affect how they are now, and how they respond to their present life. Their world is a result of carrying, or being dependent on, the past. So the result of craving to be solid and ongoing, to be a being that has a past and a future, together with the current wish to resolve the past and future, are combined to establish each individual's present world as complex and unsteady. This thirst to be something keeps us reaching out for what isn't here. And so we lose the inner balance that allows us to discern a here-and-now fulfillment in ourselves.

When our world isn't internally bound by shadow-fears, hunger, and clinging, our true potential becomes available and we experience a sense of groundedness and balance. In this firm balance, the need to have and be doesn't take hold so the pathology of thirst abates, and, instead, we experience aspiration and compassion. Accordingly, there is a transmutation of thirst into the wish to help, to be forgiving and compassionate, and to bring forth strengths to meet a situation. Where there is this inner strength, people can go into war-torn areas, and into places of deprivation and despair with the desire to offer themselves in service—and experience great love and joy. So the state of mind we experience isn't dependent on external conditions. A compassionate mind, a heart of warmth and strength, can arise in miserable circumstances when we have found that inner balance. It turns our world around.

On the other hand, what really crushes our spirit and makes our world dark is the sense of being trapped and powerless, and having no choice. So cultivating the way depends on remembering there is a choice, and making the right one. That way we can find balance, we can be with the process of emotion and thoughts and other people's actions as they are, and we can let go of being someone in that, or out of that. That's a choice we have. It's a practice that isn't confined to being in a meditation hall: many prisoners of conscience (like Nelson Mandela) find a way to let go without any formal training. If there is a sense of self-respect, a spirit that isn't bound by circumstance, then we have a basis to not grow bitter, and to survive. The world of suffering changes into a place that brings forth goodness when we can consciously relate to it, rather than identify with the circumstances we are thrown into. And we can do that, can't we? We don't have to drink the water we're swimming through. We don't have to *become* the world.

Craving Not to Be

There is also the craving to not experience the world, and to be nothing. This type of craving seems like the logical next step following the previous type of craving. But not becoming the world is different from becoming someone who doesn't relate to the world. Wanting to not be makes a problem out of existence. "I don't want to have to be here. I don't want to feel pain, I don't want to have to take responsibility, I don't like myself, other people are a pain, I want to not exist"—that's the *vibhavataṇhā* fairy speaking. And when she waves her wand, life is unfair, pointless, and miserable. Sometimes don't you wish life's hassles would stop? But the only thing that has to stop is the craving. That often takes skillful desire, the motivated effort to stop craving. Then with that skillful desire, we can rise up; we can meet challenges with the willingness to learn, to be strengthened; and we can grow more compassionate and serene.

We don't often do this because clarity isn't always in the driver's seat. The driver is blind. So we need to go into the affective, reactive, and impulsive areas of our mind to where this craving reflex arises. It's a reflex that hijacks our volitional energies. This is why the Buddha encouraged us to clearly understand the origin of our suffering, at that place we can check the hijacker.

Suffering arises, it has an origin. We can recognize that the feeling of emotional dissatisfaction begins; we were feeling pretty good, and then—we got offended, or the good time came to an end. After a little while, we feel upset, or we hanker after some new way of enjoying ourselves. The fact that the arising of suffering can be noticed means that it arises from something other than suffering, and that there is something other than suffering that notices it. Whatever arises has a cause, is created. Simply to recognize that suffering arises is the beginning of opening our mind to a deeper understanding.

If we neither contemplate suffering nor wish to understand it, suffering is not so noticeable. So one reflex is to keep shifting away from dukkha, to absorb into something else. This is the samsāra habit I mentioned earlier. But what that causes is an underlying sense of dis-ease and denial or fear of life's downside. This can amount to a blind "get it while you can!" syndrome, in which a natural state of joy or contentment is considered impossible, and happiness is dependent on having our security, our creature comforts, and our friends close by. At other times we ease the chafing of life by shrugging it off. Also we unconsciously assume that calamities won't occur—that our partner won't get run down by a truck or that our child won't be struck by disease. Most incredible of all, something in us is shocked by death: we still *feel* that sickness, death, betrayals, breakdowns, and failures are an outrageous deviation from the smooth flow of life. This is what the Buddha called unknowing, or *avijjā*—the heart's contraction to a level where the range of birth's potential is difficult to accept. During a lifetime of many small disappointments, betrayals, threats, and the rest, we develop a tough skin over our sensitivity, and a feeling that happiness is something we have to seek out. Eventually, there is so much hide protecting the heart that the innate joy of being alive becomes inaccessible. Although this unknowing is a buffer that the psyche uses to protect itself from suffering, it actually drives the dukkha deeper into our heart, affecting our ability to be open and easeful with life. In this way, unknowing and craving create what we consider reality to be.

It's a trap that we don't *have* to create for ourselves. There is another reality that the Buddha realized. With craving and unknowing abolished, he found happiness in the purity of his heart, and he called that purity "the Unconditioned." It is unconditioned because it is not dependent on circumstances, and one who realizes that, experiences nibbāna. It's a place where volition rests. There's no one in the driver's seat and no more journeys.

For the average person, however, happiness is dependent on making it happen. We keep doing things for as long as we can in order to alleviate or not face stress. But the avoidance of suffering is not the cessation of suffering; dukkha remains as a distinct potential. Even the attempt to stay free of dukkha is a kind of stress—the stress of defensiveness and the anxiety that someone might rob or attack us or that some insidious virus might be gnawing its way through our immune system. The average Westerner living with material adequacy is still always prone to anxiety because there's the possibility of losing our partner, our job, our health, our standing in the community, our dignity, or sense of well-being. No one whose happiness is dependent on a fragile tissue of circumstance can afford to relax and be at ease. Societies where people have a lot of opportunities and possibilities for pleasure are generally frantic, anxious, or neurotic. And if we only depend on fortunate conditions for happiness then we become quite selfish and deluded, refusing to accept that there might have to be some limitation to our good fortune. The right to pursue our own happiness can get distorted into the right to do whatever turns us on, no matter what the effects might be on others. It gets distorted, for example, into feeling that we have the right to use as much of the earth's resources as we'd like, to have whatever we want immediately, and to live a life of ever-renewing pleasure and vitality. This happens in the same way that, for an alcoholic, the gratification of desire only leads to more and more need, not to its elimination.

When there is an inability to relate and respond wisely to the downside of life, or even to accept that it might exist, we take dukkha deep into ourselves and bury it there—where it is difficult to extract. From not living in accordance with the changing rhythm of life, from expecting it always to be bright and positive, we create a specter that haunts the heart and affects the ways we view and live our life. We make dukkha an ultimate truth that we run away from by taking for granted and absorbing ourselves into the upside of the sensory world. We get drawn into the many things there are to watch or taste, and our mind especially offers a vast potential for sensory enjoyment. Although many people would hardly consider the quest for mental stimulation to be a sensory activity, in the Buddhist analysis it is; we delight in intriguing ideas or in being aroused by tales of stirring adventure. Then again, we can alter our consciousness completely with drugs. So the sensory world stimulates us to get propelled into many states— either by blind volition or conscious intention, all of which are accompanied by feelings, so it feels "real." This is the conditioned reality of births—we experience "being born" into the sensory realm. And since we do it over and over again, no birth satisfies us for very long.

Penetrating Craving

Let's go through the basis of craving to be and to not be again with more detail. First we have *bhava,* becoming. We try to become something in order to feel that we are making progress. This is *bhavataṇhā,* the craving for "becoming" or "existence," as it is also translated. It means the desire for some "position" in the temporal or spatial world that consciousness projects. We "feel" that we are an immaterial entity, either regarding experience, affected by it, even imperiled by it. And this felt self seeks to become in control of, or able to understand and direct, the life experience: we do things now so that we can "be" in a better situation in the future. We study in order to qualify for a good job, to have a stable family life, or to have love and security and an adequate supply of sensory happiness. This all sounds reasonable enough; but it often entails overriding the experience of the present. People work themselves hard and become very stressed chasing the dream of ease in the future. Yet all the time that immaterial felt self can never be solid—how could it? And the amount of stress that the self undergoes in order to achieve its unachievable goals makes it necessary to raise the expectations of the great things that the future will provide.

People also lie and cheat to get ahead, and after years of cheating and manipulating others, feel disappointed that life still doesn't live up to their expectations. How can it? There are the laws of cause and effect at work, and they operate according to the state of their intentions and actions. The way a person acts in the present determines how they're going to feel and the kind of situations they'll tend to find themselves with in the future. If someone is an aggressive, unscrupulous go-getter, they develop a sense of wanting more, and associate with the kind of people who fit into that way of operating. Naturally all this will reinforce the drive to get something in the future and be greedy in the present. So that's the effect—people become how they act. That is how it is—we are a "how" rather than a "who": a play feelings and states that are never solid.

The process of becoming operates on many levels—it doesn't necessarily have to manifest as big-business competitiveness or a pathological longing for security. Wanting to be projects values and wishes onto everything. Notice that often when we are doing a mundane chore, for instance, that our attitude is frequently one of wanting to get it done, wanting to have finished it in order to *be* peaceful, to relax, or to enjoy ourselves. . . . We want to be a feeling. Rushing along to be something in the next moment, we fail to open and appreciate this moment—that, too, is craving to be, and that too is dukkha. The laws of kamma indicate that if you operate in that way in this moment, the same momentum takes you through the next moment, coloring your awareness of the present with its moods and perceptions. You want to go to a show, so you hastily take a shower, change your clothes, abruptly cut off a friend who just phoned, leap into the car, find out that you left the keys in your other jacket, rush back to the house, trip over the dog in the hallway ... the scenario proceeds to the traffic jam, the lost temper, and then finding out that the show has been canceled anyway—which was what your friend was phoning you up to tell you. Just notice: a mind filled with craving does not appreciate anything.

When we get tired of running around and tired of sensory stimulation, then the craving to be nothing, to not be here, manifests. These terms are not to be taken as absolutes. They apply to mind movements that may be momentary or only vaguely perceived. *Vibhavataṇhā* is the itch to get rid of something, to get out of it all. This is often a repressive influence, or simply an attitude of not wanting to be bothered: "I don't want to see this." It is also that force in us that denies our pain and sorrow or makes us want to annihilate ourselves in sleep, drugs, or with suicide. It often results from the other two forms of thirst: if sense-craving and the craving to be are followed blindly, they leave us in states of mind that we dislike and therefore avoid being aware of. So we try to annihilate that awareness, even if it means destroying ourselves. What people don't realize is that *vibhavataṇhā* leads to birth too; birth in a negative state of repression or self-denial in this world—or in another life. To summarize, the craving to not be hinders purification of our mind by making us unwilling to be with, attend to, and hence fully understand, the various unenlightened habits that we have to work through.

Our mind moves extremely fast, and craving creates so much movement that it is difficult to see what is really going on. Sometimes desires augment each other: you want to become something so that you will have more happiness on the sensory plane; you want to get rid of your habits so that you will become a more productive human being; you would like to have a really comfortable meditation cushion so that you can become a wiser, more compassionate being. Sometimes they fight with each other:

I want to get rid of my disgusting sensual appetites, or maybe I should get into beer and TV to get rid of my attachment to purity and show that I'm not obsessed with becoming enlightened. And so on . . . *I want.* That's how we promote the sense of need, the feeling of impoverishment, and needless suffering.

Notice that the Buddha makes no moral judgment here. He does not tell us not to be this way or to cut it out; in fact, he doesn't say we even *are* that way. He just says that there are these energies at work. Remember, the first noble truth points to the suffering that arises from trying to encompass existence in terms of self. (It's like a hernia trying to heal the body.) As soon as we start saying we are this way, and we should be another way, self-desire has slipped into our mind and has pushed us out of balance. So the language of the Buddha's teachings is deliberately impersonal. This way, we don't get ashamed or defensive, and we are encouraged to calm our heart, to steady it and slow its movements. This calming takes the edge off of the thirst of taṇhā and is one of the essential aims of meditation. Based on that, we have a greater possibility to investigate the way things are in a more open and objective light. True enough, the particular quality or feeling of the way things are at any present moment may be nothing special. However, if we cultivate attention to what is arising in the present, in whatever form the present moment takes, our mind begins to reveal its own buried treasures: sensitivity, confidence, and serenity. In other words we establish a thirst-free relationship to the senses. And that gives us both poise and understanding.

5

LOOKING AGAIN AT THE SECOND NOBLE TRUTH

The Blind Driver

———

"Bhikkhus, there is a noble truth concerning the arising of suffering."

———

Let's look into this again—there's more to the origin of suffering. Certainly craving causes us to suffer, but that's really just part of it. The rest is due to ignorance—well, due to ignorance and about eleven other factors. What this means is that if we were really clear, this confused thirst wouldn't take over. To clarify this point, the Buddha gave a teaching on the twelve factors that support the arising of suffering called dependent origination. This teaching shows us in detail how suffering gets created and perpetuated—and also offers pointers on where and how it can cease.

Dependent Origination

Dependent origination is a profound teaching on how consciousness operates. It presents a series of twelve linked factors that shape and drive the heart, and thereby push us "unconsciously" into suffering. With the aid of this analysis, we can become conscious of this process and break the links in the sequence. It's almost like cutting an electrical circuit. Anywhere we break it will cut the current and bring about release. The terms and connections may seem baffling at first sight so I have drawn up a table for reference, and then I'll go on to explain it in more depth.

Table of Dependent Origination

PĀLI	ENGLISH	EXPLANATION
avijjā	ignorance, unknowing	not understanding the full meaning and implication of the four noble truths
sankhāra	kamma-productive mental tendencies or "activities"	habitual activities of mind that are aligned to self-view
viññāṇa	discriminative awareness or consciousness	the activity of the six senses, acting in a dualistic way, defining the subject as distinct from the object
nāma-rūpa	name-and-form	feeling, perception, contact, volition, attention, and their objects

salāyatana	the six senses	eye, ear, nose, tongue, body, and mind
phassa	contact, impression	the mental impression of a thing, which arises dependent on feeling and perception
vedanā	feeling	painful, pleasant, neutral bodily or mental experiences
taṇhā	craving, thirst	instinctive desire—to have, to attain, to get away from experiences
upādāna	grasping, clinging	leaning or feeding on sensual or mental experiences
bhava	becoming	solidifying awareness into a fixed state of mind, one that seeks permanence
jāti	birth	the experience of being a separate entity in a temporal context
jarāmārāṇam soka-parideva dukkha domanassupāyasa	aging, death, sorrow, lamentation, pain, grief, and despair	the sense of ego-loss, through physical death or the breaking up of the psychological foundations of self

The current that propels the mind into suffering is made of two inter-connected forces: ignorance and craving. In dependent origination, these forces act as the necessary conditions that support each of the twelve factors. However, the connection between the factors is not one of an inevitable causal sequence. For example, water is a condition for ice, but by itself doesn't *cause* ice—that also depends on temperature. Then again having ears is one condition for enjoying Bach fugues, but it's not inevitable that having ears will bring a Bach fugue into your mind. In a similar way, the conditionality of dependent origination carries the *potential* for dukkha or its cessation. The essential point in this notion is that not all of these conditions in the sequence are inevitable; they can be changed, or not given a basis for arising, and will thereby bring around a release from suffering.

Ignorance

The sequence of dependent origination begins with the condition of unknowing or ignorance (*avijjā*), which in Buddhist iconography is depicted as either a blind man or someone wearing a blindfold. This is the driver of the bus to dukkha. If you have to choose the one determining factor for suffering, it's this ignorance. People tend to take "ignorance" as pejorative, but it more precisely refers to a lack of gnosis or insightful seeing. It is summarized as "not understanding the four noble truths"—or, perhaps more accurately, not understanding their implications. That is, as long as there is the condition of ignorance, the mind still expects to find an experience that is completely satisfying and feels disappointed when things "go wrong." There is a parable of a man eating a bag of chili peppers one by one, weeping at their fiery taste as he does so. When asked why he continues to eat the peppers, he replies, "I'm looking for the sweet one." This is ignorance.

The Buddha said that it is impossible to find the origins of ignorance. However, with experience, we can see that ignorance is increased by willfully ignoring the way life is and substituting wishful fantasies, based on the viewpoint of a self imagined to exist within the five aggregates. So the current of craving is switched on by ignorance. The principle of dependent origination is that this view—its origins and results—can be seen as dependent on many linked factors, all with ignorance as their foundation. The sequence of dependent origination works in two directions: when ignorance arises and we act on that, suffering follows; when ignorance ends, so does craving and every kind of inner pain, shadow, and stress. In the analysis then, we look out for where we can break the linking of ignorance and craving. The uplifting aspect of understanding dependent origination is that it brings the ending of dukkha down to one practice—that of replacing ignorance with wisdom.

Ignorance is a mental *inclination* of ignoring; it's not just a passive quality, although it may occur through a programmed impulse rather than as a clearly conscious choice. If it were not something that we were inclined toward, there would be no way of stopping it. However, a lot of the time we are not conscious of ignorance (one thing about ignorance is that we are often ignorant of it!). Reactions appear to happen automatically, without the awareness of where the motivation lies. So the general encouragement is for us to develop awareness to the point of knowing our mind, so we can check and even uproot the automatic and reflex operations that create the suffering of our world.

The inclination to not notice, to ignore, arises dependent on dukkha, or more exactly on the unconscious craving to have a fixed position, or to be filled by sights, sounds, mind-states, or feelings. We want to be solid and we don't want to have to change our momentum or appetites. We don't want to know about things not fitting in with our wishes, although there's no reason to assume that life should or could ever be the way we'd like it to be. So ignorance affects our perceptions—the way we "see" things. If we're honest, we may notice prejudices, errors of judgment, definite biases toward seeing things "my way." Also ignorance distracts—then there's craving again: what we don't *want* to know about is ignored. Our mind may filter out flaws in a loved one's behavior, for example. Sometimes it is more conscious. They say the captain of the Titanic was informed of icebergs floating in the sea in front of his ship, yet he chose to ignore the warning and went straight into them with the resultant death of many people on board. Notice that there was an element of choice in this tragic "accident."

Many accidents are caused by people not being attentive, thinking about something else with a chain saw in their hand, doing things automatically; and that inattention is due to our mind wanting to be somewhere else. Sometimes ignorance is deliberate and willful; sometimes it could be prevented by being more attentive; sometimes it's ingrained in the ways we perceive things and requires insight and the courage to undergo personal change to remedy. However, ignorance is always activated by some element of conscious or unconscious desire. Therefore ignorance and craving form the central current that conditions this sequence.

Activities and Programs

As long as there is ignorance, actions tend to become automatic, compulsive, idiosyncratic, related to "my way of seeing things" rather than to the needs of a situation. So ignorance colors our consciousness with programs, or habitual drives that orient around self. These habitual drives, or programs, are called *sankhāra*. Just like any computer program, sankhāra can be active or latent. And in much the same way, they sit in our "hard drive" as potentials for action. They are energies that carry the codes of action (kamma), and which generate activities of body, speech, or mind. When they are active, they support thoughts and emotions and bodily reflexes; having done so in accordance with love or fear or determination, they are then stored as latent programs ready to fire off again. So sankhāra are headed by volition, the impulse to do. We're always creating. When we speak, we create words and concepts. And the result is we create ourselves in our own or another person's mind, and so it is with our actions.

Ignorance conditions these habitual programs and makes them into "activities" of a self. (I want to do whatever I want.) When there is ignorance, they also form a self out of our gifts or shortcomings. We expect results, we expect progress for ourselves or for others we have identified with. We defend and justify our actions or assign to them a significance that they may not have. Alternatively, we may be highly self-critical. This "self-view" is another habitual program, a sankhāra that means we fail to realistically sense the true worth or effect of actions and thoughts. The bias of self exaggerates our actions in terms of good or bad. It also obscures awareness of the motivation behind our actions or the conditioned and changing nature of the energies and perceptions that feed them. With ignorance, we keep leaving thumbprints on our experience: action becomes habitual activity and starts to form our identity.

Do you find that your life has repeating patterns in it, similar scenarios with different people involved? We seem to go through the same emotional cycles around different events, and we have recurring patterns of thought—the same memories, the same habits—so we think, "That's the way I am." Habitual activities, even thoughts in our mind, are elements that forge and shape our kamma, and hence our apparent self. Any identity, good or bad, is subject to stress, frustration, sorrow, and death; if the kamma is unskillful, there are a lot more problems along the way, such as inwardly having feelings of guilt and fear and even eliciting the hostility of others to prove that we're bad. Alternatively, we may perform in ways to cover up or redress previous actions, again acting from self-view. Thus more kamma is established, strengthening the sense of identity, good or bad. This is the proliferating effect of sankhāra.

By generating skillful volition, we can create activities such as wise attention that give rise to understanding. Then we can understand motivation as coming from energies such as greed or love, rather than as coming from an existing self, and we are able to find the still point of reflection and pull out of the blindness. That freedom gives us the opportunity to act and speak in unbiased ways—in the way of Dhamma rather than of ignorance. We can turn our mind in another direction—we have choice. But we need to exercise that choice and direct our consciousness in order to stop the unconscious slide into suffering. To put it another way, the Buddha says:

> Bhikkhus, what one intends, and what one plans, and whatever one has a tendency toward: this becomes a basis for the maintenance of consciousness.
> (SN 12: Causation 38)

Sixfold Sense-Consciousness

Having cultivated skillful volitions, wholesome intention, we then have the support to use wise, insightful intention to penetrate and dismantle blind craving. This is the long-term process of contemplation that we'll return to throughout the book. It begins with supervising the sense consciousness (*viññāṇa*). The sense consciousness, based upon the six sense organs, is the agent through which mental formations manifest, though it is also shaped and directed by them. Dependent upon habits, reflexes, and viewpoints that have been created by action and experience in the past, our mind's consciousness jumps like a monkey through seeing, hearing, thinking, tasting, smelling, and touching— running around this way or that. Consciousness can also be defined in terms of how it is propelled.

Interest and attraction toward a sense object is consciousness rooted in greed. Generosity is consciousness rooted in nongreed. Aversion to a sense object is consciousness rooted in hatred. Nonaversion to a sense object is consciousness rooted in kindness or compassion. Mind-consciousness may experience a great deal of confused, wavering activities around its sense objects of thought and emotion. This is consciousness rooted in delusion. But when our intentions and mind-states are clear, this is consciousness rooted in nondelusion. So we can switch channels. Consciousness may be refined and present to varying qualities and degrees, from just above coma, to sleep, to wakefulness, caffeinated highs, alcoholic wooziness, and ecstasy. It can also be directed to the refined absorptive states arising through concentration. Obviously if we direct consciousness to greater clarity and well-being, this will be for our welfare. However, our mind's ability to direct consciousness gives us another reward.

Since consciousness can be directed, we can recognize that whatever comes into our mind—deliberately or not—is what we are aware of. Also we can acknowledge that consciousness only exists and is present in the moment that it passes through our mind. So consciousness is not an ultimate entity that has a past and a future outside of what is being experienced in the present. The nature of what we experience in the present moment—

what is seen, heard, smelled, tasted, touched, or thought—changes, and we can deliberately change it by looking elsewhere, or through changing our attitude. What this means is there is nothing solid, substantial, or essentially "me" or "mine" about consciousness or its objects. Consciousness arises dependent on sense-contact and inclinations, it is not an independent self. Yet no sense of self can be created apart from some object, some mind-state, attitude, or impulse. If we really get this point, there is liberation right here.

Name-and-Form

So how does consciousness happen? Consciousness always works in terms of name-and-form (*nāma-rūpa*). Something only has presence (that is, gets established as a conscious experience) because there is the sense of contact. Contact depends on something being contacted, like food contacting our tongue. From that contact with form (*rūpa*), all sorts of feelings, and perceptions (or impressions) arise. These form a heart-definition of what a thing "is": "Oh, yum, candy!" What it is, is actually what it is to *us*—we might present an Amazonian tribesman with a computer and he would see a box. So as feelings and impressions designate something, they—together with contact, volition, and attention—make up what's called name, or *nāma*. *Nāma,* therefore, is a composite of feeling, perception, contact, volition, and attention—the factors that pick up, define, locate, and react to the data of consciousness.

Our entire world is made up of name-and-form. Even "formlessness" is a designation of a kind of indefinite form. So the world of form only has presence for us because of consciousness, and how we perceive it is very much affected by the mind-states, attitudes, and feelings that we have. When an architect or a builder sees a house, a different set of perceptions arises than when a homeless person sees it, or a burglar, or an animal. In a way, we build our own world—and *our world builds us.* What we are conscious of molds and determines the perceptions and attitudes we have. If you were attacked by a dog when you were a child, you would probably have some difficulty perceiving dogs as loyal friends. So out of consciousness and name-and-form, the sense of self arises.

Six Sense-Bases

The thing that profoundly affects consciousness, with whose rhythms and energies we are very much engaged, is the body. The body is also made up of the nervous system, which is the physical base for consciousness. To be present in the sensory realm requires a functioning physical body, so consciousness both depends upon and directs physical form, and it is infused with attitudes, perceptions, and activities based on bodily survival.

So human consciousness is programmed by bodily life and this means having sense organs: eyes, ears, and the rest of it, including the mind. Body consciousness constantly registers the pain that is a warning of injury to the body, and it registers the pleasure that is a signal for the preservation and development of the body. Then mind-consciousness kicks in and makes a "me" out of the experience. When there's ignorance, consciousness remains fettered to this restless sensory realm, because of how it is felt as "me." "I" appear to be a mental consciousness within a physical form, trying to seek solutions or remedies to disagreeable experiences or to get as many agreeable experiences as possible. Even if "I" am trying to get out of the physical form into some ethereal realm, "I" am always designated in terms of bodily presence or absence because when ignorance is in the driver's seat, consciousness is programmed to a self-view. That is how we got born, remember?

Sense consciousness normally takes our mind toward objects or to thinking about what we can contact through the physical senses. However, in developing mindfulness, attention can be trained to look back into the mind, to focus on the intentions and reactions that govern conscious thought, speech, and action. When you see something, you are aware of the seeing, and you reflect, "How am I seeing that?" If you're thinking or feeling something, rather than just acting upon it impulsively, you reflect, "Hmm, how do I react to that?" So what we can discover is that there is this one factor—volition—that is the push of our habitual tendencies, the shaper of mind and the governor of intention. When we react or act from a reflexive or compulsive base, this volition is based on ignorance and it *drives* us into action. Therefore a key point is to become aware of the volition—the push of believing what we think, do, or say.

Who's driving this thing? To focus in this way is to notice what our attachments and compulsions are, and where our sense of identity is being created. It's a way to investigate who we are, beyond our fluctuating and often unsatisfactory self-image.

Contact

The sequence of dependent origination continues through contact (*phassa*)—the senses operate through contact. Apart from the physical necessity and usefulness of having contact, the inferred self needs a mental impression of that contact to maintain its presence—self always exists in contrast to otherness. But self's need or preference changes—and that changes the nature of contact. For example, sometimes we get bored with the same old tastes, sounds, sights, people; but then sometimes it's nice to be in the presence of the familiar, as with those loved ones. So are familiar people boring or reassuring? The crucial contact that defines them is the mental impression.

If you want to look into this, sit where it's quiet and close your eyes: the natural inclination to make contact will bring up mental images characterized by feelings. These will most likely be taken as aspects of yourself and you'll find various reactions occurring and will get very busy sitting still. However, the practice of sitting quietly with your eyes closed in meditation is useful in that, with steady attention, you can realize that all this mental stuff is something that can be watched, and that it is therefore a series of objects—not the subject, not self. You only experience contact because of feeling and perceiving something. And since what is felt or perceived must always be an object, how can you ever contact a true subject, or self? That understanding in itself takes some of the drama out of the show, and as the mind stops feeding on contact, it steps back into balance and quiets down.

Feeling

Contact links up to feeling (*vedanā*). And right there, in witnessing contact, we can choose to act or not. We can direct or terminate craving. Something strikes visual consciousness and a feeling arises that is either painful, pleasant, or neutral. It is said that the body only experiences painful and pleasant feeling; the eye, ear, nose, and tongue only experience neutral feeling; and the mind experiences all three. However, the mind will *interpret* neutrality as pleasant (calm) at some times and painful (tedious, dull) at other times. And in normal consciousness, people are dealing with mental feelings based on perceptions. For instance, people can derive pleasure from doing extremely stressful things to their bodies (like athletics, break dancing, and mountain climbing)! When taken to the extreme, this can be a real problem: the mind's values or perceptions (*saññā*) can get so distorted that we can actually derive mental pleasure from bragging, abusing, and fighting—even though these are abrasive and violent feelings in mind-consciousness. Powerful emotional pleasure may arise out of being attractive, even though attractiveness can be stressful in terms of cost, artifice, and competition—and it can be quite dangerous if you attract the wrong kind of person.... Then there are the feelings associated with winning, being excited, and so on. The pleasure is not due to our mind as a sense organ (which may even crack up under the strain) but to confused perceptions. The most consistent determinant for feeling is whatever sensation or perception makes "me" feel important, or powerful.

Craving

When there is ignorance or unknowing, we don't accurately assess what we are feeling. Much of the time we are in contact with our perceptions because they can create images in accordance with desire, and they can trigger such powerful volition that we become carried away. So this takes us to the next linked factor, craving—which is *taṇhā* in its fully conscious form. Feeling links to craving. We mainly perceive this as craving for something desirable. If what is felt through the senses is not desirable, or if it brings up aversion, the unawakened instinct then creates a fantasy that is attractive. One of the most bitter aspects of the unawakened life is that when you have enough physically, your mind creates fantasies to crave. Nowadays in Western culture, our normal reality is composed of fantasies vividly portrayed on television, in movies, novels, theater, and advertisements. The pervasive fantasies of mass media and popular culture may seem harmless enough, but the contact with them and the feelings they induce unconsciously affect our values. People end up voting for a fantasy, being governed by a fantasy, using fantasy money, having fantasy enemies, and chasing fantasy goals. The only real element left is suffering, but that is repressed or not acknowledged because it doesn't fit into the fantasy. In the brave new world, everybody's happy; ignore the rest.

Again, our mind can be developed in terms of calm and discernment in order to witness and cut the current of craving. This link between feeling and craving is the easiest to break because here the craving is conscious. So we can witness and understand that pull; it is something that we can watch in order to know its ethical quality. We can switch on the light of wisdom. We can act on skillful desires with clarity; we can respond to the signals of bodily need; and we can let go of desires that are born from greed, hatred, or delusion. Then we are operating from wisdom rather than ignorance, and we can turn the energy of desire toward investigating our mind and bringing goodness into our world.

Clinging

Craving to have—or to annihilate—links up to grasping or clinging (*upādāna*). Like volition, clinging is a function of natural bodily life— babies do it with good reason—but with ignorance it becomes a compulsive mental activity. And clinging to the wrong things is a frustrating, stressful, and dangerous experience: clinging to sensory experience with ignorance is always going to let us down, because there's no having enough, and all sensory experience is unreliable. It changes and ends. If we hang our life expectations on the sensory world, it will take us to despair; it's like climbing a mountain clinging to a fraying rope. Holding on in itself is not categorically without value. For instance, those who wish to awaken hold on to the teachings and the practices that lead to liberation. The actual problem with holding on is ignorance—clinging blindly. When there is no ignorance, we can hold on to things as physical necessities or hold on mentally to workable conventions, responsibilities, or commitments. However, a blanket "no holding on" statement is something that could be used to authorize opportunist shifts of loyalties and the dismissal of rules and precepts. Loyalty becomes clinging when it is based on self-view: *my* team, *my* country—no matter what. But when there is clear and steady discernment into nonself and nonownership, that basis drops away and clinging ceases.

Becoming and Birth

When there's ignorance, clinging acts as a base for becoming (*bhava*). Out of craving, we attach to some object and then see it as a way of development or fulfillment. However, there is a weariness in having to sustain the sense of development. You can liken becoming to the fate of Sisyphus, whose punishment in a Greek hell was that he had to roll a huge boulder up to the top of a mountain. It took him a long time to get this vast boulder up the slope and whenever he got close to the top, it would break loose and roll down to the bottom. Then he'd have to go down and roll it back up. That's becoming. It never quite gets there. Instead it leads to the eleventh factor, birth (*jāti*). But such a birth is not the promised birth of fulfillment—rather, it is the experience of oneself as someone who's not quite there yet.

One of the problems on the spiritual path that we walk on as unawakened aspirants is the sense of trying to *become* something. It's normal, because we have been doing that all the time with every pursuit that we have taken up. And the pursuit of ultimate well-being, of wisdom, enlightenment, or whatever, really engages our becoming instincts. We always feel that we are not yet right. If only we try a little harder, we might get the boulder to the top of the mountain. Try a *little* harder, and we'll get there. Where? Who's driving this thing?

And yet, as an energy and if skillfully handled, becoming can be an aspect of Dhamma—in the form of cultivation. We do "become" more attentive. Wise instruction teaches us about humility, patience, and the need to be with the present moment. So we practice becoming without the self-view. We practice developing generosity, kindness, and alertness. Wise "becoming" is called *bhāvanā,* which means causing skillful factors to come into existence. It's a cultivation of the path, not of self-view. If cultivation is always coming from self-views, we get caught up in the sense of failure, or the other kind of becoming—wanting not to become (*vibhāva*), wanting to annihilate our desires and weaknesses. When there is ignorance, the forces of becoming get us "born" as fanatics, starry-eyed devotees, or tight-lipped zealots.

And whatever we get born into deepens the kammic, self-producing tendencies. So when that birth ends—when we've given up on Buddhism and have become a Sufi, or we've given up Sufism and have taken to Gestalt—if we haven't cut the links of craving and ignorance, we're even more preoccupied with ourselves and our problems and our importance. So death in ignorance—that is, not waking up when your current "world," relationships, occupation, or body ends—takes you into the possibility for more dukkha.

Aging, Death, Sorrow, and the Rest

This naturally takes us to the twelfth factor of dependent origination: aging, death, sorrow, lamentation, pain, grief, and despair (*jarāmaraṇam sokaparidevadukkhadomanassupāyasa*), a list that offers a comprehensive, if stark, summary of the consequences of attachment to birth. Yet it's not that becoming, birth, and death are inevitably filled with suffering in their own right. Death can be freed from anxiety with the ending of the self-view. We can even use death as a meditation object. We can bring to mind the perception of death and consciously let go of the future and of what we think we belong to. This is a useful daily meditation to calm and clarify our mind. We can also witness the ending of any experience: there will be a moment when there's "not knowing"—a moment of space or emptiness. Normally the ignoring habit immediately starts up again and sends a mad monkey racing to initiate the sequence. The whole thing flashes by very quickly. But to let our mind notice and give its full attention to the ending of a sound, a thought, a mood . . . is an opportunity to recognize a state of being that is both empty and yet vibrantly present. The ending of things offers a peek into the truth of cessation.

The analysis in terms of dependent origination shows us that the origin of this suffering process is compounded out of craving and ignorance. There's a blind driver with his foot on the gas pedal. And the remedy that the Buddha points out begins right here, in the *knowing*. In the context of the second noble truth, we are knowing craving—not craving to know. Cessation is not destruction or annihilation of any actual "thing"; it is the "arrest" of an activity so that it is seen clearly and ignorance does not condition volition into kamma-forming and identity-forming activities of body, speech, and mind. This takes some doing as we will see. However, the promise is that thoughts, feelings, desires, attachments, and suffering can be held in that knowing until they are, as the Buddha said,

Headed by mindfulness, surmounted by wisdom, have deliverance as essence, merge in the Deathless, and terminate in Nibbāna.
(AN 10: 107)

6

THE THIRD NOBLE TRUTH

Switching Off the Dark

"Bhikkhus, there is a noble truth about the cessation of suffering. It is the complete fading away and cessation of this craving; its abandonment and relinquishment; getting free from and being independent of it."

Having highlighted the origin of suffering, the Buddha goes on to speak about its cessation. The Buddha taught by describing how to put his teachings into practice, about skillful action that leads to the end of the unskillful action that is based on blind craving. In other words, he taught about kamma affected by wisdom rather than ignorance. His description of the results was much more sparing, at least in the Pāli Canon's account of his words. This teaching is like a toolbox that is offered to someone who wants to do the job and considers it worthwhile. It's not a teaching that everyone finds immediately inspirational. One result, and perhaps even the purpose, of such an approach is that it doesn't arouse a lot of craving—

you are not promised something in the future that is painted in such rosy terms that you get greedy and ambitious for it. But he does say that this practice leads to the complete ending of dukkha. Isn't that good enough?

This approach was radically different from the one pursued by most seekers at the time, who were concerned with the quest to find a true immortal self. One of the Buddha's discourses, the Brahmajāla Sutta (DN 1) goes through sixty-two views held by the seekers at the time concerning the world and the self (the cosmos and its hernia). These views ranged from speculations around whether or not the self and the world are eternal or partially-eternal. They include such interesting options as "neither-conscious-nor-unconscious postmortem survival," and "the self that experiences nibbāna, or ultimate peace, through indulgence in the senses in the here and now." All of these were based on interpreting states of consciousness seekers had experienced in their meditation in terms of self. And when the focus is set to find self, then every experience is interpreted in terms of self. The Buddha called such a focus "unwise attention":

> This is how he attends unwisely: "Was I in the past? Was I not in the past? What was I in the past? How was I in the past? Having been what, what did I become in the past? Shall I be in the future? What shall I be? How shall I be? Having been what, what shall I become?" Or else he is inwardly perplexed about the present thus: "Am I? Am I not? What am I? How am I? Where has this being come from? Where will it go?"
>
> When he attends unwisely in this way, one of six views arises in him. The view "self exists for me ... [the view] no self exists for me ... I perceive self with self ... I perceive not-self with self. ... It is this self of mine that speaks and feels and experiences here and there the results of good and bad actions; but this self of mine is permanent, everlasting, eternal. ..." This speculative view, bhikkhus, is called the thicket of views. ... Fettered by the fetter of views, the untaught ordinary person is not freed from birth, aging, death, from sorrow, lamentation, pain, grief, and despair.
> (MN 2: 7–8)

So as to the quest to find who you really are, or the speculation as to whether you have Buddha-nature, the Buddha would say, "Don't go there. It will set your mind spinning its own shadow, trying to nail it down."

On another occasion, when asked what was the root of all things, the undying essence or source, he commented that it was the fascination with conceiving oneself. That's the foundation of the world. And why does one do that? "Because he has not fully understood it," was the Buddha's remark (MN 1). So his recommendation was to look directly at the dynamics of consciousness, understand the world where you can access it in terms of your experience. From there, see how that depends on some sense of being a solid observer, or a participant, some kind of self. And how from that position comes a restless need, a search, and a jungle of views to get tangled up in. His policy, then, was not one of annihilationism, but a radical refusal to go beyond what can be immediately, purposefully investigated to bring around the end of suffering. And that quality to be investigated is craving—craving to have or to be filled with some sense-data, craving to be, craving to not be. All of these drives can never be completely satisfied.

The Spiritual Faculties of Mind

In some ways, the Buddha's presentation is rather daunting—there's plenty of talk about suffering and hindrances, not much about joy and bliss. But you have to want to engage in Buddhist practice from a very realistic perspective and be prepared to undertake some work and develop some skills.

This aspiration, this willingness to make an effort, is the entry point to experiencing the Dhamma. In one of the Buddha's maps of the path, this aspiration is called faith (*saddhā*) and it is the first of five spiritual faculties. The other four faculties are: applied energy (*viriya*), which is based on our "can-do" instinct; mindfulness (*sāti*), which is based on our ability to pay attention; concentration (*samādhi*), which is based on our ability to bond our mind to an object; and wisdom (*paññā*), which is the ability to discern and discriminate. These five faculties are clarifications of fundamental instincts or energies that we all have. We already use these faculties, often in confused ways, for example, when faith is confused, we fixate on aspiring to attain wealth, status, or understand beliefs. These faculties become *spiritual faculties* when they check samsaric habits rather than reinforce them. Then they abolish craving and clinging, and merge in that freedom that is called the deathless.

Although faith is the first of the spiritual faculties to arise (when someone feels inspired by a teacher or a teaching and is motivated to practice because of that)—generally the first faculties that people consciously develop are applied energy and mindfulness because they come more readily into the focus of our "action-oriented" mind. In this respect, the energy I'm talking about relates to governing where the mind is going. Volition, or intention, is therefore a key element of energy. For example, we could place our mind on the sensations of breathing moment after moment. This practice is one that establishes "mindfulness," the ability to steadily bear a theme in mind so that the restless habits of the mind die down.

These two faculties—energetic application of mind and mindfulness—can be applied to everything we do. And when integrated with wisdom, they become factors of the eightfold path. With wisdom, we can apply energy and mindfulness with "wise attention" to objects and concerns that don't stimulate craving, hatred, and speculative views. In everyday terms, this often means being more selective about media input and who we associate with. Being more discerning puts wisdom to work. Then in meditation, settled composure or concentration will arise. And as our mind settles and its energies unify, it begins to feel calm, joyful, and bright. This is one aspect of how we keep craving in check, basically by making our mind enjoy a simple here and now experience that is not bound up with sensuality or identity issues. And from this application, in accordance with the principles of kamma, of cause and effect, happiness and ease arise. Even more important, right concentration supports the furtherance of wisdom—it holds that focus of wise attention steady and takes it into areas of our mind where underlying reflexes and biases occur. When we see the stress that comes through unconscious habits, wisdom shows us where to let go.

An innate basis of faith develops dependent on the other four faculties. It grows in a healthy way when we establish mindfulness and discernment to what we are inspired by. Everyone has faith in something—that there's some happiness to be found in the world, that we can manage the day. It is vital: when people get seriously depressed, their loss of faith is what makes them suicidal. However, although it is so vital, you can't force faith to arise—it has to arise based on having faith *in* something. And it strengthens if that something is reliable. The most stable basis of faith is likened to a Threefold Refuge, also called the Triple Gem. It rests in the Buddha—the recognition that an Awakened One can arise from human roots and lay down a teaching in this world; it rests in the Dhamma—that there is an order, a balance, a truth that can be experienced by applying oneself to the teaching; and it rests in the Sangha—the ongoing "community" of committed disciples. Development occurs when we apply ourselves to experience this stable basis of faith.

The first occasion where this faith may arise and be developed is through meeting a teacher. A Buddhist book can be helpful, but to see someone living the Dhamma and responding to life in terms of that way is precious. Now, evaluating teachers can be tricky. Sometimes you meet teachers and sages who have a lot of personal charm. Sometimes they are wise and trustworthy, sometimes they are not. There have been several disastrous incidents of famous sages salting away millions of dollars in Swiss bank accounts or seducing fourteen-year-old girls. On the other hand, I have met teachers who said little, looked insignificant, and yet exemplified a life of great purity, kindness, and insight—even if they couldn't give rousing talks. The quality of their practice will inspire trust because of their ethical standards. So ethical standards create a context in which faith can arise. In Buddhist monasticism, for example, even the most attained teacher is expected to live in accordance with the Monastic Code as laid down in the Vinaya, one of the three main collections of Buddhist scriptures. This provides a communally held standard of personal modesty and sensitivity to other people and supports an environment in which no one is out to prove they are or aren't anything. In any community or relationship, you have to learn to just be part of the "us," to give up the wish to have others be the way you want them to be, and to relinquish the occasional deep urge to get out of it all and do your own thing. So when in the restrictive setup of a monastery (where there's no entertainment, no dinner, no sex, no money, and people are living with routines in a shared situation) and you notice how free, relaxed, and yet on the ball a teacher is, that gives you faith. The only way that someone can be free under those restrictions is if they've given up a good deal of craving and personal agendas.

So you gain faith in the Dhamma through mindfulness and discernment—not through attachment to the teacher, but through seeing how he or she operates. And that will give you confidence in the path—you see how the Dhamma works in terms of the things a person talks about, topics that are useful and relevant to peace and freedom from craving. You notice their manner isn't loud and demanding, or boastful. They wear their attainments lightly and don't show off. You notice that they don't need a lot, and don't need to have disciples and be a big shot. You notice that they live peacefully, happily with themselves. So you begin to get a feel for how living free from craving and free from the view of self is personally pleasant and enriching. Contact with a person like this may kindle some faith in yourself. You may think, "They are human and have come to be this way through the Dhamma; it has made them happy and clear. Surely I can at least attempt this practice-path." As the Buddha says:

> And how does there come to be gradual training, gradual practice, gradual progress? Here one who has faith [in a teacher] visits him; when he visits him, he pays respect to him; when he pays respect to him, he gives ear; one who gives ear hears the Dhamma; having heard the Dhamma, he memorises it; he examines the meaning of the teachings he has memorised; when he examines their meanings, he gains a reflective acceptance of those teachings; when he has gained a reflective acceptance . . . zeal springs up . . . he applies his will . . . he scrutinizes . . . he strives; resolutely striving, he realizes with the body the ultimate truth and sees it by penetrating it with wisdom.
> (MN 70:23)

Incidentally, Buddhist monks and nuns are not supposed to talk about their attainments. This rule was established in order to prevent cults arising based on people's personalities, which attract the wrong kind of interest. Even if the monk or nun is a very wise being, statements about their attainments would draw more attention to their personality than to the practice. There is a natural inclination in that direction anyway: most disciples at some time want to emulate their teacher. This need not be encouraged; it's a process that everyone has to go through (suffering a lot on the way) until there is the realization that there are no real role models. Each of us has to work with our own mind and habits, and the way Dhamma expresses itself specifically and individually.

So Dhamma-practice is a personal thing. We each can only go as fast and as deep as our own development will allow. It's not difficult to know in theory what we should let go of and how mindful and wise we should be—but no mind can be what it imagines it should be and what it actually is at the same time. So the humbling and earthy quality of walking the path of practice is that it involves meeting stupid lusts and petty grudges, things we think we should have dropped years ago. We have to meet them head-on, not from some attitude of who we think we should be, but with the spiritual faculties of faith, energy, mindfulness, concentration, and wisdom. We have to clear out our own backyard, and these five spiritual faculties will take us deeper so we can get to the root of our personal issues. Then, when we truly meet things with heart and spirit, the Dhamma is revealed to us intimately, and it allows us to let go of our attachments. Experiencing the Dhamma in this way can certainly affect our character—maybe we drop some regrets and become more open, or we might let go of an assertive personality and become quieter. Don't worry, our personality is still there—there's room for our individual face in the whole way of things. The point, though, is to not hang on to it—our own or anyone else's—as some central feature to guide us.

The theme of this third truth is "abandonment and relinquishment." Sometimes we refer to it more colloquially as "letting go." It doesn't mean abandoning the precepts, the Dhamma, or the teacher. "Letting go" means intimately knowing the pull of craving, and abandoning that craving in our own mind. With that you find a kind of psychological space, a nonpull, nonpush, nonjudgment poise that offers you a free choice rather than a driven reflex. This is the space of letting go. Letting go of self, of craving, of opinions, of moralizing judgments, of speculation . . . all of it. As a teacher of mine, Venerable Ajahn Chah, commented: "If you let go a little, you get a little peace. If you let go a lot, you get a lot of peace. If you let go completely, you get complete peace." A statement like that is human, obvious, and profound. It gives me faith, faith that the Dhamma can be practiced by human beings; faith that the practice is based on letting go; and hence faith in the ultimate teacher, the Buddha, who first offered these teachings. As he puts it:

> The faculty of faith . . . energy . . . mindfulness . . . concentration . . . wisdom . . . when developed and cultivated, have the Deathless as their ground, the Deathless as their destination, the Deathless as their final goal.
> (SN 48: Faculties 57)

We learn by getting a feel for craving and a feel for letting go. Ideas can be confusing. Sometimes the craving to get rid of (*vibhavataṇhā*) lies under a certain stiffness and defensiveness of manner: a "don't bother me" quality or a tendency not to face up to what is going on and learn from it. We'll have thoughts like, "I can't stand these confused people, I'm going to set them straight" (according to my idea of what they should be, of course). This kind of craving and drive is personally agitating and oppressive for others. We can quickly become a righteous, interfering pain-in-the-neck. Trying to get rid of other people's problems can have the same contradictory effect as trying to get rid of your own: both well-intentioned aims go astray when they affirm that problems actually belong to us. That is, by concentrating on them in a negative way, we unconsciously affirm their reality and lose our perspective of the situation. We see ourselves as flawed, rather than recognizing the impersonal and changeable nature of flaws. What is essential is to affirm and encourage the nonproblematic side of our mind—the experience of nongreed, nonhatred, and nondelusion.

Whenever we try to get rid of our sense of self, we unwittingly reinforce it. If we believe that compulsive habits and desires are "me" or "mine," we may feel we are *this* kind of a person who has a lot of weaknesses and has to do a lot to get rid of them in order to become enlightened or to be a true disciple of the Buddha, and so on. We assume that getting results, or even giving up and abandonment, are always and only about *doing* something with body, speech, or mind. Certainly at times we really have to apply persistent effort to check and work our way out of an addictive habit. And yet the final piece of letting go, the place that the doing takes us to, is the place where volition, having carried spiritual strengths into the knot of craving, has done its work. This takes a ripening of faith so that we have trust and confidence in awareness. At this point, even skillful volition can cease. This is the place of abandonment, of not-doing.

So there is an enrichment, a gathering of spiritual faculties, that is necessary for abandonment, and that leads to the deathless. This enrichment makes "abandonment" feel quite different from "getting rid of." Abandonment means abandoning a constricted view of life. With this, we avoid the pitfall of wanting our mental activity in the present moment not to happen, the craving to reject or annihilate oneself, the urge to not have to deal with the confusion and the passion of it all. Because no real wisdom, no real and lived understanding of how our world can come into balance, will arise without meeting dukkha and meeting the craving that throws life out of kilter. If we don't understand dukkha, we can't undo it. So abandonment, unlike the craving to get rid of and not be here, has to be accompanied by faith, wisdom, energy, mindfulness, and concentration. From that place of enrichment we can meet and come out of thirst and clinging, and open to a here and now that is clear of fantasy.

The first thing to check in with and bring forth is what we already have—and that's faith, not action. When and how do you have faith in yourself? Ask yourself, "What keeps me going?" "Why do I meditate?" Or even, "When there's no compulsion and no rewards, what is with me in the present moment?" That openness to being present is where faith comes from. Then that faith can be directed to aspiration, to the sense that there is a way out of dukkha. And we can sustain our faith with moment-by-moment wise attention and mindfulness of what is pure and clear in our mind. These then act like a pair of willing and capable hands that can hold the corruptions and the confusions of our life carefully, and can abandon its causes. This is the function of energy. And as we do so and live out the practice and its resultant well-being, we may, without even knowing it or trying to, become a source of faith and encouragement to others. Happiness and a firm, calm mind speak for themselves.

The Buddha said his teaching was for those with little dust in their eyes; what is needed then is a recognition that we have eyes, and we can see. We're not just a mass of pathological drives and ignorance. There is a light that sees the dark for what it is. It shines most clearly not when we're looking for the light, but when we're eager to switch off the dark. We *can* know, and we can have faith in that. We can know that suffering arises; it's a dynamic that we can notice happening, it's not inevitably bound up with the way we are. We can observe and learn. We can develop spiritual faculties to realize the purity that is based on abandonment—because with abandonment there is the experience of the mind at rest from craving. This is cessation.

7

THE FOURTH
NOBLE TRUTH

The Great Way

"Bhikkhus, there is a noble truth of the way leading to the cessation of suffering. It is the noble eightfold path: namely, right view, right intention, right speech, right action, right livelihood, right effort, right mindfulness, and right concentration."

Having an outline of the results and the general direction, we now get down to the "how to do it" section of the discourse. What's the system? The answer may come as a surprise.

The Eightfold Path

Just as the arising of suffering is a compound of ignorance and craving, and the ceasing is a mix of doing and not-doing, likewise the path isn't made up of a single track. It consists of eight interconnected factors. Even though it's called a path, it challenges the temporal and spatial metaphors of "I'm here and I'm going to get there." We are presented with a path out of suffering, but it's not about going to another location. It's about widening and exploring our psychological space, to include it all. All? Yes, the actions, the roots of actions, the handling of actions, and the place where actions cease. Outside of that, is there any place that hasn't been covered? In that scope is there any such thing as specific "time" or limited "place"? And without them is there any place where a separate self can hang out?

The eightfold path has eight limbs but it is only one path, not eight paths going in different directions. It weaves the general understanding of cause and effect into guidance over the way we speak and act and make a living; it blends the application of effort with the balanced composure of concentration. It starts in the resolve and consideration of our own mind, goes out with a sense of scrupulousness and integrity in our relationships with others, and penetrates the workings of our unconscious reflexes and assumptions. It's a mandala of interconnected factors that support and moderate each other.

You can't isolate just any one aspect of it and call it the path, because it's the wholeness of it that is important. Without that understanding, we tend to look for the one technique that will get us out of this mess, the one thing to do that will bring about a cure—and we don't notice the driver behind that one thing. And as you may have recognized, from the preceding passages, drivers tend to have blind spots. For starters they get stuck in their seats. Now, that said, let's begin with one thing, the thing that the Buddha said was the most important.

Right View

The path is established not on a technique, but on an understanding. The path begins with right view (*sammādiṭṭhi*). Right view can be summarized as looking at experience in terms of cause and effect. In the words of the Buddha:

> There is what is given and what is offered and what is sacrificed;
> there is the result of good and bad actions.
> (MN 117:8)

Cause and effect is at the heart of the path. In the formulaic presentation that is used in the Pāli Canon, right view is specifically set against the moral nihilism and predeterminism that was prevalent in the samana community at the time, which basically involves affirming or denying the existence of the world. Essentially right view says we can purposefully live in relationship, but not entangled with this world. This connects to the Buddha's understanding of kamma, that there is valid and meaningful action, and it has consequences. That is, even if you are not exactly clear about what you're doing and why you're doing it, you can feel the generosity, the cruelty, the greed, or the forgiveness well up in you and you follow that impulse with bright or dark results. To follow those impulses brings results. If you're tuned in to that, aware of that impulsive energy, a pragmatic form of wisdom arises: you know that bad things make you feel bad and good things make you feel good. This may sound obvious, but we don't always get it! Seeing the need to tune in to cause and effect is right view.

Right Intention

Right view is the foundation for right intention (*sammāsankappa*), the second factor, which means you take responsibility for your impulses and inclinations. With right intention, you align your action or program with three psychological roots: the intent of renunciation (of simplifying needs as distinct from following wishes), the intent to abandon mean-heartedness and indifference, and the intent to abandon cruelty and dismissiveness. Often the last two intentions are presented as "kindness" and "compassion." Yet the negative forms are actually more generous, if less inspiring. There are times when my kindness amounts to just not holding on to the negative impression that I have of someone (including myself). It doesn't always seem that sweet and radiant, yet it gets to the point: I feel the tightening and the stirring of ill-will in my chest; I know that this will do me harm and do others harm, and breathing in and breathing out gently, I release that tightness as I relax around the image of the person that's annoying me. The practice involves some effort, mindfulness, and letting go. And with that, I recognize that "the person who is annoying me" is really just an interpretation of behavior seen from "my" position. If I realize that and see other aspects of the person—and if I find out the pressures or the habits that this person is bound up with—I feel no inclination to make their life any worse, and I certainly have no interest in making my life miserable with ill-will.

This factor of right intention is not just a matter of thought, though careful consideration will take you there. It's not idealism, but a way of directing attention to the impulse-energy of volition as it arises in the heart at any given moment. This takes wise attention, which is often helped, as in the above example, by sensing what's happening in your body. There's wisdom in right intention. You investigate and notice your pulse rate pick up, your temperature rise, or you feel tightening in your chest, or the sinking in your stomach—that, clearer than any thought, is going to indicate what the heart's volition is doing. Bodies can't cover up, deny, and lie the way that thoughts can. So when you feel your thoughts start to race with "He shouldn't" and "She's always doing that" and "I'm going to set those guys straight once and for all," wait. Do yourself a favor and breathe out and breathe in a few times, and check what's happening in your body. Then ask yourself: "How does it feel, now? Is this the kind of state I want to live with and develop?" If you follow it, you're going to live with and develop it, and reap the results for sure. The Buddha put it this way:

> Whatever a bhikkhu frequently thinks and ponders on, that will become the inclination of his mind.
> (MN 19:6)

Right Speech

The third factor is right speech (*sammavācā*), which is connected to right view and right intention. It's good to study your own speech—it gives you an idea of how you think, and in what emotional pattern you see yourself in the world. Does your speech tend toward the apologetic? Does it seek reassurance? Is it aimed at directing other people? Is it used as an introduction, an invitation to share, to listen, to be in something mutual? Quite a lot of everyday speech is barely connected to anything more than the need to release some turmoil, or the wish to form some kind of bond to another person, and not necessarily on a mutual basis. Some of it is just an outflow of nervous energy, and some of it attempts to create a cheerful atmosphere: "Have a nice day." Sometimes it's a placatory gesture to excuse entering someone else's space or taking up their time: "Sorry, excuse me" or "Thank you for your patience." When we have that nervous twitch and feel awkward, or something hasn't gone according to plan and we assume we've blown it, or fear recrimination, or it's gone quiet and we feel a little tremble of worry about the atmosphere—speaking happens. But how much does anyone listen? Really listen, or check out whether things are OK with another person? And how much do we look into our own heart and mind and get a sense of where we're coming from? Speech (and that goes for writing too) is the most common and frequent form of contact. So in speaking, it's wise to leave some room for discernment and reflection. Ask yourself: "Where am I coming from, and who am I talking to?" "Is this the right time, and the right place?" This takes some effort, an effort to check in, as well as some mindfulness.

With speech, the training standard for Buddhists is fourfold: (1) to refrain from lying, exaggerating, knowingly creating a false impression; (2) to refrain from harsh speech, swearing, and insults; (3) to refrain from gossip and talebearing; and (4) to refrain from pointless "babble." At first maybe it seems that silence is all that's left! But an inspiring description of right speech comes from the Buddha:

> "He rejoices in peace and speaks words that make for peace . . . such words as are gentle, pleasant to hear, kind, heart-stirring, polite . . . at the proper time he will speak words that are worth remembering, well-grounded, purposeful, and helpful."
> (AN 10:99)

Right Action

The fourth factor is right action (*sammākammanta*), which refers to bodily action. Here the definition is again couched in negative terms: to refrain from destroying living creatures, from taking what isn't given, and from sexual abuse. This should be easy enough, shouldn't it? But consider if for one week, or even one day, everyone just refrained from killing another human being—that would be pretty amazing. So yes, it seems easy enough, but wait until the pressure's on. Therefore one of the main directions in meditation is to investigate the heart, the place of unconscious or latent impulses, and to get to those "action-station" buttons that can trigger violence. This is where wise inquiry takes over from calm as a theme of meditation practice. When our mind is settled, we connect with the heart, and maybe even bring up a theme or an image that will trigger a reaction. Then when the reaction occurs, we witness it, create psychological space around it, wait with it, and eventually allow it to discharge. Any reaction is just a program. It's volition on automatic pilot. If we give ourselves the time and space, we come into manual steering. If we go to where it's directly felt, if we widen and soften, we can let the reaction go, and a wise response will arise. As well as right view and right intention, this process will entail right effort, right mindfulness, and right concentration.

Right Livelihood

Right livelihood (*sammā-ājivo*), the fifth factor, is a big topic for many people because of the financial pressure to gain employment. Refraining from dealing in arms, drugs, liquor, and sex are good guidelines that help to keep you associating with good people. For monastics it's about living on alms-food, and being content with a set of robes, a bowl of food, and a roof over their head as a standard. And in all cases it's about not hassling people for donations. But for those in business, the Buddha gave advice on how to use their assets: to look after family and friends; to put aside some savings; to give some away to worthy causes; and to avoid wasting money on drink, gambling, and fooling around. Following this advice is going to keep your integrity and clarity alive. This may seem like common sense but when the craving hits, it isn't so common.

Probably the biggest single obstacle to right livelihood is being too busy. Busyness pushes against these factors of the path, and sometimes brushes our better nature aside. A friend of mine told me of an event at a main London railway station, where during the rush hour, somebody broke down on the platform and just couldn't go on with his day. Seeing the scene from afar, and moving toward the man, my friend was amazed to see people walking around or even over him. These were people who I'm sure had families they cared about, but in that moment, the pressure of time was blinding them. So how can we not be too busy? I also have a friend who had nervous breakdowns and suicidal depression, and after a couple of decades of high-pressure work, he eventually got enough help to understand that he didn't need to try harder to pull himself together; he needed to downshift. He sold his house, reduced his needs, and now lives happily with his feet on the ground. Although he had identified so much with his work and supporting his family, his family members are happy that they have a living, sane person with them and they have adjusted to a simpler lifestyle. So what keeps us alive? And if the company goes bust, what then?

Right Effort

The sixth factor is right effort (*sammāvāyāma*). It has four aspects: (1) to prevent the mind from being overwhelmed by ignorance; (2) to cut away or ease out wrong views and habits; (3) to dig the soil for cultivation of what is good; and (4) to maintain vigilance over the path. Effort sounds like a grunt-and-gasp kind of practice, but it all depends what you're tackling. The spiritual faculty of energy is necessary—which is going to be richer if you aren't burned out from making a living—but you don't need a jackhammer to crack a nut. Sometimes soaking it in water will do, so try putting more energy toward practicing with kindness and patience. Sometimes it's a matter of looking more carefully at where an opening is. Use inquiry and wisdom. No amount of hammering will ease your mind out of despair and grief, so try faith and compassion. Using your energy carefully is right effort. In order for it to be "right" effort, it has to be connected to mindfulness that can bear our current mind-state in mind and allow a wise response to occur, rather than a prejudged program of "I need to hammer away to get rid of my defilements." Energy has to be sustainable. For this reason, it's good to assess if there are things you're doing that you don't need to do, so that your resources don't dissipate. Even as you meditate, you can ask yourself, "What am I carrying that I can put down?"

Right Mindfulness

Effort then is to support and be supported by the seventh factor, right mindfulness (*sammāsati*). Mindfulness has become a buzzword that is used to cover a whole range of attention and cognition. Although much of this is skillful, it isn't necessarily mindfulness. And there are aspects of mindfulness—namely its connection to an ethically based intention—that can get missed out on. Right mindfulness isn't just clearly noticing the presence of something without an opinion. That is attention, another factor of mind—which is, of course, good to develop. Mindfulness is richer: it carries and steadily bears the wisdom of right view and right intention, a wisdom that is innate in humans and produces, for example, an ethical sensitivity.

The root of the Pāli word *mindfulness* refers to the act of remembering: it refers to that moment when we cast our mind out of the current drive and into "let me see" mode. It is the movement into an open space. However, whenever I cast my mind in that direction, there's an intention—what am I looking for? Is it a way to break into someone's house or a way to look into the roots of my mind-state at the moment and learn? So there are different ways of using that space; and there's a difference between wrong and right mindfulness. Right mindfulness is supported by right view and right effort. That is, it can be wisely cultivated and deliberately sustained. And mindfulness helps us to learn: cultivating it gets us in touch with how our mind rests on a sense-impression or an idea—with greed, or kindness, in a clear or flustered or compulsive way—and it gives instructive feedback on the effects and the feel of these different kinds of volition.

Right mindfulness can be directed to the inquiry as to what is the most skillful basis for action in any situation, or it can be used to steady and investigate the mind. The Buddha said that right mindfulness can be developed by meditating on the body—being attentive to breathing in and out, walking, stretching, standing, lying down; by maintaining awareness of physical and mental feelings; by being attentive to the general state of mind—whether it's moody, depressed, relaxed, elated; or through maintaining awareness of the innumerable array of mind objects—thoughts, energies, doubts, joy. . . . It can be extended to cover everything we do; this is why it is a supremely useful application of mind.

In itself mindfulness has two aspects—it is firm and fully aware. It is firm because it continues to bear something in mind beyond the original burst of interest or function. In this respect it supports right concentration, but it does not require a high degree of tranquility, since it is working readily on the ordinary level of consciousness. Yet it creates enough concentration to enable its second aspect, full awareness, to survey what is borne in our mind and to feel it out. Mindfulness with full awareness is the kind of attention that sees phenomena arising and ceasing in consciousness. Then its focus settles to look into the basis, the change, and the owner of experience. What is this thought, emotion based upon? Who owns this bodily feeling that I assume is attacking you? And where is the way to stop craving, fighting, identifying, and suffering over this? Its ability to support inquiry is what makes mindfulness such a transformative practice. When the mind-states that you take as constituting "your self" are experienced as something passing through consciousness, the sense of identity goes through some radical shifts. Then right mindfulness naturally supports wisdom and abandonment.

Right Concentration

The eighth factor is right concentration (*sammāsamādhi*), which I emphasize is not the concentration that furrows your brows and generally puts you under pressure. Maybe *concentration* is the wrong word, perhaps *collected* or *gathered in* would work better, because what is being referred to here is not an effort, but one of the results of that effort. It is a heart whose energies are not scattered and jangling, but calmly and gently suffusing the body and mind. Although that's not to say that effort (or mindfulness) is absent either. Consider doing a headstand; getting upside down and balanced takes effort and mindfulness, but once in the pose, there is a balance that is restful. Mindfulness is present to be watchful of the balance and any fluctuating tendencies that will cause you to lose balance. And there is a residuum of effort to maintain the pose, which decreases as you become more assured in your balance. Right concentration is something like that, but happier. In fact, the immediate precursors to right concentration are rapture or uplift (a buoyant state of mind), and ease (a contented feeling). Right concentration is also couched in wisdom and abandonment. It arrives through seeing through and abandoning the sullying effects of what are called the five hindrances.

The Five Hindrances

The five hindrances are sense-desire, ill-will, lethargy, restlessness, and doubt. The main work of the previous path-factors is to set up the conditions that will not aggravate or feed the hindrances, and to establish the means that will dispel their tracks and pathways in the heart. Some of the time the hindrances remain latent; you don't experience ill-will as long as things are going the way you want them to go. And you don't feel the push of sense-desire until you stop the movement of music and TV and dinner and so on. But when you've had enough of that and want to find some inner quiet, then the hindrances start knocking on your door for food. They are programs born of unknowing and craving, the ones most readily encountered when we meditate, and the ones that are cleared through right effort and right mindfulness. They are the nitty-gritty of meditation. And we'll look at them and how to clear them later. But one comment I'd like to make is that they're nothing personal, even though they scream that this is what you are. Then I'd also add that clearing them will change your life: the Buddha likened the effect to that of getting out of jail. When these are cleared, your mind easily concentrates and the wisdom that has been operating in every path-factor can penetrate deeply into the matrix of unknowing and craving.

It's possible to suppress or curtail the hindrances, and often that is a strategy to support their clearance. You push them away to get some breathing space and to regenerate with calm; right concentration can do that. It can take our mind out of contact with external sense-data, and when it ripens in absorption (*jhāna*), it can stop the thought-process altogether. It's rather like switching an engine off in order to look more closely at a car's functions and driveshaft. Concentration refines our thoughts so they become impressions and calm energies. It shows us how our mind holds an object—and how in stepping back from the craving in its grip, our mind feels peaceful, even blissful. So concentration gives wisdom a greater opportunity to work at the basis of the hindrances—the unconscious craving to have, to be, or to not be.

The basis of the hindrances doesn't come from sense-phenomena in themselves, or the actions of other people, or a low-energy state; it's the shadow that carries the emotional conviction that I am in need, that this is mine, and I want things to go my way. This conviction gets firmed up by the tangle of beliefs that it creates: that, for example, sense-desire will make me happy or that ill-will can get rid of irritating things. "I am" and "I will be" are the unconscious grab bars of the hindrances. One way of looking at the hindrances sees them as tangled and unresolved energies that need to be held carefully and straightened. But the mesmerized self can't do that. Instead we need to shift to another way of looking at our mind and its phenomena. This shift comes as wisdom operates from a different perspective—that of understanding the four noble truths—and with the collected energy of meditation.

Mundane and Supramundane

There are three meditation factors of the eightfold path (right effort, right mindfulness, and right concentration) that encourage mental, verbal, and physical action to work in a supramundane way. *Supramundane* means sensing, understanding, and relating to experience without the biases of self-view. While *mundane* refers to our ordinary way of operating: I refrain from harmful speech, I cultivate right livelihood, and I associate with good friends, *supramundane* refers to whether there is stress and craving, or mindfulness and wisdom in your mind. In this respect right view as a path-factor is the view that considers things in terms of the four noble truths. It takes the principle of examining cause and effect and turns it into examining the cause of dukkha and what brings about its ceasing.

This perspective has its effects on the intentions and motivations of your life. And of course any position that you base your identity on. You want to cultivate the ways that lead to freedom from the demands of the activities, so you find that giving up self-positions in terms of body, speech, and mind supports that. Instead of "I am a manager, mother, or community leader, therefore I should be always on top, ever giving, a continual source of inspiration," you look into where your mind takes a stand and suffers. More to the point, you review how in any given moment or scenario you can bring forth the resources that you have, and acknowledge them when they're not there. It takes truthfulness, courage, and kindness. When a response comes from clarity about what is happening, rather than from who you think you should be, you act in accordance with Dhamma in terms of thoughts, speech, and action. The consequent balance and freedom from doubt and regret validate that moment-by-moment practice.

Using terms like *mundane* and *supramundane* does immediately set up a value judgment, "Who wants poky old humdrum mundane? I'm going for the supramundane." Well that view is so steeped in ignorance, self-view, and becoming that it isn't going to achieve the mundane, let alone anything supra-. The mundane is the path to the supramundane, it is the means of unifying all the resources that will catalyze other factors that are specific to meditation, and which open the supramundane. These factors are known as the "seven factors of awakening": mindfulness, investigation, energy, rapture, tranquility, concentration, and equanimity. And it is these factors, not our wishes, that usher in a letting-go in terms of the most fundamental mental action: the act of placing attention. Normally governed by a blind driver, attention can be consciously directed and moderated, and can even be freed from being placed. Then, as we will see, it is experienced as an "unsupported" awareness outside of time and space—and outside of suffering. So there is a path to the supramundane, and it has to be firmly established through meeting, addressing, and cultivating these four noble truths. Then this brings about an integrated life that is assured of freedom, of "merging in the deathless and terminating in nibbāna."

8

FACING THE WALL

"There is this noble truth with regard to suffering: in this way, bhikkhus, vision, insight, wisdom, knowing, and light arose in me about things not heard before. This noble truth with regard to suffering is to be thoroughly understood: in this way, bhikkhus, vision, insight, wisdom, knowing, and light arose in me about things not heard before. This noble truth with regard to suffering has been thoroughly understood: in this way, bhikkhus, vision, insight, wisdom, knowing, and light arose in me about things not heard before."

The Buddha goes on to deepen the significance of the practice of the four noble truths. He begins by analyzing the first noble truth in a pattern of three stages: acknowledgment, motivation, and result—or view, practice, and full understanding. This pattern is then repeated in each of the other noble truths. In each case, the first stage is a fuller reflection on the importance of bearing the meaning of the specific truth in mind; the second stage demonstrates the way of practicing with that truth; the third fully penetrates the significance of that truth. Together, the twelve stages define the process of awakening through the four noble truths.

Wisdom is the thread that connects each stage and each truth. In the case of each stage of each truth, understanding is described alike as "vision, insight, wisdom, knowing, and light"—all these are aspects of the wisdom faculty that is turned toward penetrating dukkha. So the very consistency of wisdom at all stages presents the truths and awakening in an interesting way: could it be that the mind that can see dukkha is operating in the same liberated mode as the mind that can see the cessation of dukkha? Since it appears to be so, we get the sense that awakening is the process of taking the same wisdom faculty through the stages from acknowledgment to fully experienced understanding. Wisdom—the unbiased acknowledgment of dukkha—is first initiated, then it is motivated: this dukkha must be understood. Then wisdom bears fruit in accomplishment and result: thus dukkha has been understood. Yet it's the same wisdom, insight, and light operating throughout. Therefore, in speaking of the way, the Buddha says it is one of deepening realization, but the essence of that realization is not delayed in time:

> One who sees suffering also sees the origin of suffering, also sees the cessation of suffering, also sees the way leading to the cessation of suffering.
> (SN 56: Truths 30)

So the clear acknowledgment that "There is suffering and it is to be understood" carries a powerful and transformative insight: the dukkha that we experience, if wisely attended to, is capable of being penetrated. It reveals that dukkha doesn't have to close us down or drive us into rage: it's not absolute, and therefore it can be dismantled, or not created.

So, bearing this big picture in mind, let's look at the first noble truth again. The text reads, "There is this noble truth with regard to suffering: in this way, bhikkhus, vision, insight, wisdom, knowing, and light arose in me about things not heard before." So is knowing suffering some kind of attainment? Most of us don't feel very inspired or liberated by the state-ment "There is suffering"; after all, what is enlightening about that? Lib-eration seems a long way off from the experience of dukkha.

However the clue is in the expression used. The formulation of the words is slightly unusual: it's not the way that the average person would formulate the experience; he would probably say, "I am suffering" or "She is suffering," and so forth. In such a case, the unstated implication is that something has gone wrong for that person and that they shouldn't be suf-fering. The instinctive view of suffering is first to see it all in personal terms, and second, to postulate nonsuffering. That is, when "I am suffering," the world, the flu, or the broken car is hurting *me*. Actually these things have no personal aim or intent. It's just that "There is dukkha." That's the way it is. And as for the imagined world where dukkha doesn't occur, as for "This shouldn't happen to me; it's not fair"—this is the way it is, and it's perfectly fair; it, or something like it, happens to everyone. So is it possible to widen the perspective beyond a self-view, out of expecting ourselves to be successful, productive, understood, appreciated, and healthy? Yes it is, by going into our turmoil and defensive resistance around natural limi-tations, and widening our perspective. It's just dukkha. If we can do this, then some basis for steadiness, compassion, and light can appear.

To summarize, this first step in liberation of dukkha takes the natural characteristic of dukkha and sees the mechanism that converts it into "I am suffering." Then there is light and a chance to penetrate and disman-tle this mechanism. With reflection, we may assume that, ultimately, we cannot get rid of "suffering"—that we can merely temporarily alleviate our problems through medicine, counseling, aid, and amusement. These methods of alleviation are fine and so on, but are not a total solution. Yet the recourse to them is so instinctive that even to question that recourse brings up the response: "You mean, you can just coldheartedly sit back in a state of inertia and say, 'There is suffering,' and that any attempt to do something about it is just unawakened desire?"

Not so. The approach of the Buddha's teaching is to see where we can give up the defenses, distractions, or complaining that the existential duk-kha normally evokes in us. And for this, I'd recommend acknowledging and giving up not external supports but defensive and distracting ego-activity. The escape from dukkha that we can achieve in the ego-based way is accompanied by either running, fidgeting, and scrambling, or by hardening, defending, possessing, and tightening up. We run or we build a wall. Try to feel when these occur—then steady yourself, hold gently, and let your sense of being soften. Dukkha is not to be blamed, cursed, or agonized over; dukkha is to be understood.

To see if the method works, give it a try—not on the suffering that we can get rid of temporarily, like mild discomfort or hunger, but on the dukkha that we can't do anything about. For example, bring to mind the dukkha of aging and death (things we cannot control); or the dukkha of being separated from what we love and having to face what we dislike (a pattern that we can alter in detail but not in a fundamental way). Try to stay steady and open without thinking of something else, and let the agitation or the shrugging off pass through you. Be aware of your body, and breathe in and out slowly and deeply. Give your mind and heart time to find a balance. It will feel wider, clearer, and firmer than before.

What happens when we approach any predicament with close attention to this feeling base? As human beings, we have to get old and die. The perception of that feels one way. We may get agitated by this thought or shrug it off—that's "running." We may feel frightened, and tighten up—that's a "wall." Now when we acknowledge these instinctive reactions, isn't this acknowledgment, not following those reactions, conducive to getting a handle on dukkha? Doesn't this give rise to a "knowing of the way it is" and hence the possibility of being able to relinquish it? Isn't the "way it should be" just one more wall? And when we relinquish that, when we have no notions of how things should be, doesn't that make us clear and sensitive, more fully alive? When we maintain this direct clarity and openness, a strength of heart is available that we forget we have.

What becomes apparent is that the pain of death and grief is really the pain of that wall and that running, the pain of not wanting it to be this way, not wanting to be experiencing these feelings. And the real internalization of the dukkha comes through trying to be separate from these feelings, having a wall against them, or trying to get rid of them. When we can accept uncertainty about the future, separation and loss as a natural part of life, then the real soul-destroying sense of alienation that the wall and the running create does not arise. When we realize that we're all subject to dukkha, then the pettiness, the jealousies, and the grudges disappear. And we find, sometimes to our surprise, that we can cope with life's changes. Then in the peace of not suffering, and with the presence of knowing and clarity, there are new, real, and relevant possibilities of what we can do. So instead of feeling hopeless and agitated in the presence of suffering, we can be with it in a clear and healing way.

I recall people hearing these teachings in monasteries and Dhamma centers, and meeting others who had come to the realization that "There is dukkha." The response is generally: "So it's not just *me* who feels like that!" Sometimes people even feel elation at having come out of the dull cocoon of confusion and being able to let go of the self-questioning: "Why *me*? Why did I get this bad deal?" Having birth traumas, being damaged as a child, being jilted, losing a job, being betrayed, getting sick, having your mother die, getting shortsighted, going gray, losing your husband, being manipulated by your boss, and the rest of it . . . is dukkha. But when these are seen as nonpersonal—as aspects of a common experience—there is an opening of the heart to something more serene, less demanding, and more compassionate. Our "own" stuff doesn't seem like so much then.

On the other hand, I also hear people say, "Life's great! I'm going to Hawaii, and I'm going to have a good time!" We don't always recognize that the constant need to be entertained, to progress, or to be appreciated by someone is a sign of not being fully at ease with ourselves. Again, our instincts leap to the defense, "What's wrong with going to Hawaii, getting ahead in life, or having a loving relationship?" There's nothing *wrong* with those things, in themselves. But relying on this sort of happiness makes us fragile. Ask yourself, what does your happiness depend upon? What happens if—or actually, when—that isn't available? See what I mean? Now we can only know for ourselves whether or not we're clinging and dependent, but what helps in this respect is to notice if we're running or shielding or trying to fill an apparent hole in our sense of being. None of this works because the hole is actually a block, the block of ignorance. Trying to fill it is the wrong strategy—all the creature comforts in the world only add more padding around the stuck place. And running or defending certainly doesn't clear the blockage either. What is needed is to handle it and relax its constriction and numbness, and we can do this in a very direct way: notice the instinctive strategies, pause, ground your awareness in your body, widen and soften, and give yourself time.

Another way of not seeing dukkha clearly is to see it as an unchangeable experience, feeling stuck with it and giving up on ourselves. This not responding to dukkha is resignation rather than acceptance. When we lack an understanding of dukkha, we may take on a kind of despair about the human predicament—when will we ever get rid of the social injustices and the violence and the unfairness? And we may think, "Give up, it's hopeless." That's another wall, another shield around the heart, more ignorance.

To open up to the understanding that "There is dukkha" is a radical step. The common myth that is perpetuated in society is that the normal person is happy, balanced, and integrated—otherwise there is something wrong with them; maybe they're mentally unstable. We're even alarmed by unhappy people. Everyone in the media is smiling and cheerful; the politicians are all smiling, cheerful, confident; funeral homes even make corpses up to look smiling, cheerful, and confident. Meanwhile, however, perhaps you're not smiling and you don't feel cheerful and confident. You know you can't live up to any of the images of the model person. You don't have the right appearance or status symbols, your performance doesn't cut it, you're out of touch with the latest trends, or maybe you are just poor—someone whom society doesn't want to acknowledge. Unhappiness in Western culture is often treated as a sign of failure. Others think, "They're not happy, maybe they didn't do enough. And maybe they'll want something from me, so better steer away from them."

But "There is dukkha" brings us all together. The rich often suffer from the fear of losing their wealth and security—or even from the guilt of being affluent. The poor frequently suffer from material need and from the degradation of being treated as second-rate. The young have the dukkha of feeling they have to conform to the authority of those who are older; they also have the dukkha of being restless, and of not having an established role in life. So they have the dukkha of needing to prove themselves, of having a lot of sense-desire, and of being anxious about the future. The middle-aged often experience dukkha through the increased pressure of responsibilities, having a position to maintain, getting stuck in habits, losing some of their vigor and initiative, and being anxious about the future. The elderly may experience dukkha through not being able to keep up, losing status or a valued role in society, feeling unwanted, dimming of the sense faculties, and also being anxious about the future. Then there's always the regret we might have at any age over past actions, the limitations of body and mind, and the sense of needing to find some meaning in life. So there is dukkha, but isn't it a relief to know that *it's not your fault*—that there's nothing wrong with *you*?

Then you have the confidence to know what dukkha you can shift. Suffering becomes a block in our sense of being when any position is taken as an identity—when *how* you are becomes *who* you are. It's the difference between "an enslaved person" and "a slave." As long as circumstances are taken to be identities, we adopt the degradation or superiority, the conceit or paranoia, that each entails. Then the dukkha of circumstance becomes a permanent feature of our heart and mind, and affects our attitudes and actions. Is a poor person, for example, someone who has little money, or is a poor person someone who does not have "as much" compared to society's model for a happy human being? Isn't the experience of suffering compounded by the experience of being rejected, which leads to feeling inadequate, bitter, and depressed?

When I was on pilgrimage in India a few years ago, I met many people with very little cash and only a few old clothes. However when they had spiritual values to orient around, they didn't carry poverty as an identity so they weren't suffering from it. I met a Sikh temple attendant who lived in one room with his wife and four children. Their only furnishings consisted of a bed, a stove, and a cupboard. They were not embittered or depressed; far from it. They were in touch with something more reliable than material good fortune. There was the dukkha of lack, and yet not of suffering. That's the way it is; the social model (at the village level at least) is not the person who is happy because of what they own, but who lives according to his values and principles.

I'm not advocating poverty, but encouraging a wise and grounded response to any circumstance. Again, not seeing life in terms of just "me" is that wiser perspective. When there is understanding and a set of values that encourage sharing, then the limitations, the needs, and the lacks of any given life can be acknowledged and effort can be put into using material supports with compassion. This is also true in cases of deprivation; surely a major contributor to this is the greed and exploitation of others, which has its source in identification with material prosperity. If we could all accept the experience of limitation on our resources and comforts, if affluent people's standard of living were not so high, there would be fewer people who felt, and actually were, "poor." Maybe with more sharing, there would be less severe physical deprivation. Instead of creating golf courses in the desert, or seeing air-conditioning, two cars, and countless television channels as necessities of life, we could try to accept limitations to our material circumstances and acknowledge "There is suffering."

This acknowledgment doesn't require that everyone should feel wretched; rather, it's a matter of learning to know and accept that this earthly realm is one of limitation. When we wake up to how human life on this planet actually is, and stop running away or building walls in our heart, then we develop a wiser motivation for our life. And we keep waking up as the natural dukkha touches us. This means that we sharpen our attention to catch our instinctive reactions of blaming ourselves, blaming our parents, or blaming society; we meditate and access our suffering at its root; and consequently we learn to open and be still in our heart. And even on a small scale in daily life situations, such as when we feel bored or ill at ease, instead of trying to avoid these feelings by staying busy or buying another fancy gadget, we learn to look more clearly at our impulses, attitudes, and defenses. In this way dukkha guides and deepens our motivation to the point where we'll say, "Enough running, enough walls, I'll grow through handling my blocks and lost places."

Acting upon that motivation takes resources like faith, energy, mindfulness, concentration, and wisdom. And its culminating effort is that of bringing our dispassionate awareness to bear upon how, where, and when the hurt really is. This takes us into a heart that always tries to find a place within the five aggregates, that wants to be a solid personality, wants to feel comfortable, wants guarantees, wants something to hold on to—but just can't get it. Nothing really sticks. But isn't that good news? When we understand this, we can stop suffering over being the misfit, and shift our attention and intention beyond being a thing, having a position, and going places. We can witness our life with wisdom; then there is the realization of that which is knowing and insightful and which brings forth a response of compassion rather than frustration. That shift is the essence of liberation. Dukkha has been understood.

9

ABANDONMENT

Stepping Out of the Fire

"There is this noble truth concerning the arising of suffering: in this way, bhikkhus, vision, insight, wisdom, knowing, and light arose in me about things not heard before. This noble truth of the arising of suffering is that it is to be abandoned. . . . This noble truth of the arising of suffering is that it has been abandoned: such was the vision, insight, wisdom, knowing, and light that arose in me about things not heard before."

After the declaration above, the Buddha then repeats the threefold analysis that he used for the first noble truth to explain the second noble truth. The theme here is abandonment. The insight of the second noble truth is that there is an origin to dukkha; that the origin can be penetrated by abandonment; and, in its third and final aspect, that it has been penetrated by abandonment. Here, it's important to bear in mind that abandonment is not "getting rid of"; it's not an unpleasant medicine that we have to take until we are cured. Abandonment isn't just done for a certain length of time until we have let go enough and can find something better to hold on to. True abandonment, instead, is a result in itself; it becomes a joyful, fruitful way to live. It's the easeful abiding place of the wise, the place of emptiness that allows the world to arise and pass without our grasping on to experience. As long as we hold on, we want the world to be the way we think it should be, and we want the things we love not to age, wear out, decline, or change from the state we like or have grown accustomed to living in. That is not possible, and the more we hold on, the more we suffer. Abandonment is the end of that suffering.

To acknowledge that suffering has an origin is already a form of abandonment of sorts. It means rather than thinking, "I am the victim of a frustrating world that refuses to conform to *my* wishes," we acknowledge that suffering is an inevitable part of life and it is something we take within ourselves by the way we react to circumstances. We have to recognize that often it's our misguided drives and opinions that have to be abandoned, rather than the circumstances themselves. Getting a flat tire on the drive to work is one kind of suffering or dukkha, but getting angry about it is the kind of suffering we can avoid. And we do that by abandoning our impatience—and the fallacy that there's a perfect and reliable plan, system, or machine. Abandoning these opinions rather than repressing them is an insightful process.

People should not steal and lie. Let's not quibble over the topic or the opinion—in most cases it has truth in it. These actions are bad and they make life difficult for all of us. But just look at how we can feel so exasperated, angry, and even violent when other people do wrong. Notice how we make ourselves stressed and vindictive—and assume that all that is because of someone else. Have you ever seen people kicking their cars or bashing their TV because they don't work? But those objects have no malicious intent, they just break down like they're bound to do. And from bashing the car to beating the irritating kid isn't a great distance.

We tend to personalize everything. Why everything gets at us and makes us so angry is because of something our mind is doing—but to acknowledge that entails giving up some position of "me" and "my emotions" that are right and justified. Now, I'm not saying that abandonment means not feeling anything—that attitude really drives people into dangerously repressed places. The way is about seeing how things get under our skin and chafe our heart; it's about abandoning the action of taking in dukkha. That takes penetration—looking into our mind and seeing clearly how it works. It means that where the contact and feeling occur, instead of reacting to irritation or pushing it away, we abandon that personal standpoint. We widen our perspective into being aware of how we are feeling, and with that clear and steady awareness, we can watch the mental process very carefully. Like this:

> Dependent on the eye and forms, eye consciousness arises. The meeting of the three is contact. With contact as a condition there is feeling. What one feels, that one perceives. What one perceives, that one thinks about. What one thinks about, that one mentally proliferates. With what one has mentally proliferated as the source, perceptions and notions tinged by mental proliferation beset a man with respect to past, future, and present.
> (MN 18:16)

To get to the point more directly: nothing can truly affect you except your psychological and emotional processes—the push or grab that occurs in the mind with the experience of contact. All that charge and push is a volitional formation, called proliferation, whereby from one feeling, one psychological twitch, a whole cascade of emotions and thoughts rush out in a chain reaction. The above discourse goes on to teach that when this proliferating process is checked, it "is the end of resorting to rods and weapons, of quarrels, brawls, disputes" and so on. So abandonment means not believing that how things are felt and perceived to be is what they actually are, and that they are not a necessary cause for action. In other words you feel the panic—but instead of reacting, you widen your awareness through the palms of your hands and the soles of your feet and breathe out and breathe in, slowly. Otherwise if the action of perceiving and thinking get charged, they proliferate and fill our inner space. They put the pressure on until we get overwhelmed—and react. For example, a friend of mine told me of an incident involving a dance in a barn that caught fire. The perception "fire" caused most people's minds to flood with emotions that blocked clarity. Everyone stampeded for the door—everyone except my friend's grandfather and a couple of his friends. The three of them looked around for a moment and considered that since the barn was made of wood, they could break through a wall. They did exactly that and they were the only ones to get out alive.

Abandoning Addiction

Naturally it's helpful to abandon our bad habits. But sometimes the perception of a smooth, comforting glass of scotch, or of a really tasty super-sized burger hits our mind—and a fantasy grabs our heart and drives us into action. And the process itself, of being emotionally grabbed, is so addictive, that when it's not happening, we can get bored and depressed. Then, grabbed by *that* perception, our mind proliferates into thinking thoughts like, "I'm at a dead end," "Life is a waste of time," and "I'll meet the man of my dreams." This proliferation is addictive. It gets very dangerous because with the loss of self-confidence and self-respect comes ignorance and further addiction. For instance, an ex-serviceman was telling me about the way he'd used alcohol to relieve some of the extreme tension caused by the fear and aggressive conditioning of army life. He'd drink to get rid of the stress, then he'd go to bed in a befuddled state and wake up the next morning feeling ghastly and confused. The anxiety over what happened last night and the need to try to pull himself together for the morning was so stressful that he'd reach for the bottle of vodka or scotch under the bed. Soon that, too, became a habit. Abandoning the stressful lifestyle would be the best remedy; or if not that, then he could discharge the stress through meditation. The point to acknowledge is if suffering isn't checked where it catches hold of our mind, our conscience goes, self-respect goes, sense-restraint goes ... and we're in big trouble.

But to abandon addiction, we have to penetrate the mechanism whereby our mind leans and feeds on sensory phenomena. That seeming support and nourishment, is the source of getting stuck. Leaning or feeding on is called clinging or grasping (*upādāna*) in the characteristically stark language of the discourses. The term *upādāna* is often associated with the behavior of fire. The Vedic understanding is that fire is a potential, a divine energy, that was ever present in a nonmanifest way but that could cling to or feed on substances like wood and so become manifest as flames. The Buddha picked up this image and turned it into a powerful statement about how the senses relate to their data. There is one notable instance in which he addresses a group of fire-worshipping ascetics:

> All is burning... the eye,... ear,... nose,... tongue,... body,... mind are burning with the fires of greed, ... hatred, ... delusion,... with birth, aging, and death, sorrow, lamentation, pain, grief, and despair...
> (M 1:21)

The Three Fires of Greed, Hatred, and Delusion

The metaphor of fire is a striking one. The Buddha used it because he was talking to a group of fire-worshipping ascetics, but the origin of suffering—the perception and idea that we need to have something, become something, or get rid of something—has the power to get any of us heated up. It's our mind's relationship to the senses that is the problem. When that relationship is marked by the three fires of greed, hatred, and delusion, they consume our attention and produce a lot of smoke—so much that we don't see the fire. Our consumer society has standardized wishes and expectations to the extent that we call them rights and expect them to be fulfilled—even though the level of consumption of the earth's resources in terms of energy and raw materials is too high. Craving is burning up the planet, even though this planet is our home and source of food. Craving also generates rich and poor, have and have not, and along with that there's jealousy, fear, resentment, violence, and hatred. This very hatred diverts massive resources into armaments, but the source of hatred isn't addressed. That's the fire of delusion, the really smoky one. And ironically, a good proportion of consumer-delusion is actually created by the need to take a break from the stresses of a consumer society. So it goes: the three fires support each other and screen off the possibilities of fulfillment and happiness issuing from a mind that is contented, settled, and clear in itself.

However, our mind doesn't have to be on fire like the external senses; the senses are bound to feed on sensory data because they are bound to the slow, consuming flame of bodily life, functioning in order to support bodily needs and instincts. We can't train our tongue to not take in flavor, but our mouth only gobbles up food because our mind urges it to. It's in our mind that we can feel the heat of the three fires of greed, hatred, and delusion rise, often just over issues and opinions; and that's where we also have the possibility of reflecting on and stepping out of the flames. For that we have to avoid taking a stand for or against an issue. We have to take the sense of self out of the picture, and acknowledge the process. This shift allows for the dawning of wisdom: suffering can be witnessed, I don't have to engage in it. Then motivation arises: if I can witness the process of taking in, then maybe it could be understood and abandoned.

As a practice, this process can be summarized. First of all there's the matter of view. This means acknowledging, for example, that the anxiety over your daughter's future, however reasonable, is causing you suffering. There's a tightness in your chest, an unsettledness in your belly, a tendency to go into red alert whenever she seems stressed over her exam results. Now the point is not to say, "I shouldn't worry" or, "It's a natural concern" but just to acknowledge the feeling of anxiety. Then there's the practice: you are actually experiencing anxiety as it is happening, as an embodied feeling, with no should or shouldn'ts about it. The next aspect is to steady your awareness around that feeling and let go of interpreting it, dismissing it, or trying to fix it. Just be with that feeling. Then breathe into the feeling, widen and soften your awareness. Relax a little, give yourself time; ease the energies associated with that feeling. Then tune into the spaciousness, the empathy, and the direct clarity of the awareness of that feeling and let the feeling do what it needs to do in order to be felt. This will allow the feeling to shift, you'll sense something like a sigh or a breath of fresh air—and you'll find yourself realizing: "I was pretty much the same at her age. She'll be OK." Without losing the sense of empathy for your daughter, you'll have dropped the agitated state your mind was concocting. To put it simply: acknowledge the mind-state that goes with the topic, put the topic to one side and be aware of the feeling and energy, then widen your awareness with spaciousness, empathy, and clarity.

The motivation has to be guided in terms of penetrating the "how" of suffering. Otherwise the desire to find a way out of suffering turns into craving to find and have and be something, and we get driven into obsessive mental activities. We can even generate suffering over *how* we go about learning and practicing. We can find ourselves endlessly shopping around for the right meditation or retreat setting—the right diet, bodywork, enough relaxation, a spacious and sympathetic teacher to relate to, eclectic spiritual teachings from which to select the one that is exactly suited to our specific personal tastes, and a format that does not require giving up what we don't want to relinquish. Teaching approaches and styles differ— sometimes even within Buddhist traditions, different teachers emphasize different aspects of Dhamma. It can get confusing, and some teachers expect their students to not read books from other teachers or attend their retreats. So is it (1) pick and choose to find out what works for you, or (2) give up everything else and surrender? We can become obsessively restless and choosy, or fixated on "the only way." The way to navigate this is to notice if what you commit yourself to, or the *way* that you commit, leads to further perpetration of "me" and "mine" and "myself." Does it lead to abandonment or to thoughts like, "I can't practice here," or to "I can't practice anywhere else"? If we're getting less flexible, less spacious—there's clinging. If we're endlessly shopping around, our obsession takes another form—and we can see how our views and strategies flare up to defend it! We might say, "It's my right to choose." On the other hand we might say, "This is the only way. It's the authentic tradition." Maybe so—but where's the heat coming from? And what leads to abandonment?

The sign to watch out for is the gobbling, the continual feeding of our senses or the rabid quest for ideas and "quick fix" solutions. It's not that we shouldn't eat, taste, see, hear, and have ideas—but that urge to cram things in comes from ignorance and takes us over. When we withdraw from sense-contact, when we meditate, that urge intensifies around mind-states. In fact any old mental junk food will do. Then if we don't have a particular obsession, the likelihood is that we will find a whole lot of concerns and opinions running around in our mind and putting the pressure on. We will find ourselves saying, "I've got to get this done, I really need to have one of these." I personally have spent hours on retreat designing and building monasteries—not that I have any building skills at all. Actually the building isn't applying pressure, it's the craving that is throwing up mind-stuff, looking for something to get stuck into. Hence it riffles through the garbage pail for a few bones and crusts. Craving in terms of the external sense is a good teacher—but if you don't learn from it, then the mind puts aside sense-objects in favor of the big delusions: the views, opinions, and notions of the world, the truth, and what I *really* am.

Working with My Mind

I had only a brief introduction to meditation before I entered a monastery. So I had a sudden over-the-edge kind of jump into a full-on Dhamma domain—renunciation, precepts, solitude, and meditation—in Thailand no less, where I couldn't even speak the language. As the weeks passed and turned into months, the view into my mind became mesmerizing. My ability to concentrate improved quite a bit, but still with the soporific effect of the hot climate and the hour after hour of being in solitude, I couldn't hold my energy onto the meditation theme. Thoughts would start by drifting slightly . . . I wondered how long I should sit, whether or not to move when my body hurt (to be sensitive) or maybe to sit it out (and be resolute). Here's what it looked like inside my mind at times:

> Sensitive or resolute, which is better? Maybe I'll endure for a while, and will eventually build up a greater ability to tolerate pain . . . but it would be nice not to have it, and it's natural not to want pain . . . whoops, better get back to concentrating on the breath, the mind is wandering. . . . This is not as good as yesterday . . . temporary setback . . . apply resolution. . . . Breathing in . . . note the sensation in the abdomen. . . . Breathing out . . .

flowing out through the nostrils. . . . Wonder how long before you don't feel pain? . . . It would be nice to go for a walk now, stretch the legs, I could do that mindfully, yes . . . but that's giving in, you sneak! . . . Maintain discipline . . . one hour sitting, one hour walking . . . wearing out the forces of craving. . . . How long does this go on for? . . . It's only a half hour since I sat down. . . . It's evening, cooking smells in the lane outside, dinnertime . . . normal people are enjoying themselves doing normal, blameless things like having a meal, pleasant company, nothing wild or crazy. . . . Yes, when I get out of here I'll be much more restrained, I've learned my lesson . . . no more wild scenes . . . and . . . what was her name? . . . Whoa! If it was all so great, why did you leave it!

(Mindfulness to the rescue again! And then resolution) . . . get back to the breath . . . breathing out . . . amazing how far your mind can travel in a matter of seconds . . . scientists reckon that the alpha rhythms of the brain travel at . . . how many cycles per second? . . . Maybe I could do this whole thing much easier with a biofeedback machine; definite improvement on these primitive Asian meditation techniques . . . one flicker away from concentration and you get a bleep! Maybe when I get back to England . . . now SHUT UP! That's it, cutting through delusion . . . breathing in . . . breathing out, here and now . . . easy now . . . lighten up on the thinking, just bare awareness . . . like a naked ascetic: bare awareness, yeah, like that, good one, eh? It'd be nice to live on a tropical beach where you didn't have to wear all these robes . . . but what's the point? . . . Get down to it! Right, a half hour more and I'll call it quits for the day, give myself a little treat . . . like what! I guess I could walk round the hut and look at the moon. . . . Big deal! . . . Easy now, "nibbāna is the highest happiness," here and now, open to the moment . . . don't repress. . . . That's better, flowing along real smooth . . . you don't have to live as a monk to do this, it's just nonattachment, living with a smile. . . . Taoism's the answer really, then you can have

music and sex in a nonattached way. . . . Who are you kidding!
Breathing in . . . then long, slow breath out, deep and slow . . .
nice, and only twenty-five minutes left. . . . Oh my knees hurt!
How long is this going to go on for?

I could see my mind gobbling up everything all right. And that offered
one insight: the unrestrained following of impulses, cramming the mind
with anything that comes along, has to be abandoned. But in the here and
now, the results of my past actions were playing out. So what to do at times
like this? One of the benefits of living in a Buddhist monastery—and one
of the torments—is that you have the example of the Buddha and also,
generally, other people with some peaceful, loving, and wise qualities. The
benefit is that you feel it must be possible to work this dukkha out in a way
that is not brutal or repressive; the torment is not being able to find that
in yourself. At a certain point, the path out of suffering seems to take you
back into it again. The conflict between what we should be and what is
actually going on in our mind seems to create as much dukkha as blindly
following our desires. Eventually something has to shift.

The point, which is a growth point for many practitioners, is in acknowledging, meeting, and handling the five hindrances: the fires of
sense-desire and ill-will, the thick smoke of lethargy, the burning sparks
of restlessness, and the flickering and sputtering of doubt. There are means
of pushing them aside: first you keep returning to the meditation theme.
Then if that doesn't work, it's time to think clearly of the disadvantages,
the decay, or the unattractive aspects of what you are pulled toward; or it's
time to develop kindness (or at least not to move into aversion) toward
what you dislike. When dullness clouds your mind, walk up and down,
keep your eyes open, widen and stretch your attention span to dispel lethargy; with restlessness, stay in your body and breathe out. When doubts
arise about the future or whether the practice works or whether you have
the capacity or are a complete mess—break through that jungle with a
fresh "don't know mind." These techniques work, in time. But at times,
my mind just seemed so helter-skelter that it was impervious to just about
any kind of instructions I'd give it. And those hindrances often didn't

come one at a time. Like too many patients entering a doctor's surgical room at the same time, the whole crew would tumble in together fighting and wrangling with each other. Eventually all I could do was sit back and watch the show.

Surprisingly enough, that provided an access point to abandonment. Because it became very clear to me that this was not "my" mind. If it were mine, I could control it. If it were mine, it would have finite, knowable boundaries—but this mind just seemed to have an infinite amount of extendable space for delusion of every kind. And I began to realize that most if not all of its contents were not mine. There was a street scene from the late '60s; there was a rock concert from the early '70s; there was a view from on top of a truck bouncing across Algeria; and so on—all the stuff of sense-impingement from the past, and a few fantasies about the future. There was nothing I could call "me" in that view; just a struggle to get on top of it or make sense out of it all—and I'd just let go of that. Now there was a strange coolness in that way of seeing things.

Sooner or later there's a point at which you have to drop the self-view. It starts with beginning to look at your dukkha in an impersonal way: this is the mind, or this is the mind being driven by habitual actions. It's not the case that you can stop being driven through just any idea—if we cling to ideas, they create their own drives in terms of "I should be this" and "I'm going to get to that." Instead we touch into letting go of self-view through directly knowing "This is how it is." We can see there is the suffering of an uncultivated mind, fed on sensory stimulation, wrong views, and delusion for a couple of decades. How much anguish do we want to make out of this? It means meeting phenomena directly. And for myself it meant abandoning some pretty well-established positions. "I'm going to do it" is one of them; "I can't do it" is another; and the list went on through every kind of self-view about: "I'm not worthy or good enough," "It's not good enough for me," "I have a lot of kamma to work out," and "I have to get rid of self." But none of those strategies put out the fire. At the same time, there was nothing else to do in that little hut in Thailand. I couldn't shrug the whole thing off so I just had to sit back and watch, and feel and be with it all. Funnily enough, that took the heat off, and I began to sense some inner space that wasn't touched by the hindrances. One aspect of craving had been penetrated and abandoned, and it opened up the space for some understanding to inch in a little closer to where the fire was burning.

Now I'm not saying that mine was a great attainment or the full flowering of abandonment or the end of the story. But it gave a hint that abandonment is a continual possibility, not just an end-of-the-line release that may occur after twenty years of practice. It was about stepping back, about seeing the mind-states just as they were, about letting go of self-view. From that letting go of self-view, I could find the space to intuitively "hear" what was needed: patience, kindness, and humor, and then came the wisdom, "Take your time, we have to bear with this." It was strange that simple, cool wisdom seemed to dawn from some part of my mind that I'd not been in contact with before, something that my mind could be touched by and could respond to. And from that place, I could find an approach that would gradually settle the hindrances. For me, it's generally a process of feeling the underlying energies of the hindrances, and connecting that turbulence or stagnation to the steady energy of breathing in and out. The breathing seems to sort things out. Sometimes I might use other strategies to counteract passion or negativity, but all of these approaches are applied from a different place, from somewhere less driven, less self-obsessed with "me getting enlightened."

Abandonment is not suppression or rejection. The motivation that's associated with it is an unwillingness to hold on to assumptions and habits that are causing dukkha. With the presence of seeing or knowing, there is that which sustains the mind by itself. In that sphere, there is no need. Through encouraging investigation and thereby activating our innate wisdom, these noble truths lead us to something incomparably more worthwhile than this mass of dukkha. They give us back to our wisdom, rather than push us into dependency on a technique, a teacher, or a place. That is why these truths are fine, noble, pure, and rare.

What they encourage is an objective investigation into how our senses work, and the dependency of our mind. They point out that if dependency isn't understood and abandoned, we suffer. But if it is, if we can just let our eyes do the seeing, and our mind do its thinking—we don't have to create a self in there to get roasted. Don't you find "cessation" an attractive option? It just means to stop setting your hair on fire! This is the training in abandonment. The Buddha says:

> Thus, Bāhiya, you should train yourself: In what is seen, there is only the seen; in what is heard, there is only the heard; in what is sensed, there is only what is sensed; in what is thought, there is only what is thought. . . . Then for you . . . there will be no "there," where there is no "there" . . . there will be no "here" . . . and because both extremes are not, this indeed is the end of dukkha.
> (U 8)

10

REALIZATION

Absolute Honesty

"There is this noble truth about the cessation of suffering: in this way, bhikkhus, vision, insight, wisdom, knowing, and light arose in me about things not heard before. This noble truth about the cessation of suffering is to be realized. . . . This noble truth about the cessation of suffering has been realized: such was the vision, insight, wisdom, knowing, and light that arose in me about things not heard before."

Here the Buddha talks about realization, about making the spiritual ideal into a felt reality. The word *realization* is the translation of Pāli words based on the root word *sacca,* meaning "actual," "true." The Buddha encourages us to see things directly, without bias, to be absolutely honest. So one of the phrases that is used in describing the practice-path is, "To clear the mind of bias and to insightfully see how things have come into being." It reminds us that the path is not about seeing something in particular; instead, it's about seeing clearly. And we have the potential to do that, a potential that has to be realized. We're not just a mass of suffering, denial, and passion. There's something in us that can witness, something in us that doesn't get caught in the emotional turmoil and heat of the three fires of greed, hatred, and delusion. If there wasn't, how would anyone ever get enlightened or get free? Yes, something in us resonates with the sense of "Buddha" and feels inspired to practice a Dhamma taught by such an enlightened one. However, maybe because this freer mind isn't locatable, and isn't emotionally understood, we lose touch with it. Instead a current runs out of the mind that is strongly felt and it grabs hold of sights, sounds, and ideas. This is the basic current of craving that generates the five hindrances and all our suffering.

Of the five hindrances that I've referred to, the sneakiest one is doubt. It doesn't come in with the loud music or the heavy effects of the others, but it forms one of the ten "fetters"—or major obstacles. And it is this doubt, this not realizing the Dhamma in oneself, that is the major fetter that gets dismantled at the first stage of enlightenment called stream-entry. I know what you're thinking: Stages? Fetters? Well, here's another list—in Buddhism we worship lists rather than gods!

The Four Stages of Enlightenment

The map of enlightenment presents a process of clearing away major obstacles to freedom in four successive stages. That's interesting because it indicates that enlightenment (or awakening) isn't about becoming something; it's not an addition, but a subtraction of the unnecessary clutter that's dragging us down. This clutter is really not at the level of addiction to peanut butter, but is at the level of being addicted to major views or assumptions that we orient ourselves around. That is, we often find and establish ourselves through our personality, our ability to maintain a socially acceptable face to the world. Along with that, we also orient our mind around a set of beliefs or daily routines. All this is something that gives us a sense of knowing who we are, and we feel lost or embarrassed if this cognitive structure gets shaken. And yet this entire structure is learned and acquired, and it does get shaken by external pressures or psychological stress. So to keep creating yourself around how you look and what you believe in is a source of instability, stress, and suffering.

Then again, we instinctively orient ourselves around feeling: feeling good, "I'm OK, I want to be with that" or feeling bad, "I'm shaky and challenged." And in a subtle way, we also orient ourselves around a sense of being, "I am awareness, I am knowingness." This doesn't seem to be a big source of pain, but for one who meditates, even this "I am" is experienced as a constriction, a restless need to be something, and a temptation to adopt the conceit of, "I am beyond it all." So these are the three levels at which the fetters occur: the cognitive or personal, the feeling or instinct, and the ontological or essential.

These fetters can be broken through in four stages of awakening: the first three fetters are centered around a conscious and cognitively based sense of self. These are the ones we'll be looking at in more detail, and breaking through them is called stream-entry, which is the first stage of awakening. Having put aside this sense of self, the other three breakthroughs clean out the remaining fetters. The second breakthrough, called once-return, weakens the fetters that bind our mind to sensory feeling with either interest and attraction or irritation and resistance. This stage is called once-return because if you lessen these two attachments, the rebirth current is so little moved by sense-data that it only produces one more birth. You only look back once at the peanut butter jar as you walk past. The third breakthrough is called nonreturn and it means that you don't look back at the sensory world as it passes through your awareness. So it's good-bye to a birth in terms of sensual incarnation. Finally the last stage of awakening breaks through the remaining fetters, which are the attachment to subtle meditative states (even formless meditative states), conceit (having a notion of being something), restlessness (trying to find or hold what that might be), and ignorance (not fully opening due to subtle holding on or forming a position or a state of being). One who breaks through all of the fetters is rightly called a true worthy one, an *arahant*. (Not that they'd call themselves that, of course.)

Breaking Through the First Three Fetters

So there are a total of ten fetters that fall away through four successive breakthroughs, or stages of enlightenment that cause levels of ignorance to peel off. As I mentioned briefly, the first three fetters (or types of ignorance) that drop away at stream-entry bind our cognitive assumptions—the way that our thinking mind is set up to interpret experience in terms of self. The first fetter is personality-view. This is the superficial aspect of self-view, the belief that the socially conditioned creature of habit who mutters in our head is actually some essential being. When you look at it like that, it seems crazy to hang on to this moody, insecure being, but a lot of the time, that's the program that's calling the shots. The second fetter is doubt, which arises when we don't see the Dhamma intimately. We may have a conceptual understanding of it, but we don't see our own light. And the third is an attachment to customs and systems: our daily routines, our cultural values, our Buddhist tradition, or the meditation technique that we use. At stream-entry all these fetters fall away.

Stream-entry is the beginning of being completely composed on the path. With that level of clarity, there is no longer the instinctive need to hold on to any image, physical or psychological, as one's self. Someone who's "entered the stream" relates to their body as a part of nature. Similarly, they no longer look at someone else's physical image as an expression of their enlightenment—or lack of it. Even more to the point is that they regard the bundle of learned habits, emotional patterns, and attitudes as an acquisition, a product of conditioning, and of old kamma. Stream-enterers are not trying to make the world fit their personality, nor are they trying to abolish their personality. "Personality," after all, is a psychological body that is formed through contact with the world. It's important because we act through that. But through the process of wise attention and inquiry, we can watch how our personality functions, know where to check it, where to encourage it, how to heal it. A certain degree of detachment, as well as insight, is needed in order to respond, kindly, to personality as a worthwhile organ for interaction. After all, we're living in a society where we have to be a "someone"—so be it wisely!

With stream-entry, one no longer has any doubt that the path is based on purity of body and speech, and that it leads to fruition or full awakening. Doubt about whether or not one is capable of cultivating Dhamma, or about the value of that Dhamma, does not arise. With this mature understanding also comes a more balanced attitude regarding the use of techniques, conventions, and practices: one can use them sensibly, avoiding the extremes of either slavishly following them or rebelliously rejecting them. Finally, doubt, uncertainty about the Dhamma, is quelled because through applying himself or herself, a stream-enterer has sensed "the deathless," nibbāna. All that affects and purifies the personality.

We'll get back to the deathless in due course. However, on considering these three fetters that are to be removed, you can see how they work. Personality-view keeps the attention and mode of operating all tied up with sense-input, daily events, personal history, idiosyncrasies, and foibles. So naturally we might not feel that confident—we might wonder, "How can this take me to nibbāna?" Or we might get messianic and sense that our personhood is a manifestation of the absolute. Believing that, because our personality's stuff is all we see and hear, that that's all there is, we naturally enough ask a lot of it, or try to shape it up with some nice, clear-looking structures. And if we have a lot of doubt then we cling like crazy to those structures. We want everything worked out in advance according to the system. We get upset if things don't operate at the right time in the right way (also known as "my way"). We passionately defend our way, our culture, or our religion as the best and the truest or the only way. Fundamentalism, which is an extreme form of this type of clinging, gets very constricting. For example look at royalty and the protocols they have to observe. At an official occasion, the kimonos that a Japanese princess has to wear are so delicately arranged that she has to remain motionless for hours in order to avoid disturbing them. And since she can't go to the bathroom, that may also mean not eating or drinking for hours prior to the ceremony.

Most of us cling to the structure of our daily routines, and for meditators, we often cling to our meditation technique. People can hold on to strong views about where one should watch the breathing—at the nose-tip or abdomen—even though the Buddha never specified a precise spot.

In fact he said simply that one should be mindful of breathing (which is a process not a thing). So it's probably up to the individual to find out what works. But when there's clinging, or wanting to cling to some technique, that undermines our own wisdom faculty, our innate sense of knowing. Subsequently we might be inclined to reject techniques—which isn't right either. The way out is to be honest: for example, when breathing in and out, just simply be aware of breathing in and out. We don't have to lay all kinds of meditation structures over it.

Honesty and Wise Seeing

Being honest about our clinging leads us to inquire as to what keeps us bound to these unsatisfactory ways of operating. And with that sense of inquiry, as we step back from engaging in the fetters and just look into them rather than condemning or justifying them, we find some intimate wisdom, clarity, and light. We know there is no point in operating through these forms of clinging because that either supports the wall that we build against life, or keeps us running on automatic. However, every time we step back and review ourselves, there is a steady "This is how it is" kind of wisdom—a wise seeing—that lessens the personality-view. After all, there's nothing so uniquely "me" about having a personality with its foibles and limitations. This is everyone's stuff.

These two—the ability to step back, and the wise seeing—go together and support each other. They ripen in abandonment, in complete letting go. They are part of our innate potential; we can bring them into play, but a lot of the time we don't. The life-view of getting things and getting ahead moves in one direction, and stepping back doesn't seem to be in accord with that view. It's nonproductive, so we don't have time for it. But what we begin to realize is that if we don't step back, time has us. We're on the run, on the treadmill of work, career, and getting ahead; on the vehicle of getting what we can out of life, a vehicle that's driven by a blind driver. But if we can't afford ten minutes, or even five minutes to step back, that blind driver is going to stay in the driver's seat. If we can step back, and not be anything or be nothing—not adopting some view that life's a waste of time, but just curtail getting wasted by time—then there's room for a subtle inner light to dawn. For a moment we *can* stop putting the pressure on, and stop running to find something to be filled by. That moment of ending dukkha can be realized.

Stepping back—out of past and future, out of pulling this way or that way, out of finding answers or coming to a conclusion—is a subtle action of mind. It's like an outbreath, a deflation of being, becoming, and needing. The Buddha referred to this shift of perspective, this moving out of gear, as "unattaching" or "nonattachment" (*viveka*). I experience it as a shift, rather than as a philosophical stance that I adopt. It begins with stepping back from the pull into sense-pleasure, and it generates a quality of dispassion in our mind. Dispassion about experience and dispassion about how we are or aren't cools the fires that get kindled by personality-view—the "Will I succeed?" "Will I be popular?" turmoil that drives teenagers in particular into deep anxiety and depression. Consider how much of the day or year is already booked before it starts with things like, "On Fridays I do this"; "Come July we'll go on vacation"; and worse, "I have to go to the office party because it's expected of me." Nonattachment to customs and systems can help us to step out of the routines to find the time to sense ourselves afresh. It gives us a chance to realize, "Here I am, I'm a being, not just a doing." All those forces of other people's opinions, of fulfilling social roles and objectives—they're not me, not mine, and they change. Right there is a glimpse of freedom. This ability to step back has to be realized, because it checks the compulsive volition of craving, or of trying to become something. It gives us something clear and peaceful to center our life around and so it lessens the potential for suffering.

Nonattachment arrests some of the biases and in that space, the light of wisdom, of seeing clearly, can come forth. Wisdom, like nonattachment, is innate—but it too needs to be activated, brought forth, and realized. Then when it is brought into the context of suffering, wisdom supports letting go—and it points to the way out.

This theme has been touched on throughout this book. But it must be said that although we get intuitive flashes of knowing, we have to cultivate right view and right intention to clear access to it and allow it to grow and become fully conscious. And we have to further cultivate mindfulness and concentration to take that knowing into the blurred and compulsive knee-jerk reactions of the blind driver. One fundamental process that brings wisdom to light is the practice of being absolutely honest about what's going on. This is done by establishing mindfulness with reference to body, feelings, mind-states, and the mental phenomena, both positive and negative, that are relevant for purification and for enlightenment.

Mindfulness and Concentration

The practice of establishing mindfulness is outlined in two suttas known as the Satipaṭṭhāna Suttas, or "The Foundations of Mindfulness" (MN 10, DN 22). These texts describe how, being clearly conscious and having a sense of ardency, we focus on bodily processes as they are—most readily on breathing in and breathing out. We just keep returning to that rhythmic process of breathing, as we might return to a theme in music, even while there's a whole lot of other noise going on around. Even simpler, we abide "contemplating body as body"; for example, when walking, just attune to the experience of a body walking. This practice is about focusing, staying with and not adding anything to the process. Furthermore, we are encouraged to know a hating mind as affected by hate, a deluded mind as affected by delusion, a developed mind as developed, an unsurpassed mind as unsurpassed. Even the hindrances are to be contemplated in this nonjudgmental way: noticing greed, hatred, dullness, restlessness, and doubt—when they are present, under what conditions they arise, how they can be abandoned, and the way that prevents them from arising. Above all, through mindfulness and concentration we get to sense that although our mind is affected by love and hate, it can stand back from those affects. Sensing this, the domain of nonattachment can widen.

This brings us back to the same mental mode that we developed with the contemplation of the four noble truths: a direct, steady witnessing of what creates our views, opinions, judgments, and passions. It's not that we aren't doing something about the problem by meditating—the "knowing it as it is" approach requires both a keen attention and the restraint to not get pulled in to the show. No comment about the show is being made. The monologue of self that normally attends our actions and thoughts like the audience in a theater, alternately hissing and booing at the villains and cheering the heroes, is steadily reduced each time that we bring our mind back to the object of contemplation. The theater empties, and so there is less reactive energy looping around in our mind and triggering off more reactions. And we begin to notice the silence and abide in that. Energy is withdrawn from the proliferation of feelings and perceptions around mental and physical objects, and the hindrances fade out. But the energy, purified and untangled, remains. So when there is attention without self-conscious bias, our mind begins to clear in a light and peaceful way. As it clears, it feels uplifted, and as it does so, it feels refreshed and at ease. And so it settles into concentration. The knowing also goes with it, witnessing subtler forms of stress and attachment. Knowing initiates release. Nonattachment deepens into the nonclinging that breaks the fetters.

Mindfulness and knowingness, or full awareness (*sampajañña*) as it is initially sensed, can become a common factor for our everyday life. As the Satipaṭṭhāna Suttas point out, this full awareness can even be present to the point of knowing when mindfulness isn't present. So although mindfulness is set up and established, knowingness is part of that innate wisdom faculty. It can be present in any circumstance that is headed by right intention, and it can be directed to cover each moment of experience. So in one way, this knowing is beyond circumstance. However, we do have to support the conditions that allow us to consciously engage it. Its fleeting nature is actually the fleetingness of our dwelling in it, mainly because we're not always interested in being awake. Being awake doesn't usually seem so important—until, of course, you feel dukkha.

But if we can square up to it, if it doesn't blow us away, dukkha can be understood, or maybe "stood under," opened up to. If we can follow the process of feeling and attachment through to its (bitter) end, after the love and the despair and the tears and the blame, we will come back to the knowing. The knowing is dispassionate. Dispassion then is to be fostered as a way of connecting honestly, letting things speak for themselves without claiming or denying them. And yes, we have that potential for dispassion too—but you can't create it out of nowhere, it too has to be realized.

While this knowingness still feeds back to a mind that hasn't acknowledged it, all the interpretations that get made are in terms of self. "I'm doing well"; "I'm happy"; "My mindfulness is strong"; "My mindfulness is weak." This connection, then, is one that provides wood for the fire of grasping to take hold of. And in that case, we attach to the system that is making us feel calm, or we have a sense that we've made progress and feel we know how much further there is to go—or we may even think that we're fully realized beings because we can witness the thoughts in our mind without getting stirred up by them. There is still a notion that I have been in some state, I am in another, and I wonder what comes next? This type of thinking is a foundation for doubt and self-view. For realization, knowing has to disconnect from leaning at any level. The clearest way to do this is to focus on the object and on anything that we "know" as changable. And as we take that focus deep into right concentration, there is the realization that holding any state as lasting is dukkha. This loosens up the holding on to mind-states, as well as the very dependency, the self-view, that wants to grasp a mind-state. When there's no holding, and no leaning or inclining, awareness is broad—and no one owns it.

Not holding on to any state is tough to do because we're not honest a lot of the time, which is because of fear, the fear of losing our self-image. The social pressure to get ahead and win is so ingrained that we're anxious about failure, about losing our position or livelihood. This anxiety about doing becomes anxiety about being, because in a driven life, doing *is* being: you're supposed to be doing and you're assessed by it. But anxiety about being isn't something we want to own up to—because we should be confident, happy, and successful. Otherwise, there's an anxiety about losing our friends. Furthermore if we direct that honesty into our heart and mind, we're uneasy about being with the anxiety, the sadness or the bleakness of a mind that we've neglected. No wonder we lose touch with its innate wisdom and warmth. Just letting our mind get filled by any old sight, sound, thought, or impulse that the world throws our way, then pressuring it to come up with the goods at any given time—that's no way to treat a mind. It's like you give it the wrong food and expect it to keep raising its level of performance.

So we need to be honest about the fact that we can end this dukkha. We need to be honest that it is necessary and that there is a way to accomplish this goal, if we have the courage and the know-how. Anxiety about being can make us elevate the path to an out-of-reach place, saying, "It's beyond someone like me." But the question is, Where does suffering stop for you? Aren't there those "no-pressure" moments, or those "feeling welcome" scenarios, or those "This is the way I am, and that's all I can be right now" acknowledgments that you can experience some degree of freedom? In terms of the path, we're looking at freedom as a one-moment-at-a-time experience. When the driven sense abates or stops, even for a moment, when craving to be is relinquished, what is left, what is present? Is there a person, an image of who "I" am, was, or should be in our heart? Or is there just "cessation," a rest that isn't dead or asleep?

This cessation that Dhamma-practice steers us to comes in stages— that's why it's good to know about four breakthroughs and ten fetters. And also that even if a fetter remains, we can be on the path toward breaking it. It's not that the whole bondage drops away in one shot; liberation is a gradual process. So we look at places where we stop suffering, and try to sense what brings that about. We have to bring it down from some "way out there," "ultimate" position to realizing that it's something you do that you need to do more of, more often. The Buddha wouldn't have taught it if it were out of reach. Realizing the ending of some suffering in oneself, and what was absent when that occurred, gives us direction, gives us encouragement, and gives us back our authority.

The other main obstacle to being honest concerns not really acknowledging our aims and means. The bias to get and to become, or to sense that we can never develop at all—all that finds a way for us to lose aspiration. Sometimes people feel that any aim is an egotistical search, like we're a dumb donkey chasing the carrot that always moves ahead because it's dangling on a stick strapped to its head. Well, we have all kinds of aims—aims to eat, enjoy ourselves, and so on—so why not use the aiming energy of our mind for inquiry into well-being? To look at where we struggle and how that stops—that's an aim. And wouldn't that be supported by a means of steadying our mind? On the other hand, people can get stuck in the self-view of "I can't do it," which is based upon assumptions about doing, and that there's a need to push hard. But doing Dhamma isn't always an uphill struggle, and effort isn't always like lifting weights. Effort is skillful when it is moderated with calmness, kindness, and patience—and is applied one moment at a time. Perhaps this is why the Buddha called his teachings a path: to walk it, you have to establish a foundation, take that step, realize and dwell in the results—*then* the next step becomes clear. He explained it as a natural process:

> Bhikkhus, for one who is virtuous . . . there is no need to wish: "May freedom from remorse arise in me." Bhikkhus, it is in accordance with Dhamma that freedom from remorse arises in one who is virtuous. For one who is free from remorse, there is no need to wish: "May joy arise in me." Bhikkhus, it is in accordance with Dhamma that joy arises in one who is free from remorse.
> (AN 10:2)

And similarly joy is the foundation for rapture, rapture for calm, calm for contentment, contentment for concentration, concentration for insight, insight for dispassionate realization, realization for liberation.

Sometimes even attainments become sticking points. You want more, or wonder if this is *it*. There is a story of the Venerable Anuruddha, a renowned bhikkhu who sought the advice of the arahant Sāriputta. Anuruddha had developed some remarkable qualities, which he described to Sāriputta: he had the "divine eye" with which he could see the ten-thousandfold world system. (That is the entire cosmos of heavens, hells, and human realms.) He had great energy and resolute mindfulness, yet he said his heart was not at peace. The Venerable Sāriputta replied:

> Well, Anuruddha, as to your statement about seeing the ten-thousandfold world system, that is just your conceit. And to

your statement about being strenuous and unshaken and so forth, that is just arrogance. As to your statement about your heart not being released . . . that is just worrying. It would indeed be well for the Venerable Anuruddha if he were to abandon these three conditions, if he were not to think about them, but were to focus his mind on the Deathless element.
(AN 3:128)

The Deathless

So what and where is "the deathless element"? What does the phrase "realizing the deathless" refer to? Is it a thing, a mind-state, something sublime, even formless? Is it that gentle radiance that we might experience now and then when our meditation is going right? Naturally enough, our tendency is to seek out and create perceptions about the "deathless" that foster our sense of being or feeling something. But all that is part of the experienced world, and it arises and passes. What the Buddha pointed to was in a different domain—where seeking and being something can cease. The domain of letting go, and the sense of not-leaning. One time, talking to his disciple Ānanda, he described the range of consciousness from that of the sensory realm on to more and more refined states of perception. And in summing it up he compared all of that to the result of not clinging:

> Here Ānanda, a noble disciple considers thus: "Sensual pleasures here and now and sensual pleasures in lives to come, sensual perceptions here and now and sensual perceptions in lives to come, material forms here and now and material forms in lives to come, perceptions of forms here and now and perceptions of forms in lives to come, perceptions of the imperturbable, perceptions of the base of nothingness, and perceptions of the base of neither-perception-nor-nonperception—this is as far as personality extends. This is the Deathless, namely the liberation of the mind through not clinging."
> (MN 106:13)

So rather than posit some absolute truth, the Buddha pointed to letting go. And that means being absolutely honest about what's here. Knowing is a given that needs to be realized and made use of. Nonattachment is a given that needs to be realized and brought into action. Together, and supported by other path-factors, they can take us out of anxiety and craving to the point where a deep relinquishment of being anything can take place. So the deathless is not a given, not some ultimate self or True Nature; it is just that full connection to the way it is—that really there is no place in the vast world of time, space, or mind to hold on to. That domain of no location, where wanting and losing and hankering and doubting end, is only entered by cultivating a path to that ending. The path doesn't create it, so beware of getting fascinated by the signposts and the paving stones and who laid them and which are the nicest. Just do some honest, unwavering walking: that, as the Buddha continues to remind the Group of Five, is the path that is to be cultivated.

11

CULTIVATION

The Wheel on the Road

"There is this noble truth of the path leading to the cessation of suffering. . . . This noble truth of the path is to be cultivated. . . . This noble truth of the path has been cultivated: such was the vision, insight, wisdom, knowing, and light that arose in me about things not heard before."

In teaching this last noble truth, the Buddha says that a path is needed. In other words, we have to keep going, even after a flash of not-suffering, and relate whatever breakthroughs we experience to an ongoing course of practice. So an overview, a map of the path, is very useful. And we should find a way to keep going when there still is suffering; we should find a way to relate to that too. Here again, a map of the path is handy. When you hear mention of five hindrances and ten fetters (which give rise to relief, joy, and clarity, when they are let go of), you want to check in with that map. Ask yourself, "How am I doing? I'm in a pretty good (or confused) space—now what?"

So it's helpful to keep checking in with the map of the path—in order to cultivate it. To use another analogy, we need an instruction manual. Dhamma practice entails processes akin to breaking soil, planting seeds, weeding, watering, and giving it time. You need a manual to say which process is relevant at which time. However, wherever we're at, we pay attention to our mind and feed it with faith, energy, mindfulness, concentration, and wisdom. Out of those factors, the way to cultivate our practice will arise. Furthermore we cultivate letting go with reference to attainments, hindrances, and defilements. In brief, the wisdom of nonclinging is the main thing to develop.

There's a moving account in the Pāli texts of a bhikkhu called Khemaka who had broken through not just the first three fetters, but also the fetters of residual sense-craving and ill-will. He was therefore a nonreturner, one who doesn't get born again into a physical body. Still, he hadn't completed the path, and he knew it. The account tells of how, even though he was seriously ill at the time, he made a point of dragging himself over to a place where a group of elder monks were debating, to participate in the discussion by defining how he *wasn't* completely enlightened. In his case although the obvious forms of clinging had vanished, and he didn't attach to any of the aggregates in particular, still he could a sense a lingering sense of "I am," the smell of "*being* enlightened." And being wise, he knew what to do. Here's what he said:

> Suppose, friends, a cloth had become soiled and stained, and its owners give it to a laundryman. The laundryman would scour it evenly with cleaning salt, lye, or cowdung and rinse it in clean water. Even though that cloth would become pure and clean, it would still retain a residual smell of cleaning salt, lye, or cowdung that had not yet vanished. . . . The owners would put it in a sweet-scented casket, and the residual smell of cleaning salt, lye, or cowdung that had not yet vanished would vanish.
> (SN 22: Aggregates 89)

In essence, Khemaka handed his practice and realizations over to the path. Rather than proceed from any kind of "I am" position, his furtherance was based on continuing to witness change and not-self with regard to the aggregates. In his case that would include perceptions of enlightenment, states of consciousness, and the very volition that sustains the practice-path. He knew that all that ongoing stuff is not me, not mine.

Khemaka's example, and that of many others, teaches us that cessation comes periodically; it's the same process of abandonment, but it has to work through the levels defined by the four stages and the ten fetters. Khemaka had let go of all but the last three fetters—conceit, restlessness, and unknowing (or ignorance). Conceit here isn't pride but is the residual notion like a smell, that there's an "I am" around somewhere, though it can't be placed. So the first major cessation—of the obstacles to stream-entry—and the many minor fallings away of obsessions and stuck places, are only the first, though precious, fruits of the path.

Having insights and then making too much of them can be an obstacle to letting go. At certain times of intense practice, a sense of realization may dawn and our mind can become very clear and peaceful. That clarity may last for a few minutes or even days; but the greater clarity is to have the clarity about cessation and how it fits into an ongoing path. Otherwise we can overestimate or underestimate the insights and releases that occur. Some people still try to understand the meaning of a mystical experience of oneness that they had a decade ago. In a sense, that extraordinary experience has subsequently spoiled their practice because they continue to remember the experience and focus on wishing to have it again, or they wonder whether it was really valid and where it went. The uncertainty makes it difficult to start afresh.

Sometimes people turn up at the monastery claiming to be arahants and bodhisattvas (those who've put aside final enlightenment to help others). The arahants are difficult enough—they don't want to fit into the routines and help out, and they expect special treatment. But the bodhisattvas are even worse, because they feel obliged to tell you how you've got it all wrong, and they want to set up a teaching program to help you get things right. We had a bodhisattva at our monastery once who couldn't tolerate anything cooked in a Teflon-coated pan or any processed foods like white sugar or white rice. Eventually he left.

Not everyone becomes so deluded, but sometimes we do have valid insights into not-self and experiences of cessation that nonetheless get distorted. It's like if you set the feet of a ladder on a box of matches, climb on the ladder, and have someone kick the matchbox away, the ladder only jolts down a couple of inches, but in that moment you get the same sense of falling as if you'd dropped a long way. Release is like that. So you have to watch for the long-term results. Ask yourself, "Is anything picked up? Is there anything left to take hold of?" And then continue as before. It's not that the insight or the release isn't true, but the problem is that feeding and clinging are such residual habits that we feed on the memory of the moments of release. Or there's an attachment that forms around witnessing. As the Buddha put it:

> Here bhikkhus, some recluse or brahmin, with the relinquishing of views about the past and the future, through complete lack of resolve upon the fetters of sensual pleasure, and with the surmounting of the rapture of seclusion, unworldly pleasure, and neither painful-nor-pleasant feeling, regards himself thus: "*I* am at peace, *I* have attained Nibbāna, *I* am without clinging." ... And that too is declared to be clinging on the part of this good recluse or brahmin.
> (MN 102:24)

The self-view affects our activities, motivation, and sense of achievement. It can be extremely helpful then to live in a way that constantly asks something of you and trains you to relate to the here and now without self-consciousness. This takes cultivation, in meditation and in the more random flow of daily life—where we can't always find the space to be above it all. Our bluff gets called when we put our Dhamma-wheel on the rocky road.

So rather than having a one-off experience that just gets stashed in one's identity cupboard, respect for the path makes us willing to be put to the test in meditation and also in the "no-control" world of limitations, restrictions, things going wrong, and unexpected things happening. It's particularly revealing to see how one's mind works or reacts when we're out of a tranquil and controlled situation such as a retreat, and are getting our buttons pushed. Whether it's our health or pressure at work or the blame of others, the sure practice is to refer the experience to how suffering operates, and how to let go of it:

> He attends wisely: "This is suffering"; he attends wisely: "This is the origin of suffering"; he attends wisely: "This is the cessation of suffering"; he attends wisely: "This is the way leading to the cessation of suffering."
> (MN 2:11)

The Buddha described his own experience of fully awakening in a particular way. It wasn't just a momentary flash but a thorough review of the way the mind works, and, with each realization, the Buddha later commented: "But I allowed no pleasant feeling that arose in me to gain power over my mind." So the bliss of release at each stage wasn't grasped at—he maintained a focus on the path established by the understanding of mental kamma, cause, noting results but not getting absorbed into them. The severance of each fetter comes when fundamental constraining activities (*āsava*) stop at each level of awakening. *Āsava* means something like toxic seepage; it's translated as "outflow" (as from an abscess), or "influx" (as from a leak in a sewage system), or "taints" (to describe the bias that they place on the mind's awareness). The language is striking in its intensity for a good reason: we don't take this stuff seriously enough. However, like a leak in a dam, *āsava* are of the nature to create further and more damaging floods; they open up the hairline cracks for a whole lot of mental and emotional stuff to come gushing out.

The Buddha described three outflows, three ways in which the mind rushes out in avalanche mode. These may be listed as: the outflow of sensuality (*kāmāsava*)—a trajectory based on the sensory "description" of reality, the outflow of becoming (*bhavāsava*), and the outflow of ignorance (*avijjāsava*). The mind rushes into those modes of activity the way that water heads toward the sea down a gradient. So although there is volition, no conscious effort is necessary. Because of this, by and large the outflows seem selfless and go unnoticed. People deny they were angry, they say they were being firm and making things clear. Or in spiritual circles, they come up with lines like, "It was anger, but there was nobody being angry" or, "This isn't attachment, it's just sensory appetite happening as a natural energy." But what's the good of *that*?

Outflows rest on underlying biases that remain as latent tendencies in consciousness, rather like a dry riverbed in a dry season. Then when the rain of irritating contact, or of attraction, pours down, we have a flash flood. It may not be deliberate; it may come from a place that is beyond or beneath our personal selfhood—but that doesn't mean that there's no kamma and no result. People still drown, and with each flood, the riverbed deepens. Because of this we have to maintain path-factors to keep the flood in check.

The outflow of sensuality is based on the empty feeling of that riverbed and its interest in being filled by sights, sounds, tastes, touches, and so on. When there is wisdom to assess the experience, we can acknowledge that the mind is only filled by sense-data for a while. Then the wisdom of nonclinging can arise, the wisdom that knows the mind as distinct from sense-objects. This wisdom, as it flows through the mind, makes what used to feel "empty" now feel bright and calm. This uproots the bias toward sensuality. No matter how flooding the sense contact, nothing fills a mind that has the bias toward sensuality. The outflow of becoming is powerful. As a latent tendency it works as the quality of mind that looks toward the future and wants things to be solid. This tendency is uprooted as the wisdom of nonclinging refers to the sense of time. Time as a sense is not numbers on a clock, it's the pull of becoming. When this wisdom reviews that, it sees that there is no end, no achievement in time, only the pushing onward. It sees that there's no solid ground, only mirages. The wisdom of nonclinging itself is the only true ground. And that's timeless, here and now.

Ignorance rests on the tendency to not see. In brief, this fetter is uprooted by the wisdom of knowing the path. It is the path that uproots the biases, not some self. In ways that may be more obviously apparent, ignorance outflows as the unwillingness to notice and respond to cause and effect, the push that takes us into addictions when we know on one level that they don't make us happy, or the flash that starts the violent reflex that we should know doesn't solve problems. Ignorance stands on the edge of uncertainty or the prospect of facing unpleasant feelings, and pushes us to do anything to stay out of that darkness. But ignorance *is* the darkness because feelings come and go; life goes on uncertain as ever, and will terminate at an unpredictable time. If we could develop a mature response to dukkha, we would be able to switch off the empty feeling and its darkness.

These are strong pulls when they're flowing. So it's generally the case that when they're not, we look carefully into our mind for any underlying biases. This may not be that hard to do—in fact it may be difficult to know where to start! But when you consider that flash flood of dependent arising, and how it depends on the twinned factors of unknowing and craving; or when you contemplate the five hindrances—and how all of them amplify with the sense of "I am"—you recognize that you need a team of factors and not a self to deal with them. You use the wisdom of investigation to look at how you can set unknowing and craving apart, by acknowledging, "This is the pushy bit, this is the craving, and this is the knowing of that." And by acknowledging these things, the links get weaker and weaker. So the wisdom of nonclinging is to be strengthened and applied by the "factors of awakening": mindfulness, investigation, energy, rapture, tranquility, concentration, and equanimity. These are factors you can trust more than your biased ego. We apply factors of the path to bring these factors of awakening into being, then we strengthen and refer our experience to them and let them work on us.

There's wisdom in knowing how to develop these factors of awakening. In practice this comes down to maintaining mindfulness and investigation around the arising and passing of sensations, feelings, interpretations, impulses, or mind-states. (This is another way of describing the five aggregates, as we experience them in meditation.) Then, through steadily holding your mind in that inquiry, clinging starts to stand out because it is unsteady. And in the place of clinging, calmness develops. Through developing calm, you experience the qualities of ease, spaciousness, and inner silence, which gives you a reference point to know when clinging arises. You come to know clinging by how it feels: a certain tightening in the body and mind. And you come to recognize the voices through which it speaks: in thoughts of righteousness, self-pity, and sneakiness. And as you contemplate clinging, you get the basic understanding that it isn't owned: the sense of "I" arises as a result of the clinging moment, rather than before it. There isn't the decision: "I think I'll cling today, see how much suffering I can create for myself." So it's not that, "I have a lot of attachments, and cling a lot." It's just that the origin of clinging has not been seen. Clinging is an action, not a person. This understanding encourages us to find a way where we can stop that grasping reflex.

Two other factors of awakening, rapture and tranquility, are also important qualities in meditation. They help to relax the mind's grasp, because they address that sense of needing to be filled. In this way they help to ease up one of the big issues of self: Can I feel good? They arise through sensing the space of the mind when the hindrances lapse, that absence of pressure. But you have to know where and how to look for them: not as something that you do or get, but in the background. Often rapture begins in the body as an easing up of tension, which can be focused on and its sense of release can be spread throughout the body until the overall feeling is light and buoyant. People may experience rapture in terms of an inner light, or a sense of awe and silence. The Buddha's recommendation is to stay grounded in the body:

> A bhikkhu makes the rapture and pleasure born of seclusion drench, steep, and pervade this body, so that there is no part of his whole body unpervaded by the rapture and bliss.
> (MN 119:18)

The pleasantness of rapture can be destabilizing—a rapturous mind can come up with fascinating lights and spaces and moods—that's why the advice is to ground it in the body. But more than the pleasantness of the feeling of relief is the shift in volition: rapture and tranquility relax the sense of self as doer. You *do* the attention and the focusing, but rapture and tranquility are *born* of nonattachment. You don't *do* them; they come to you, when the mind is settled in its meditation theme. The experience is rather like being a boat that's beached in the sand as the tide comes in: first there's a gentle touching by some uplifting quality, then gradually things start gently rocking until the boat is afloat. So we can let go of "self as doer," without having to be "self as rigid" or "self as collapse." And then: What does that feel like? How is that quality of openness, or noninvolvement, furthered? Tranquility gives you the ease and sensitivity to really check that out; there's the need to develop this so that the thoughts based on "me trying" give up. There is trust in the process of meditation. Then as mental and bodily tensions relax, concentration (*samādhi*) arises. It's easeful, firm, and brings a sense of unification. The powerful incline, the gradient that ties us toward sense objects, is quelled.

One of the great benefits of concentration is that it holds calm and ease and knowing at the level of the mind that is often unconscious or bound up with reflexes. This is where the biases and latencies lie—at an involuntary level where we're "not ourselves." And so it takes factors that are not about "me trying" or "me doing it" to penetrate that; to go down to that prepersonal potential in the nerve endings, and step back from those ingrained biases. This is why we need all the factors of awakening, not just some mindfulness or understanding.

Then equanimity, the final factor of awakening, holds a dispassionate space. It's more than just a check on emotional reactions—equanimity as a factor of awakening entails sensing and dwelling in the stillness without owning it. Through equanimity, volition is released from claiming anything. This is a giving up whereby nothing need be said or done. So, as the text puts it, the factors of awakening are to be developed "based on seclusion [nonattachment], dispassion, and cessation, and they ripen in complete release," (SN 46: Factors of Enlightenment 1).

The Ten Perfections

And then, there's maintaining the path outside of meditation. In this respect, the persistent cultivation of "perfections" (or *pāramitā*) has evolved into a main theme in Buddhist cultures. Perfections are ways of generating good kamma so that when practicing in daily life, the mind is trained to release unskillful thoughts and deepen into transcendent ones. They help us to keep the path in mind on the mundane level, so that we're prepared for those moments when we get flustered and squeezed and can't just dip into samādhi. Two main sets of texts and teachings—called Theravāda and Mahāyāna—group these qualities differently; what I'll describe here is the way that they're expressed in the Theravada tradition, as that's my own practice tradition.

In Theravada, the pāramitā are listed as generosity, morality, renunciation, wise discernment, energy (or vigor), patience, truthfulness, kindness, resolution, and equanimity. All these ask us to bring forth skill from our heart in response to what we experience, and it's a response that has letting go of greed, aversion, and delusion as its aim.

Generosity is about sharing; and not just in material terms. It's a whole attitude to life. We share resources of money, time, skills, and energy because of the sense of interrelatedness that is the bedrock of life. We're all in this together, everything affects everything else: consider other people's welfare as you'd like them to consider yours—this is how to transcend self-view on a mundane level. And when we act from that sense of interdependence and create good kamma, the result is that we feel good. So everyone gains. The giver feels joy and the receiver feels the effects of kindness. Through the practice of perfections a sense of innate value—in oneself, in others, but mostly in the blessing of skillful action—arises. This does go against the Western "anti-ego" notion that you shouldn't feel good about your own actions, but not feeling good about your actions just generates a cynical or sad ego. So by referring to actions and results, the teachings on pāramitā bypass self-view in what they do and how they're understood. It's not what we think we are, it's what we *do*.

All the perfections follow that principle. They speak for themselves. Morality leads to self-respect and the trust of people around us. Renunciation draws us out of the grip of the materialist energies that control much of society. Discernment cuts through the blur of feelings to tell us what is skillful and what isn't. Kindness and compassion are the only workable ways to live with other people. Patience—to not rush, to allow things to move at a harmonious rate—is great for the willful, "got to get it done" mind-set that accompanies obsession. In a busy, deadline-based world, always get ready to push the patience button. If we want to experience the beauty of equanimity, cultivate patience. Monastic life is great for that: being dependent on what people offer, we have to wait for the resources to turn up. Sometimes in a backwoods monastery that means going without the tool that would make a job simple, or repairing your own equipment, or washing things by hand. We may have to wait until someone with a car, or someone who can drive the monastery's car, turns up before you can run an errand. Sometimes people are late bringing food—they are stuck in traffic, or have lost their way. So we wait for the meal. It's amazing how, having burned in the fires of impatience for a while, something lets go and we feel serene. When we have resolution, the commitment to go through the fire, a psychological space opens up—we feel the space of equanimity and we get to operate in a steady and sustainable way.

These pāramitā are not always on display in the world; nor does their cultivation mean that you will become a success in worldly terms. But it might happen. A friend of mine in business told me that years ago he vowed to only deal honestly with clients—no false promises, no granting favors, no illegal fixes. At first his business declined a little, but after a while, as people realized that they could trust that what he said was what he meant, they began to prefer his straight way of dealing, and his business increased. Ethical business can make sense. At any rate, we always gain in terms of having self-respect, a clear conscience, and friends that we can rely upon. It's these things that will get us through the tough times. When the economy crashes or our health fails, when we're bereaved or blamed, knowing how to live simply and be an equanimous witness to experience is a real lifesaver. As the Buddha says:

> "When a person has assessed the world from top to bottom," the Master [the Buddha] says, "when there is nothing in the world that raises a flicker of agitation, then he has become a person free from the smoke fumes, the tremblings, and the hunger

of desire. He has become calm. He has gone beyond getting old;
he has gone beyond being born."
(Su-N 1048)

But it takes resolution—for months, and years. The practice of pāramitā doesn't really get going until we have felt the fire of greed, aversion, and delusion, and have heard the blaming and the complaining of our mind. And it doesn't get going until we have caught the whisper of the wily, "How can I get out of letting go?" voice of the mind. That will only manifest when we stick with it. Then we know the one we have to get past, and if we turn to our wisdom rather than to our craving, we can drop a big chunk of embedded suffering.

With the factors of awakening and pāramitā, we can bring wisdom and nonattachment into focus on various levels so that we don't leave any blind spots. We can discover wisdom as the basic ability to know an object, to discriminate; wisdom as knowing to look into our own mind and heart; wisdom as knowing how to step back and gain a wider perspective; wisdom as knowing the feel of kamma, of good and evil; and wisdom to review experience in terms of the four noble truths. Out of these arise right knowledge (*sammāñña*) and right release (*sammāvimutta*), the fruition of wisdom and letting go.

Because the practice-path has mundane as well as supramundane fruitions, we get to see the results in how we or other people act. A lot can be said about moral conduct and simplicity of needs, but what has also impressed and inspired me has been the clear faculties and the mental agility of great practitioners. They make it seem that life, and even spiritual life, is a kind of skill, a kind of play. I remember when Ajahn Chah visited our small residence in London, there was an artist who'd spent ages painting a stunningly lifelike portrait of Ajahn Chah. The artist showed him his work, and Ajahn Chah wryly commented, "If I scribbled all over it, would you get upset?" The artist was a meditator—he got the point and laughed.

Playfulness is a way of being that avoids the pitfall of self-importance. Play doesn't have to be reckless or distracting; it can also take us into experience in an adventurous and challenging way that uses energy, concentration, and mindfulness. And in this light we can walk and wobble along the path, rather than get frozen on a tightrope over the chasm of failure. Did you make a mistake? Get back on track. Did you have a good result? Refer to the path. The nervousness and clumsiness of self-consciousness gets consumed in the purity of the action. This letting go of success and failure means that we are able to live in the present with all the uncertainties and tangled history, without flowing out into ignorance and becoming. To put it another way:

> They do not sorrow over the past,
> Nor do they hanker for the future.
> They maintain themselves with what is present:
> Hence their complexion is serene.
> (SN 1: Devas 10)

12

THE HOST OF MĀRA

"As long, bhikkhus, as these four noble truths in their twelve aspects were not seen by me; not seen with the purest insight as they are, then I didn't teach the world—with its devas, māras, and brahmas, its samanas and brahmins, its monarchs and ordinary folk—that I had fully realized complete awakening.

"But, bhikkhus, as soon as these four noble truths in their twelve aspects were seen by me; seen with the purest insight as they are, then I taught the world—with its devas, māras, and brahmas, its samanas and brahmins, its monarchs and ordinary folk—that I had fully realized complete awakening. The knowledge and the vision arose in me: 'My release is assured. This is the last birth. There is no further becoming.'"

The Buddha, speaking to the Group of Five, points out that he didn't teach the four noble truths until he had actually put the path into practice himself, and turned the path into the fruition—letting go of all clinging.

Before you can let go of the clinging that establishes self-view, you have to get to the point where you see it as a view, not as a real thing that has to be destroyed, but as a shadow that dogs our thoughts and actions. The practice up to that point is like clearing through smoke to find out where the fire is based. And a lot of that smoke gets in your eyes. So to a sincere but unenlightened meditator, the difficulties of the mind may be experienced as a kind of swirling shadow. It's a shadow that seems to know your weak spots, a cunning shadow. This is what the Buddha called Māra.

In the texts that look at experience in a more graphic and allegorical way, Māra, presented as "he," is a demon who knows how to get us spinning and grasping. Māra is the force that identifies us with the changing conditions of body and mind. Doubt is one of his main voices, that and identifying with the uncertainties of existence: "Is this the right path for me?"; "I shouldn't have such doubts"; "I shouldn't repress doubts"; "Why am I a repressive person?" and so on. These all contribute to the sense of self, which is an oppressive, congested feeling. Even a relatively insensitive person feels shut in when these creations are coming out of the smoke. Then, having thrown us off balance and into believing in smoke, Māra urges us to smother one set of smoky self-images with another: he encourages us to drive ourselves hard to prove that we aren't lazy, to be austere to prove that we aren't greedy, to be indulgent in order to be a more fun kind of person . . . to keep becoming somebody in order to suppress the doubt, guilt, and anxiety that are an inevitable feature of the unenlightened mind. The mental congestion gets pretty dense.

For Siddhattha, the Buddha-to-be, it was the same. The only difference was that he didn't have anyone to point out and help him overthrow Māra. According to the sutta's account, the dispelling of ignorance is through penetrating the four noble truths. But in the more figurative presentations, the Buddha-to-be is presented as attempting to realize awakening seated in meditation beset not just by Māra, but by a whole horde of demonic forces and energies called the host of Māra. Māra doesn't come alone or unarmed. It is impossible to name all the constituent members of

Māra's army, but the ten generals of the army have been identified as Sense Desire, Boredom, Hunger and Thirst, Craving, Sloth, Cowardice, Doubt, Obstinacy, Worldly Gain and Fame, and Conceit. They have one thing in common—they all stampede the mind toward self-view through identification with sense-data, becoming, or the denial of dukkha.

The story goes that he had to call upon Mother Earth to witness the vast store of pāramitā the Buddha had developed through many lives to find enough ground to support his balance. Then the Earth rose up in goddess form and with water streaming from her hair, she washed away the demon host. And the Buddha could sit immovable with the awareness to know that all this stuff was not what or who he was. Touching the Earth, he said, "I know you Māra," and the disappointed demon left—for a while. It's a dramatic story, bringing to mind just how alone the Buddha was at that time: no longer part of a family, town, or caste, rejected by his fellow outcastes, and with no teacher to look to. We are fortunate that no matter how Māra and his hosts manifest, ever since the Buddha's awakening a spotlight of wisdom has been thrown on them.

It's the way that Māra speaks in our mind that gives him his deluding quality. Māra says things like: "Take it easy. There's a nice palace in Kapilavatthu waiting for you, which is much more pleasant and useful than wasting your time here." Sometimes Māra is critical: "When are you going to face up to your responsibilities, get a decent job, and quit sitting under this fig tree contemplating your navel? What kind of a seeker are you anyway, when you couldn't hack it as an ascetic?" And sometimes congratulatory: "Well, you're really enlightened now; you don't need to deal with this world of unawakened idiots." Māra is always persistent and cunning: "OK, this is the voice of delusion; but it keeps on going and you're never going to shake it off." Māra is the force that identifies us with our personal world. As he clouds our mind with memories and regrets, Māra attacks our faith that there is a way and undermines our confidence to keep practicing it. Without faith, the energy of aspiration dies; then there's no mindfulness, no concentration, and no insight.

The enlightened response to this voice of Māra is to say, "I know you, Māra—I know this is just a delusion." This is the unshakable confidence in the power of wisdom and letting go that the Buddha demonstrates by remaining cool and unmoving in the midst of the demon host. But even then, Māra doesn't give up. Even after his enlightenment, the Buddha was assailed by Māra. One example was when the Buddha had paced up and down in meditation for a great part of the night. The Buddha then washed his feet, entered his hut, and took up the lion's posture (that is, lying down on his right side, placing one foot on the other). He was mindful, clearly aware, and attentive to the thought of getting up again. Māra approached and berated him for taking a rest. Māra seemed to have a thing about resting: he tried the same approach when the Buddha was resting due to a wound on his foot. But each time, the Buddha repelled him by declaring that he was free from craving and clinging (SN 4: Discourses with Māra).

Here, Māra assumes the form of the nagging inner tyrant of the mind that is always ready to take the darkest view of our behavior, but at other times Māra's approach differs. Māra is not fussy as to how he chooses to entangle us with self-view. Māra can justify sensual indulgence as "freedom to open to the sensory realm"; he can call self-hatred "being honest and firm."

Māra is also an equal opportunity employer—or nearly so. Although he has ten generals out there in the field (the ten fetters), for the close-up work he relies on just three women—his daughters. They, however, have the strength of ten. Their names are Craving (*Taṇhā*), Passion (*Ragā*) and Negativity (*Arati*)—you must have seen them around.

I think Craving has had wide-enough coverage already, so let's get introduced to Passion. Passion is the nerve-tingler, the vein-flooder, the heart-stopper, and the brain-fuddler. She is passion for forms, passion for senses, passion for mind-states, passion for formlessness—whatever takes your fancy. When she visits, you start jumping. And how we raise her up, love those impassioned speeches, the dramatic moments, the dizzy "losing-the-ground-feeling" that lifts us to a state where rhetoric, exaggeration, recklessness, and self-absorption take over and we are empowered. It could be the guy at the dance, the football game, the trumpet note that sends people into battle, the passion for ideas that turns humans into ideologues and fanatics, or the passion for nonexistence that drives the ascetic—passion makes us feel full in ourselves. Just take a look at the myriad meditation techniques, arcane knowledge systems, ritual empowerments, and devotional exercises—it's clear we want to saturate our mind.

Even intelligence can be deluding! People can become so enamored by scientific, religious, or political ideas that they fail to notice whether or not these have any good effects. Ideas can be used to justify fanaticism and brutality toward other beings. Attachment to ideas can divorce people from direct experience where sensitivity, virtue, and peace are found. The thinking mind, if followed blindly, will make us feel that we are getting close to truth—but in fact the thinking mind is merely fascinated with the feeling of knowing and of having interesting thoughts buzzing in the mind. So delusion can be both an extremely intelligent, yet ignorant quality—ignorant of the laws of cause and effect or of what is for the well-being of others. Filling our mind with a lot of ideas can be one way of blocking out the awareness of how things are.

And in all that shifting insubstantial smoke, we will be missing the point. The point has to do with what is really our own space, our own "home." All this stuff changes: the pulse calms down, the party's over, we've won the debate, flown the flag—and now it's time to go home. And how dull and humdrum "home" can be: because while we were out there dancing with Māra's daughter, we didn't make our own space bright and cheery. When our mind values passion, it loses sensitivity to what is already here: our mind's space. It's what we touch into when there's nonattachment. It's dispassionate but there's room in there to let things pass through—and it's through this that we don't get the hangovers and the harshness of coming down, the boredom, and the feeling of not getting the action. With dispassion the mind is sensitive and enjoys being here—a here that can be open to the moment-by-moment presence of consciousness. We are already full, full of consciousness; what we need is mindfulness and the other factors of awakening to bring that into light. In the light of the fruition of those factors, consciousness lets go of its activities, its colors and inclinations, and comes to rest as "signless, boundless, and all-luminous" (DN 11:85).

So how do you "do" dispassion? Just through noticing the space around things—just through focusing on the movement of up and down, of change, and of how our senses change. Let that awareness grow. There's no point in getting all fired up as to what and where that awareness is, but every time there's that shift and exploration and gladness in the awareness of the mind itself, we attune to that which has no signs, no tunes, no buzz. And that, too, is satisfying. If it weren't, the Buddha wouldn't have gone there and he wouldn't have taught the way to get there.

Let's visit Negativity next, the crabby one. She charms us with the ability to put everyone and everything down—when we can't feel up about ourselves, putting other people down does offer a superior moment. Negativity can be witty and cutting and cynical, giving a feeling that we're outside of this. Negativity can be righteous and condemning—and even as she draws us into a place where we can pass judgment, she creates a world of other people fixed in its vision. Criminals, evildoers, and witches get formed out of people who are confused, damaged, or eccentric. When I visited a prison, it was quite a revelation to find out that the friendly person who I had an interesting talk with was doing life for murder. Combine a wretched upbringing, a gang of other young men, a few drinks, a knife— and somebody's dead. Even when you come across pathological cases, it's good to reflect that dependent on conditions, dependent on kamma, that could be you. It's not to condone any action, but just to come out of judgment and back into connection.

That's what Negativity can't do. So she leaves us out there alone in a world of idiots and criminals and weirdos who aren't like *us*. And she feeds the inner tyrant in all of us, who turns those sour attitudes toward our own actions, foibles, and less-than-ideal performances. One of her ploys is to create very high ideals of what we should be or achieve; she keeps raising the bar. No compassion, no space, no congratulations are going to come with Negativity in the mind. The way of seeing and uprooting her is through developing goodwill and compassion: to look for that which can be nourished, appreciated, or empathized with—in ourselves and in others. And we're not looking for a perfect self, but for a skillful action or characteristic.

Looking in this way brings us appreciative joy (*muditā*), an ability to be gladdened by the happiness, good fortune, and good intentions of others—and eventually by our own good intentions. I make a point of concluding each day with reflections and gratitude for a specific experience of that day: it could be that I received food to eat, or that I got a letter from a friend, or even that I managed to check myself and avoid saying something on an unskillful impulse. Humans can do a lot of damage, so notice the bad things you didn't do. Humans also have a great potential to see how things could be better, so balance that with the recognition that things could be worse. Then Negativity and Passion don't get their foot in the door. And when your door is not open, Craving can't talk you into buying her wares.

Meditation, or the domain of mindfulness and concentration, is how the Buddha recommended we can come out of the domain of Māra. Mindfulness and concentration cause us to develop bases for sensitivity and happiness that are independent of external conditions. And they help to align us to a more balanced way of operating in the world. So even if you're not intent on complete awakening, but just want a little more peace of mind, it's good to know about the host of Māra. Whenever we are meditating, a quite responsible and reasonable idea will come along and start to needle its way into our mind: "The lawn needs cutting! I really ought to get out and cut that lawn. Am I just being irresponsible by sitting here meditating? After all, the lawn does need cutting." Maybe the lawn does need cutting, but does it have to be right at this minute? But the voice of Māra goes on and says: "Well, I can't really practice now anyway with that on my mind. I'll mow the lawn now, then meditate later." Once we begin thinking in that way, we find that there are endless numbers of things that we ought to do. If we believe it, we find ourselves caught in the spin. And Māra says: "Well, I'm too agitated to meditate now anyway, maybe I'll just relax for a while . . . or maybe tomorrow . . . or maybe when I retire."

Once I had a comic strip that addressed that point. It showed, in a series of frames, a man's journey through life. In the first frame, he was a baby: "Too young to meditate" said the caption. Next a young kid, running and playing: "Too excited to meditate." Then a teenager riding a motorbike: "Too much fun to meditate." Then falling in love: "Too much in love to meditate." At his office desk: "Too busy to meditate." At home falling asleep in front of the TV: "Too tired to meditate." Elderly and ill: "Too old to meditate." Then the tombstone: "Too late to meditate." The number of times that we say we don't have time is an expression of how badly we need to take the time. As Ajahn Chah said, "Do you have time to breathe?"

Not that Dhamma practice is always about sitting still and getting into tranquility. When we reinforce the habit of blindly following our passion, our negativity, our sense of "I can't do" or "I'm not good enough," we unconsciously assert the view that the only way we can practice Dhamma is in refined circumstances or that meditating requires pristine mind-states. So we miss the opportunities that the eightfold path and the cultivation of pāramitā present. And we miss the opportunity to insightfully investigate the thoughts and drives that really affect us, the very ones that need to be understood. Game, set, and match to Māra.

But with meditation that leads to insight, we don't need to clear all obstructions or experience a great deal of calm to get started. Insight is based on looking into what underlies the way we're operating at any given moment. For example, notice how you speak. Notice the emotional biases. Notice the assumptions you make about "what others think of me." Any of Māra's daughters in there? What would it take to not give them room and board? The more convincing and habitual the mood is, the less it should be heedlessly followed. The ordinary, unquestioned habits and assumptions are the very ones that we need to see as impermanent, coming from conditioning, and not from a fundamental self. Otherwise, we're not bringing Dhamma into our life.

Of course, if the lawn does need cutting, there's a time for this. But recognize that there are always responsibilities and things to do, and many of them are based on good reasons. Then consider whether they will ever stop, and can they ever be done? I mean, can the lawn ever be finally cut? As soon as it's cut, it starts growing again; then you're back mowing the lawn. Is your life going to be a round of cutting lawns? Is this what you're born for? To work for the welfare of all lawns, or the garden, or washing the car, or fixing the house, walking the dog, and so on? Maybe there's a need to consider more clearly the amount of responsibilities that are undertaken and their purpose in the light of the truth that "it never gets done" and meanwhile you might drop dead tomorrow. We have to put in some roadblocks to check and inspect the compulsive drives. What do they assume? Is that true? What would it be like if that drive weren't there? Some of our busyness amounts to new styles of running, and new designs for shields.

When you have trained in wise attention and mindfulness, keep in touch with your inner body language. Is it tight or restless, is there running away or shielding, or is it an obsessive drive? Can you bring some openness, some compassion, and some reflection to bear on that? Can you say, "This is dukkha, it is to be understood?"

When we're coming out of the fire, we have to get used to the smoke. It gets confusing, but we have to keep hold of the view that leads out. And the Buddha summed it up as, "I know you, Māra." He didn't budge. He didn't get up and fight, or look for a cooler spot. Firm, clear knowing is the view that dispels the host. This means of insightfully knowing enables us to practice in the presence of the host without compounding more suffering. Instead of feeling alarmed, ashamed, or infatuated by their presence, we can develop the ability to see Māra and his daughters as smoke. That gives rise to an understanding that they are visitors, and not-self. With this confidence, undistracted energy arises in our mind, and, with that, zest and joy. Such spiritual factors lead to the full awakening of the mind, to true peace. Then the need for position and states of being or the search for something in the sense realm to be filled by—all the expressions of the outflows—can be abolished.

13

SELFLESS MOTIVATION

"But, bhikkhus, as soon as these four noble truths in their twelve aspects were seen by me; seen with the purest insight as they are, then I taught the world—with its devas, māras, and brahmas, its samanas and brahmins, its monarchs and ordinary folk—that I had fully realized complete awakening."

After his awakening the Buddha spent several weeks in retreat, meditating and reviewing consciousness; this was apparently the time when he systematically reviewed the process that he described in the analysis of dependent origination. In that rarefied state of mind, he was able to detect and even communicate with divinities that had sensed the import of what had happened under that Bodhi tree in Uruvela, India. According to the account, the high divinity Brahma Sahampati took a special interest in the Buddha and dialogued with him on some aspects of Dhamma. It was also Brahma Sahampati who urged the Buddha to teach, with the phrase, "There are beings with but a little dust in their eyes who are wasting through not hearing the Dhamma" (M 1). The Buddha had doubted whether anyone would be interested or would have the capacity to put into practice the level and consistency of letting go that he had perfected. As he said:

> Enough of teaching the Law
> That even I found hard to reach;
> For it will never be perceived
> By those who live in lust and hate.
> (M 1)

Regardless of how we choose to relate to Brahma Sahampati (and let's not dismiss what we don't know), the Buddha was moved by compassion and saw that some had potential. Out of a sense of empathy, of "trembling with" or "resonating with" the fate of human beings, he decided he would try to formulate his realization in terms of a teaching. I think that this capacity to resonate with others was more than a sense of sympathy and a wish to help. It was a capacity of receptivity and an ability to attune to the way that other people are, a capacity that gave Gotama Buddha his extraordinary ability to relate to a wide spectrum of beings: human, divine, demonic—and animals too. Accordingly, proclaiming that, "wide open are the portals of the Deathless. Let those who hear show faith," he decided to seek an opportunity to teach (M 1).

It's easy to understand his initial reluctance. He had realized nibbāna, and who would be interested in that? Nibbāna is held to be the ultimate goal in Buddhism, and yet even defining it is difficult. As I've said, it means something like "not blowing" or "not bound." It's not about having one's wishes fulfilled, or going to a happy place; it's not about hanging out in eternity with blissed-out deities, or a loving Father, or even in some super-chilled formless glow. In fact it's about not hanging out anywhere at all. Nibbāna doesn't have a location, or an aim. It can't be defined as a thing or as nothing—because it's not in the category of "things," even subtle things like happiness or compassion or formless inner space. But nibbāna, once rightly understood, is an attractive option. It is the ending of sorrow and delusion, and it is supremely peaceful. And by the extinguishing of the "three fires" of greed, hatred, and delusion, nibbāna gives tangible results in terms of other people's welfare:

> If ... greed, hatred, and delusion are given up, one aims neither at one's own downfall, nor at others' downfall, nor at the downfall of both, and one suffers no more mental pain and grief. Thus is nibbāna realizable even during this lifetime, immediate, inviting, attractive, and comprehensible to the wise.
> (AN 3:55)

The metaphors associated with nibbāna often liken it to the blowing out of a fire. When it is no longer burning, the fire has "nibbāna'd"—the elements on which it was based are no longer in a state of combustion. This may seem like sterility and lifelessness from the viewpoint of the fire, but from the perspective of the elements it means life and potential. That is, when the fires of greed, hatred, and delusion are extinguised, the mind is free to operate in terms of its fullest capacity.

Here, *mind* means something like "heart." So qualities like calm, clarity, and kindness are all enhanced both through the practice-path of extinguishing the fires, and through the result or Fruit, where the tinder and the sparkiness of the heart are removed. How that manifests in terms of what a nibbāna'd person subsequently does depends on other capacities—such as their intellect. It's rather like switching off the engine of a boat in order to inspect and remove its defective drives: when you switch on the engine on again, however sweetly the boat may run, its power depends on the size of the engine. Also some people only have a dinghy. The Buddha, who was a gifted speaker with great leadership capacities, had an ocean liner, with room on board for many; however not everyone who realizes nibbāna has such teaching skills. The Buddhist scriptures refer occasionally to "Silent Buddhas"—who have, like Gotama Buddha, realized nibbāna unassisted by a teaching, yet don't have the capacity to teach others. And much is the same for arahants, those who realize full enlightenment through a Buddha's

Dhamma: many do but some don't have the capacity to bring a verbal teaching across. Their presence may be a powerful source of inspiration, but they don't necessarily have the range of resonance or the capacity to guide other people's minds.

For the Buddha, his realization and resonance with other beings was demonstrated through approximately forty-five years of wandering and teaching anyone who wished to hear, a mission he carried through to his dying breath. Even on his deathbed he encouraged any of those assembled to come forward and ask questions before he passed away. And one thing he was very clear about—nibbāna is the highest peace, an ease of being that is not related to any particular circumstances and therefore not subject to change:

> There is an island, an island which you cannot go beyond. It is a place of nothingness, a place of non-possession and of non-attachment. It is the total end of death and decay, and this is why I call it Nibbāna.
> (Su-N 1094)

With that as a reminder, the emphasis that the Buddha gave repeatedly was on the practice-path that leads to nibbāna, a path that proceeds in terms of deepening letting go. The fruition of the practice issues from the middle way: based upon dispassion and cooling. The realization of nibbāna doesn't arise from getting heated up and righteous about the host of Māra; nor does it come from accepting craving, passion, and negativity and letting them blaze away in our mind; nor does it come from denying the existence of these problematic forces. It comes around through first seeing with pure insight and then responding. To practice for nibbāna means in any situation abandoning unskillful responses, and abandoning responses based on impressions of self and other. Nibbāna is realized through penetrating and putting to rest those compulsive projections of craving and ignorance through which a self is imagined. The problem isn't that nibbāna is for selfish people who want to get out of the world; it's more the case that most of us are bound up with too much self-interest and attachment to want to do it.

And yet the Buddha taught—and felt that the teaching on suffering and its cessation was the perfect vehicle because it appeals to our natural self-interest, yet can only be accomplished by transmuting that self-interest into dispassion and letting go. So to bring the mind to nibbāna requires a strong sense of motivation—a turning of craving into the desire for realization and the effort to let go of grasping. Yet the encouraging thing is that nibbāna can be glimpsed briefly before one has completely let go— so we get a taste that encourages us to continue. In its sequential deepening through the four stages of enlightenment (stream-entry, once-return, nonreturn, arahant) it can be likened to opening a channel ever more fully, of releasing subtler and subtler constrictions. So whatever the verbal teachings, the way is universal; and this understanding allowed the Buddha to teach using the worldview and terminology of the time: Dhamma, kamma, nibbāna, and heavenly realms. His method would often be to ascertain what his audience's position was and, from that position, expound a path to the experience of no conflict, or no suffering, or the deathless. So he taught the way independent of any personal position or philosophical viewpoint, presenting themes that relate to the way that human beings in general experience their lives.

Who the Buddha Taught

As the sutta states, the Buddha taught across the spectrum of beings in the world: *devas* (or deities), demons, brahmas, samanas, brahmins, monarchs, and ordinary folk. This gives us an idea of the range of a Buddha's mind, because each of those categories of being would have a different kind of self-interest, a different set of problems, and a different context within which they might expect results. And the challenges that teaching that range presented should leave no doubt of the Buddha's capacity, openness, and selfless motivation. If he'd been more into marketing, he'd have aimed his delivery at the kings and deities, those who had most power and influence. In fact although both of the two major kings of the region were disciples of the Buddha and deities held him in great respect, his teaching was most often given to and realized by ordinary folk and contemplatives. It was a teaching that readily appealed to people on the edge—the bereaved, the desperate, the gone forth; those who knew suffering. He even converted a serial murderer, Angulimāla, who subsequently realized arahantship. And as for demons—the Buddha met Māra in many guises throughout his life after his awakening, and the teaching was always the same: "I know you, Māra, there's nothing here for you."

Why the Buddha even bothered to address demons at all, let alone formless deities, was because of the depth of his understanding and compassion. He saw that all the phenomena that we take to be "me" and "her" and them are only conditioned configurations of kamma; they are only the force of becoming manifesting in gross or subtle forms. He didn't see any actual selves or solid beings that should or couldn't ever get enlightened. Realization depends purely on motivation, cause and effect. Nor did the Buddha choose or yearn to have disciples. His intention was purely to bring forth the Dhamma for those whose minds were prepared to receive it. Furthermore, understanding how conditions and minds change, he was also motivated to sow the seeds of awakening where at some time in the future (perhaps even in a future life) they might bear fruit. He never gave up on anyone: even Māra, he reckoned, was just going through a rough patch and at some mind-boggling time in the future would start to turn things around. This sense of perspective and resolve gives us all the encouragement to not give up on ourselves: to pick up Dhamma in terms of teachings, meditation practices, resolutions and vows, and to sow Dhamma-seeds wherever we can—in our own mind or in those of other people. Sooner or later there must be results.

In terms of his human audience, the Dhamma community of the time presented the greatest challenges as well as the greatest fruitions. When reading the discourses, it quickly becomes apparent that there are many occasions of bhikkhus realizing nibbāna, but there are also occasions when they were reluctant to accept his teachings. There were quite a few protests and rebellions when the Buddha introduced the rule to not eat food after midday (MN 65, 66, and 70). (In the early years of the Sangha, the monks and nuns could eat whenever they liked, the only encouragement being that as those who live on alms, they should keep their needs to a minimum.) At Ukkattha they emphatically did *not* delight in his words (MN 1), and the books of the Vinaya are mostly made up of accounts of bhikkhus squabbling over requisites, flirting with women, pressuring lay-people, and engaging in all kinds of skullduggery. To top it all, the Buddha's own cousin, Devadatta, repeatedly plotted to assassinate him. Yet the Buddha kept teaching, sometimes with fierce reprimands, sometimes with humor, but always out of compassion. And he never asked for anything in return—not even results or gratitude:

> Here bhikkhus, compassionate and seeking their welfare, the Teacher teaches the Dhamma out of compassion: "This is for your welfare; this is for your happiness." His disciples do not want to hear or give ear or exert their minds to understand; they err and turn aside from the Teacher's Dispensation. With that the Tathāgata is not satisfied and feels no satisfaction; yet he dwells unmoved, mindful, and aware. This, bhikkhus, is the first foundation of mindfulness that the Noble Ones cultivate, cultivating which a Noble One is a teacher fit to instruct a group. (MN 137:22)

Recluses and wanderers of other sects would often challenge the Buddha on matters of doctrine, particularly from their own perspectives on the benefits of asceticism, on the nature of the Divine, or on the nature of the self. In which case, the Buddha would generally direct attention back to the nature of the dialogue itself, or to how holding a view was itself a cause of conflict and dukkha, and how he had gone beyond that. He says:

> Vaccha, the speculative view that the world is eternal . . . not eternal . . . that the world is finite . . . infinite . . . that the soul and the body are the same thing . . . that the soul and the body another . . . that after death a Tathāgata exists . . . does not exist . . . both exists and does not exist . . . neither exists nor does not exist, is a thicket of views, a wilderness of views. . . . It is beset by suffering, by vexation, by despair, and by fever, and does not

lead to disenchantment, to dispassion, to cessation, to peace, to direct knowledge, to enlightenment, to Nibbāna.

... Therefore, I say, with the destruction, fading away, cessation, giving up, and relinquishing of all conceivings ... all I-making, mine-making, and the underlying tendency to conceit, the Tathāgata is liberated through not clinging.
(MN 72:14–15)

Or when being confronted by an argumentative sophist, the Buddha just side-stepped the topic of doctrine to point to the goal of putting a teaching into practice:

"What does the recluse [i.e. the Buddha] assert, what does he proclaim?"
"Friend, I assert and proclaim such [a teaching] that one does not quarrel with anyone in the world."
(MN 18:4)

In some cases, the Buddha kept silent when a question was asked, as in the case of "What happens to the self on awakening, which made no sense—it was like asking, "where does a fire go when a fire goes out?"

To kings he taught the benefits of wise and compassionate statesmanship; to householders the benefits of living ethically; and to businessmen he gave advice to live prudently, look after friends and family, put aside some savings, and give a portion to support those who had gone forth. When mothers or grandmothers were grieving over lost offspring, he gently, through dialogue, brought them to the acknowledgment of our universal mortality, and hence to an emotional acceptance of the fact. Despite the great differences between all these characters, their concerns and capacities, the value of wise reflection and nonclinging was something that they could relate to. Above all, the Buddha practiced Dhamma and nonattachment even as he taught it. Living out his enormous resolve to teach, he gave up any position in the world—apart from to know the Dhamma and to offer to those who could receive his offerings.

Meeting the Buddha in a Personal Way

This way of relating to the personal and highly differentiated world presents useful examples of how to handle our own experience of individuality, our own specific kamma and dispositions, within a teaching of not-self. Owing to the limitations of language when you hear of "not-self," you could imagine that a personality is "wrong" or to be wiped out. But rather than eradicating what is individual and particular, Dhamma practice encourages us to meet it, rather like the Buddha meeting and finding a response to anyone who came to see him. The enlightened view, or "Buddha-view," of pure insight doesn't affirm that this is what you are, or that you are something other than this. It neither blames nor condones. It's a silent teaching, offering a view into how the sense of self comes into being, and where the suffering arises in that. As a practice it requires us both to step back from adding more to the mix and from trying to build a wall against it. And so it encourages us to fully meet ourselves—with our idiosyncrasies, troubles, and lost places—in a pure way: just to know how it is. But when we know how it is, all that is no longer who we are. The turbulence or the stuck fixations of the mind fall away under the gaze of "I know you, Māra, there's no base here for clinging."

Not that it's easy; seeing our emotions and thoughts as "just that which arise" takes some doing. We learn from the Buddha's example that it takes calling into mind the strengths, patience, warmheartedness, and discernment that we develop every day. Then as our mind settles in that clear holding, the factors of awakening dissolve the knots that bind up and cause us to suffer. And when those knots start to dissolve, our hurt areas sigh and come to rest, our hunger laughs at its expectations, our craving turns into motivation—and we can respond to life with clarity and compassion. We see this is how it is; now is the Dhamma and a real and personal understanding dawns. However much we intellectually know about Dhamma, it's humbling to discover that we can only realize it through meeting the host of voices and energies that move through us. This means meeting and feeling for the desperation, neediness, and frustration that sends the mind running around like a spooked stray dog. It means not kicking that dog away, but gathering it into a heart of clarity and compassion. When there is this "Buddha-view," this heart of clarity and compassion, we can trust it to reveal and know to relax the compulsiveness, anxiety, and passion that are bound up in our world. We too can say, "I know you, Māra, there's nothing here for you." Our aggregates can function free from clinging. And as we relate more compassionately to ourselves, we can also extend that to others. And with that, our ability to accommodate and care for others then broadens and deepens.

14

UNSHAKABLE AND
UNSUPPORTED

"The knowledge and the vision arose in me: 'My release is assured. This is the last birth. There is no further becoming.'"

At this point, after describing the path the Buddha reveals and affirms the fruit—an awakening that amounts to the release from becoming. The path does not create this fruit. This knowing-release ripens within the supportive mesh of the interconnected path-factors, and yet it surpasses them. Path-factors are conditioned and depend on being brought into play. Fruit is Unconditioned, not-dependent; hence not subject to change. Accordingly, the Buddha asserts to the Group of Five bhikkhus that his awakening to truth is not just a momentary vision; it's no passing thing.

What makes him so sure? After all, everyone experiences certainties that don't always prove reliable. How many relationships begin with the conviction that "You're the one for me," only to find out a year or two later that "You're not"? If you meditate, and have gone on a long intensive retreat, you may have had those blazing realizations that this is IT, only to have to ac-knowledge sheepishly that when you went home, the glow faded, and after a few days you were back to being crabby or misunderstood again.

Conviction based on belief, affirmation, or mind-states is unreliable. Belief by its very nature needs to be constantly affirmed. Left unattended, it wilts. When religion is based on belief, the adherents must keep on meeting to tell each other how wonderful it all is, or they go out and con-vert someone—getting fresh converts boosts people's own belief to no end. But why is there this demand to believe? Does truth, or God, really need to be believed in? Can't it stand up on its own?

When inspiration initiates and promotes conviction, it fastens onto a particular feeling, mind-set, or image. In terms of images, we tend to lean upon the image that the teacher or leader presents, or the image of the group, the community, or even the place. However, we can only depend on them for so long. The sense of conviction in the clarity or the ease of a teacher may encourage us to follow what he or she teaches in order to achieve the same results; but our impressions are conditioned into our mind, and their effect doesn't last. Eventually, even in following a teaching, we have to make our way over the uneven and boggy ground of our own mind. Monastic train-ing, for instance, starts with faith, morality, the input from a teacher, and a peaceful place to live. But after a period of living and working with other people going through changes and growing pains, these aspects can quickly degenerate into fault-finding, having too many duties, and resenting people always telling one what to do. It all depends on our changing perspective. However when we want to go through the terrain of our own mind, sooner or later we have to come to terms with the fact that inspiration is part of the landscape to pass through. It's not a base for conviction.

Volition, Attention, and Contact

When observing his own landscape, the Buddha looked at the conditions of body and mind on which his life, identity, and world depend. He looked into the inherent nature of all of these conditions (not just the inspiring, fascinating, or wretched ones)—and saw that all phenomena are caused.

They arise dependent on conditions: obviously seeing depends on eyes and an unimpaired nervous system, and happiness depends on agreeable feelings. But he took that investigation down to the root conditions. Happy or sad, inspired or depressed, the structure that supports or holds this world of mind-stuff is a programmed coming together of three conditions: volition, attention, and contact. As we discussed earlier, volition means the turning of the mind, an activity of seeking based either on a reflex or a clear intention. Attention is the agent that forms and sustains focus: the mind homes in to pick up the signals. Contact means there's something to attend to—for the mind, it is an impression or feeling derived from the other senses. Together volition, attention, and contact make up the operational code of the program. This is what moves the mind. Being dynamic, our whole landscape is subject to change and can only be temporarily sustained—when we've had enough of watching the news, we're bored with this book, our mind is tired, or a reflex brings something else into our attention, our volition turns to another channel. In other words, dependent on the impressions that contact brings, volition moves our mind elsewhere.

Volition is conditioned by interest, perception, and feeling. And all these things are changing. Do you ever notice how in the global arena, this decade's enemies were our allies or were not in the picture a few decades ago? Or that the president that everyone's vilifying this year is the same one they voted in to office a few years ago? And when it comes down to our more intimate world—whether "life is sweet" or "life's a struggle" all depends on many factors, doesn't it? And there are many complexities and seeming paradoxes: The monastery's sweet furry cat is a merciless killer of birds. The horrible smell of decomposition is a sign of the healthy digestive processes of nature. An Italian artist used to fill cans with excrement and seal them up, which galleries would subsequently buy and exhibit—until they exploded. Is this a statement about the human condition, or just a can of shit? It depends, doesn't it? Just for this reason, perceptions are unsatisfactory. In fact no dependent condition can be relied upon, nor can it be a true quality, a self, or an ultimate truth. Truths that arise dependent on some vision, some special state of mind, or a belief are only relative because of that dependency. What made the Buddha's conviction so assured is that it was based upon *removing* the dependencies:

"This is peaceful, this is sublime—that is, the stilling of all sankhāra, the relinquishment of all dependencies (*upādhi*), the destruction of craving, dispassion, cessation, Nibbāna."
(AN 10:60)

Let's go into this more closely. Mental phenomena arise dependent on attention—if your mind is engaged in reading or watching TV, then maybe there's interest in acquiring knowledge, or in being filled with something stimulating or relaxing. Another motivation might be to get away from thoughts and feelings about the person next door or the future of the economy. So that attention itself—where and why we focus—is dependent on some kind of volition or intention. And for there to be a focus, an attention, there has to be something to contact, to attend to. The mind's capacity is huge: it can attend to thoughts, sounds, sights, memories, and so on. It chooses what is agreeable, or in accord with a concern or a wish or an obsession. There are hedonic and ethical features to that intention: I incline toward the pleasant, or I am moved by compassion or by jealousy. Those inclinations are latent and when something pops into attention that seems to fit, my volition gets going and attention homes in on it. This is the most obvious feature of volition—it moves out in terms of a pre-existing inclination in order to contact something that fits. Generally that volition is sustained (or not) dependent on the feeling or the impression and mind-state that arises with contact—in which case it depends on feeding, or clinging. It's not that clinging is immoral or bad, but behind this is a deeper basis for volition: the need to have something to contact. Try being without a thought or a mood for a while and you'll see how the mind seeks to land on something, even unpleasant things. It's a programmed reflex. The selecting and choosing gives rise to the impression, "I have choice"—it makes me feel a little more solid. This volition looked at under a Buddha's eye is called craving to be something, or becoming. It's not necessarily immoral, pleasure based, or disgusting, but it is thirsty. Volition makes *me*; that's why it's difficult to give up.

This dependency, the threefold bond of attention, volition, and contact, arises as mental sankhāra—as activities or programs. They give us something to be: a future, a past, a present. They inform and guide consciousness a moment at a time. This is what holds our world, and yet it is all dependently arisen. It's workable, but it can't produce anything that either lasts or stands up by itself. It's like a tripod that rests on a shaky foundation. You can't take a stand on anything that is known, seen, or experienced on this tripod of conditionality.

Yet the unenlightened mind does exactly that. It takes this dependently arisen world of form (dependent on organic substances for birth and survival and of brief duration) to be the real thing. It takes beliefs and views to be true and worth fighting over. And it takes mental states to be the true reality of my self. It's natural enough: even when you know the whole thing is mortal and finite, you've got to get a life—what else is there? Are there any other options? This is what the Buddha went forth for. He'd try to find an alternative. It took a while, because like most of us he was looking for a thing. It was only the pain and frustration of looking for states that eventually got through to him. And with a calm and level attention, he started looking *at*—investigating the no-option that we all experience: the realm of the five aggregates.

We'll come to what he found, but before that let's look for ourselves for a while. With steady attention and the intention to let things speak for themselves, let's focus on the here-and-now experience of our body. What I expect you'll find is that whatever runs through your frame of reference will change, even if you can hold it. When your mind leaps or drifts off, just bring it back to the sense of the pressure and tingles of the body. Then you can sweep your attention steadily around your body—noticing the back, legs, feet, front, head, arms—and your focus steadies. Interestingly, only one body part occupies your attention at any one time. Actually it seems we can't really focus on the whole body in any sustained way: if you feel your eyes, your feet aren't there; if you feel your hands, you'll lose sense of your throat. Normally, attention glimpses, sketches an impression, and darts off—this creates the usual sense of a composite "body." It is rather like the solid images on a TV screen, which, when you press your nose to the glass are just seen as changing lights. So let's take one place in our body, say the right hand—what's there? Pulses, warmth, mildly agreeable feelings . . . are those the hand or are they what's happening to the hand? Suddenly "the body" changes into "the experienced body," something made of changing sensations and feelings and reflexes.

Maybe then try widening the focus and feeling the overall sense of a body, say in terms of warmth or pressure. Then the sense of shape and of specific parts of the body disappears. So what we can directly know about our body, to which we are giving as full and unbiased attention as we can, is it's a flow of experiences that depend on attention, intention, and contact. Uh-oh, this sounds familiar! So am I saying that there is no body? Tell that to the doctor and she'll want to check your sanity. Or is there a body? Well, you have plenty of bodies; which one is the real one? Which one is you—the young, old, healthy, or sick body? Is your body the hand, foot, eye, or throat? Is it the sensations, twinges, or numb places? Is it the hard bits, soft bits, fluids, cavities? It all depends on how volition, attention, and contact "designate" our body: our experience-body is actually a "designation body."

We can zoom into our mind in much the same way. But, to cut a long story short, the picture's the same. None of it stays, you can't have all of it at the same time—and another thing, all of these phenomena rest on something that they're not. Bodies stand on ground, rest on chairs, or float in water. Minds rest on mind-states—eager, perplexed, gentle, or impatient—and on input through the senses. The mind isn't the same as what it witnesses, yet can we have a mind independent of it being occupied by some passing mood or thought? If we get really calm so that thought ceases, the mind rests on calm or ease. It can go as far down that track as "neither-perception-nor-nonperception"—and can depend on that. Not that this is wrong. In fact it's the path. It's what we can do and it's what Siddhattha did. Once he had composed his mind so that its attention was clear and malleable, Siddhattha investigated its supports. And he found there was a way to release them.

So let's go back to our experience-body, focus on it, and let things happen within that focus, without pushing or trying to find anything, or come to a conclusion. In that context, when we come out of wanting anything to happen, there's some spaciousness—and when a feeling comes up, try to attune to that spaciousness. Develop an attitude and energy of not-feeding, demanding, pushing away, skipping off, or proliferating around the feeling. This is nonattachment. By practicing in this way, we realize that for these few moments we don't have to solve the problems of existence, or know who we are, or what we're going to do. By being with something that we can directly attend to, not through inference or report, we can find an interesting point of nondependence. Clearly the body still depends on food, water, and air; obviously its continuing well-being depends on care and attention; but there can be a steadying and cooling of mental volition that hints at a domain and a direction that could be liberating. . . . Maybe this should be developed! So say good-bye to your family, find yourself a tree, and sit under it!

As a path, nondependence depends on application, on bearing in mind, and on concentration. The path isn't the Fruit; it doesn't create release. This knowing-release ripens within the supportive mesh of the interconnected path-factors, and yet it surpasses them. Path-factors are conditioned and depend on being brought into play. As I mentioned, right view is the first—a perspective of looking at how things depend on causes. That has to be sustained. When it is sustained within a concentrated mind, right view sees dependent arising and dukkha, and dependent ceasing and nibbāna. Given that option, the mind relinquishes the underpinnings—it "nibbānas." It is this unbinding, this removal of dependency and props, that gives the Buddha his conviction: this realization is of nonarising; there's no way that it could cease.

The Buddha's Three Realizations

In his time at Uruvela, the Buddha had three great insights, revelations, or knowledges that settled the matter for him in a way that was crucial for his liberation. The first was the realization that what is experienced as a "person" is just an ongoing and changeable manifestation of bodily and mental processes, rather than an isolated one-off self. And stepping back from the identification with that, he touched into the underlying life force or energy that it drew upon. With his extremely attuned mind, he could sense how this life force, itself a conditioned thing, existed independent of the bubbling identity that rested on it like froth on the sea. Although the identity and the body were changing and finite, he couldn't see an end or a beginning to the life force itself. And this stretched the question of being beyond the span of a single life to one of endlessly "wandering on" (*samsāra*). It's rather like the the story of a gene, or of DNA.

In that stepping back with a focused attention, there was a shift to a transpersonal overview. Recognizing that this wandering on included everyone, Siddhattha looked beneath his personal experience and realized that the direction of wandering was dependent on the mind's habitual inclinations, the activities of the mind. So he began to understand the turbulence that generated all these suds; it wasn't random, it was driven by an active cause, or kamma. Thus the second great knowledge arose: That there's "bad" and "good" kamma, led by volition. That there are energies that are disruptive or abusive and do not sustain clarity or health; and there are also energies that are harmonious, nourishing, and clearly attuned.

Then looking into these energies, he noticed there were thermals and currents that generated turbulence. This was his third great knowledge, knowledge of the mind's unchanging bias. The bias was for consciousness to lean on sense-data and on the sense of becoming something, a leaning that depended on the assumption that there was a self that could benefit, be made more happy or solid, by such means. These are the outflows of sensuality, becoming, and ignorance that I discussed in chapter 11. The result of this bias is that the consciousness that generates a feedback loop mentally interprets that feedback experience as occurring between two positions as "selves." There is an apparent "I," an agent, the active one that is doing the wandering, and a "me" that experiences the results of what I've wandered into. The turbulence generates suds. Holding on to that loop, that kink in consciousness, as a real identity is a particular kind of kamma, the one that keeps the overview of "I" and "me" ongoing and broadly consistent. Don't you wake up each morning with roughly the same old "you?" This is handy, but not liberating.

One moment gets stitched to another moment in this I-me process. And throughout that process, the designations of body and world remain. There's still the sense of pressure, warmth, movement that I call my body, and even if the details of that have changed, the designation process remains in the same locked pattern. So the inference is that there's a solid self somewhere with this—the pattern remains even though the details change. And there's still the sense of a yesterday, today, and tomorrow—even though the details of those have also changed. Sights and sounds may be different, but a visible and audible world arises, designated as the world "out there." As long as the designation process (the bias in the feedback loop) remains, the whole world could change—I could lose an arm, go blind, or have a break-down—but still there'd be the root assumption of a permanent self that this is happening to. This is the dependent consciousness. But although there is a real and functioning feedback loop, the apparent self that it creates is fiction. It may be a suitable, humorous, or nightmarish piece of fiction, but it arises through a reflex bias, an unnecessary dependency. And sometimes this bias throws the mind way out of kilter.

You may wonder what happens to the world and the self when the mind stops its outflows, stops its designation process. Well, awakening, clarity, and an unimpaired sensitivity remains. In his third great knowledge, this in effect is what happened to the Buddha. He comprehended the dukkha in-volved in this process, and in seeing the craving for designation, for being something, was at the root of it, he let go and abandoned that. He gave up turbulence, stopped creating suds. This practice didn't so much extract him from saṃsāra as it switched off the saṃsāric process in his mind—including the designation that this was "his" mind. In fact, although wisdom remained, the tripod of volition, attention, and contact was taken apart. Nothing to be aware of, no finding. All that was left was the "unprogrammed," or as it is bet-ter known, the unconditioned, nibbāna. As the Buddha put it:

> O house-builder, you are seen! You will not build this house again. For all your rafters are broken and your ridgepole shat-tered. My mind has reached the Unconditioned (*Visankhāra*); I have attained the destruction of craving.
> (D 154)

In another sutta, he described the unconditioned another way:

> When a person has gone out, then there can be nothing by which you can measure him. That by which he can be talked about is no longer there for him; you cannot say that he does not exist. When all ways of being, all phenomena are removed, then all ways of description have also been removed.
> (Su-N 1076)

Having dismantled the "I," "me," "self" programs, the Buddha could rightly say that he had gone beyond this life. And what about a future? If we accept the knowledge of an ongoing life-force, why wouldn't it keep on going? Well, of course the life-force does keep going, that's what's sustaining you and me. But the suds arise dependent on turbulence, and when that turbulence ceases . . . here and now, the push of further becoming in that individual ceases. To put it simply, there's no push to go anywhere.

Since we're talking about cessation and life-forces continuing on, you may wonder what is it that goes from one life to the next. Some people may have a problem with the idea of rebirth. People often ask, "How can anyone remember a past life?" Well, all I can say is, I have a problem with email and telecommunication: I don't see any words flying through the air, yet they keep landing somewhere in my little electronic box. Maybe I should take the thing apart to see where they're stored. And how did that entire football team shrink down and get inside your TV? And how does this get transmitted? Well, those guys don't fly through the air but a signal is being transmitted, and it is received by an instrument that is tuned in to that channel. "Rebirth" is much the same.

Interestingly the Buddha didn't speak of "rebirth" or "re" anything. He spoke of switching off the current that carries the signals, the current of further becoming. So it's not that there's a consciousness that moves from one life to the next; rather, it's sankhāra programs in the flow of becoming that generate, inform, and program a consciousness that produces another consciousness. And they do so in a pattern that contains the dominant tendencies of the mind that's been guiding it for the span of a life. There's transmission of a code. Say you're big on sports, then the sports channel is the one you'd be tuned in to. The kammic patterns that I've encouraged during this life span continue—or to put it simply, "I" get born again. But if that sankhāra ceases, if the program is cleaned of leaning and grasping, then that process isn't going to happen. This is what a Buddha has done. He switched off the power. No transmission. No e-mails or TV shows are getting sent, so they don't land. There's no more birth.

Hence the person we call the Buddha generally referred to himself as Tathāgata (Thus-Gone) in terms of the only way that designations can apply. The terms *Awakened* and *Bhagavā* (Blessed One) give us aspirants more definition to focus on, and incline us to a path and pāramitā that we can work on. The city that was called Uruvela later became Bodhgaya in honor of the great samana, and the fig tree under which he sheltered has been similarly honored and transplanted throughout Southern Asia as the Bodhi tree. Wonderfully, through these images and designations, as through the designations that we call my body and my mind, the Buddha can also be called Thus Come. Although his body and mind passed away millennia ago, the Buddha can still be with us through the practice of faith, energy, mindfulness, concentration, and wisdom. In our patience, resolve, kindness and renunciation, and in all the factors of awakening, Buddha is with us here, today. Homage to the Tathāgata!

15

WHAT KONDAÑÑA SAW

This is what the Blessed One said—and the Group of Five bhik-khus were gladdened and approved of his words. And while this exposition was being delivered, the untarnished and clear vision of Dhamma arose in the Venerable Kondañña: "Whatever has the characteristic to arise, all that ceases."

When the Buddha finished speaking, the Group of Five were delighted by the scope and the clarity of his teaching. They all gained what was described earlier as a "reflective acceptance of those teachings." But for Kondañña the experience was one of deep insight; the teaching struck a chord in his heart and there was a major breakthrough. It was his own realization, not just an agreement with what the Buddha had said. Kondañña's knowledge was through insight, not logic—he insightfully saw for himself what the Buddha was pointing to in talking about suffering, its origin, cessation, and the path to that ceasing. His "untarnished and clear vision of Dhamma" was expressed in his explanation, "Whatever has the characteristic to arise, all that ceases."

More than being a good listener, Kondañña obviously had the skills of penetrative insight to use the Buddha's words in a way that immediately brought around a major shift of perspective. But seeing that things arise and cease doesn't in itself seem that radical: every Romantic poet who writes of the passing of summer, human mortality, or the fading of beauty says the same without having an untarnished and clear insight. But in the Buddha's discourses, this realization of impermanence represents the first major breakthrough of stream-entry. The same insight is recorded at a later date with reference to the two wanderers who subsequently became the Buddha's chief disciples. One of the wanders, who was eventually known as Venerable Sāriputta, was impressed by the way a bhikkhu conducted himself with calm composure. This bhikkhu was the Venerable Assaji, a member of the Group of Five, who at this time was an arahant. Sāriputta asked him for a teaching, but Assaji, saying he was still too green to give a full discourse, only gave a brief digest of the import of the Dhamma:

> The Perfect One [another term for Tathāgata] has told the cause
> Of causally arisen things;
> And what brings their cessation too:
> Such is the doctrine preached by the Great Monk.
> (M 1)

Sāriputta was tuned in, and the import of these words struck home with the very same dawning as in Kondañña's case: "Whatever has the characteristic to arise, all that ceases." He went to tell his friend Moggallāna the news, but just by looking at him Moggallāna knew something big had happened to Sāriputta:

> "Your faculties are serene, friend, the colour of your skin is clear
> and bright. Is it possible that you have found the Deathless?"
>   "Yes, friend, I have found the Deathless."
> (M 1)

As Sāriputta passed on Assaji's words to Moggallāna, Moggallāna too had the same insight, and made the same comment that Sāriputta had previously made to Assaji:

> "This is the truth: even if that were all,
> You have attained the state where there is no sorrow
> That we for many times ten thousand ages
> Have let pass by unseen."
> (M 1)

So what did they get that Keats and Shelley missed? To put it briefly, the poets probably weren't cultivating the noble eightfold path. And so their minds weren't attuned. They didn't take the sign of impermanence inwardly and refer it to "the cause of causally arisen things"—to the way their minds created a world. This creation of a world with a self as a kind of hernia hanging out of it is something we've come across before in two ways: first in the teachings on the five aggregates and second in the teachings on dependent origination. In terms of the aggregates, reality is made up of the experience of form (one's own or something else's), feeling, perception, activities (or sankhāra), and consciousness. In dependent origination, that uncomfortable predicament is seen in terms of ignorance and craving. But ignorance and craving aren't hanging around in thin air; they're embedded in consciousness by the sankhāra aggregate.

As I've said before, sankhāra carry the codes of action in terms of body, speech, or mind. They are embodied as three things. First they are the nervous intelligence that supervises breathing (notice how your breathe rate changes when you've excited, tense, relaxed, or depressed). Second, they are intelligence that forms and activates thoughts (which also change dependent on happiness, assurance, or fear). Finally, and most importantly, they are the intelligence that forms emotions and impulses. This "mental" or heart activity normally dominates the other activities, and at any given moment it conditions our consciousness to experience happiness, stress, anxiety, love, and thoughts about what we should or shouldn't be—essentially conditioning our world. And as we know, some of that conditioning is very stressful.

That's why the Buddha found the stilling of these sankhāra to be sublime and peaceful. He saw "the cause of causally arisen things, and what brings their cessation too." Interestingly enough, cessation, or putting things to rest, comes about through sankhāra too, by the skillful volition relating to the eightfold path. For example, we can use mindfulness of breathing to steady and soothe the bodily sankhāra. This will then steady and soothe the mental activities. Obviously this stilling, putting to rest, or "cessation," doesn't necessarily mean that we are unable to think for the rest of our life. It's more that the mental sankhāra that build a world and a self—as we've seen for the Buddha, and to a lesser extent for Kondañña— take a break from formulating experience in ignorance.

So, yes, the Buddha was still breathing after enlightenment, or rather his body was—but his absorption could be profound enough to not be aware of that. Rather than having other input to block his awareness of what was unpleasant, or bring on something more interesting, the Buddha could let go of that mental activity of perceiving—and not pick up thoughts, feelings, or other perceptions.

To look into this more fully: some sankhāra (the bodily ones) are inevitable for this life. And the verbal ones are useful. Neither of those are the source of the internalized world–self dualism that most of us navigate through. This is the work of the mental sankhāra. This mind-action has several levels: first of all there's the preliminary function, which I've already described: the mind perceives and registers sense-data and organizes it all into a reality. But there's also an ethical and hedonic level of sankhāra that mediates over those perceptions, and determines which ones should be followed. This level organizes volition; this sankhāra decides what to do by referring to values such as conscience, compassion, and personal well-being. Here the mind can be led by wisdom, though this gets a little tricky because of another level of sankhāra, which is the one that carries the sense of self and self-interest. That is, although I "know" that sharing is good, sometimes I don't want to share with you because I'm annoyed or frightened—or I'd rather have things for myself.

With some training and introspection, however, we can adapt this self-interest by witnessing the results of our actions. Conscience and compassion give long-term well-being; getting high on drugs is a quick burning, short-term yield, and a downer in the longterm. Rather wonderfully, the human consciousness, if rightly attuned, tends toward skillful actions because of this ability to learn. In other words, wise programs and activities can replace the reckless ones.

Yet even here, there is still the urge to crave and cling. You may even think, "I want people to be fair and peaceful, and I get depressed and angry if they're not." But even holding on to skillful sankhāra is still suffering. This clinging is still there in the third level: it's a meta-sankhāra that takes over the functional and ethical sankhāra to provide self-orientation and a worldview. Yes, clinging in the sense of feeding on or leaning on, isn't necessarily pleasure oriented or unwholesome, but it's about creating a solid basis for self. In this (actually fragile) solidification, it's the felt notion "I am" that underlies the other forms of clinging. And even good "I am's" suffer from loss, uncertainty, and rigidity of views, especially when the world doesn't operate as we feel it should. However, this meta-sankhāra, though clung to, isn't inevitable. The possibility of release from clinging presents itself when we see the dukkha in it, and how it depends on ignorance. What do I mean by ignorance? Well, there's ignorance in not seeing that this core "self" experience is also constructed and unreliable.

Once we see where there is clinging, nonattachment begins to develop. And at this point we do see that what is to be grabbed, what has been grabbed, and even grabbing itself, is ephemeral. It all changes: this is what Kondañña saw.

With nonclinging we get a sense of our whole world dependently arising and ceasing. And seeing the impermanence of all these impressions, impulses, and states of mind is considered a good way of turning inward toward the path of liberation. So as insight penetrates, we go beneath the topics, the sense-data and thoughts, and we attend to the very structuring that brings those topics into presence. We attend to the clinging that conjures up our usual view that the five aggregates are solid. That is, when there is clinging to the experience of form, we assume shapes and textures are definite and real. We measure and assess and are moved by those attributes. But form is subject to change: What shape is a flame? How crisp is snow when the weather warms up? Feeling is inconstant too: we assess and are moved in terms of pleasure and pain, but they change too—any diminution of pleasure is disagreeable, but pleasure can't stay in a steady state. Then there are perceptions that carry a lifetime of meaning in terms of "friends" and "foes" and "interesting" and "tedious"—and they can also switch around. And there is volition, the ability to do and make. We judge ourselves very critically on those grounds. Yet, as every winner has to find out, winning isn't permanent. Our ability changes; we eventually lose it all—all, it seems, except the tendency to cling.

Clinging, however, *is* weakened by the skillful activity of meditation. For example, we sit quietly and experience the flow of feeling, the dependent and changing experience of our bodily form, and all the "I should do it" programs twitching in the mind. And through meditating, we can unhook the reactions and reflex-activities by focusing on their changeability. This practice, although based on ethics and sense-restraint, doesn't attempt to affect the topics that the mind is carrying in its perceptions and volitions. Instead it entails contemplating sankhāra as subject to change—so whatever our impulse or perception is, it's seen as just another passing thing. Dispassion then arises because we've started to disengage the meta-sankhāra of clinging. As Sāriputta put it:

> Friend Kotthita, a virtuous bhikkhu should carefully attend to the
> five aggregates subject to clinging as impermanent, as suffering, as
> a disease . . . as empty, as nonself. What five? The form aggregate,
> . . . feeling, . . . perception, . . . volitional formations, . . . consciousness. . . . When, friend, a virtuous bhikkhu carefully attends thus
> . . . it is possible that he may realize the fruit of stream-entry.
> (SN 22: Aggregates 122)

Name-and-Form

This is "entering the stream" because with that nonattachment, the mind comes into the flow of Dhamma. It starts penetrating how sankhāra operate at that meta-level of clinging. This is where the mental aggregates operate as designators in the process of "name-and-form." *Name* is the mental aggregates, by which a thing exists because I know it—it moves me; I see your face and there's a resonance. That "name" *depends* on form. But form itself doesn't happen for me without a name. The Amazonian tribesmen don't see a computer when I give them one, they see a box. I don't see the wavelengths of light that bounce off flowers and drive butterflies wild with desire. So the personal experience of form depends on it being named. This naming occurs through perception and feeling, and through the sankhāra of contact, attention, and volition. And in that setup, contact, attention, and volition "act" as a kind of tripod that holds the mind on an object so that perception and feeling arise. Then when perception arises, "I" perceive, and as what I perceive affects me, I act on that and more sankhāra arise. This is the beginning of the conflagration that can overwhelm us.

This tripod is all we have to keep "our world" going, so although you may steady it through mindfulness and put it on a firmer ground through ethical conduct and restraint, you don't directly dismantle it. What occurs instead is that through Dhamma-practice, the stream of consciousness that the tripod rests upon gets reviewed and seen as changeable, subject to stress, and not a self. Then the world and the self, the reality that the tripod supports, gets a lot lighter and more flexible. With complete enlightenment, things are very free, but attaining that freedom is a gradual process. Normally consciousness is gripped by ignorance and craving, and the first way that this grip gets released is through removing the fetters of personality-view, doubt, and attachment to customs and systems, which I mentioned in chapter 10.

To make it more concrete: imagine consciousness to be a moment-by-moment stream like water. It is both fluid and reflective. If it pours over rocks or moves between curved banks, this stream will be twisted so that there are waves and ripples on its surface; then whatever is seen on its reflective surface will be distorted. When you look at the water, you'll see your face with a crooked jaw. If that's the only way you see yourself, naturally enough you'd imagine that's what you look like. But it would be weird trying to shave in the morning, and brushing your teeth would also be a complex job because actually your face isn't like that. You would feel uncertain, and would consequently get very attentive to those actions, but unless you were to give attention to the direct, felt experience rather than to the reflection, the process would be stressful. This is pretty much what it's like when you have a personality-view imposed on consciousness: the personality-view twists how it forms in each moment. Then, although you try really hard, the face that you see never quite fits with your experience, and all that trying to make the experience line up, through holding tight or adopting systems and customs and clinging to them, makes life less than joyful.

But you can approach experience more directly. This might begin by noticing that the reflection isn't as solid as it once seemed. For example, at times, the surface is bright and clean, which causes you to look one way. At other times, the surface is oily or dirty, which causes you to look different. Suppose with that understanding, you begin to have faith that you aren't as fixed as you once thought. Then you stop gripping consciousness so tightly so that sometimes your image appears twisted and at other times it is untwisted; you start to sense that this image of "you" is a reflection that is subject to distortion. Then even if the twisting and the distortion remained for a while, you wouldn't take it as reality. Furthermore, you might very well study the container of the stream and the bedrock that the reflection is flowing over. And if every time you experienced a pull or a twist of craving, you removed a rock, pretty soon the stream would calm down and you'd get a clearer view. This is what stream-enterers have done: they have probed the stream of consciousness and have smoothed out its riverbed. They have developed ethics and compassion, have cultivated meditation and letting go, and as a result of these have released the craving that builds up around self-image and personality, around uncertainty, and around customs and systems. The volition, attention, and contact are dependently arisen and of the nature to cease once the ground they stand on is smoothed out. Furthermore, with that experience of handling consciousness, the insight arises that consciousness is not self; then the topics and energies in the conscious process can be allowed to come and go.

So Kondañña examines his experience—he looks into the looking-glass, past the reflections and smears, and notices the surface of consciousness is actually gently pulsing. The seizures that make it rigid have softened. What he has done is cool down, step back, and really look at how the grabbing action itself is impermanent. Even being grabbed changes. Can you notice? If you draw your attention back to the moment, or the "place," where thoughts and impulses are arising, if rather than taking issue with or following them, you keep your attention lightly balanced at the point of arising, the thoughts and impulses don't take hold. With that we are at the point in consciousness where volition arises to make contact. If we can rest back at that place, the grabbing needn't harden into a clenched grip. Then grabbing a pizza, grabbing the idea of letting go, being grabbed by a mood . . . can be released. This is what Kondañña knew. He could look into consciousness with clear and calm attention—and instead of seeing a person who should be conforming to this or believing in that, he would just notice aggregates arising and passing. He realized that it is the very holding that molds consciousness with a twisted surface and uncomfortable feel, and he had confidence in pursuing that insight. And such realization is in accord with the Buddha's advice:

> Stay focused on impermanence to get clear of self-view: because when you do so, you get established in the understanding that none of this is self. And when that way of seeing is fully established, self-view gets wiped away—and this is Nibbāna here and now. (AN 9:1)

Even though this talk about consciousness, name-and-form, and fetters may sound otherworldly, the results of entering the stream are evident. For starters, not experiencing things from the base of personality cools the reactions around praise and blame, success and loss. When you're bound in personality and somebody addresses you as "Fatso!" you can feel a trifle offended. However, isn't it conceivable that on hearing such a remark, you'd notice where the other person was coming from—be it friendly or malicious—and respond to that in them rather than hold their remark as pertaining to who you are? That's what stream-enterers do: their personal form isn't being held as an identity. Although stream-enterers can die peacefully, their more immediate relief is that they no longer have a lifetime career of buying into or fending off praise and blame.

Similarly, speculative views, the source of controversy and doubt, don't catch hold in stream-enterers' minds. If most people look within long enough, they will recognize that they have some kind of life-view. Some people believe there is no meaning in life; that we're just born and die and that's it. Others believe we are all sent here by God to serve, as agents of the Divine. And some people might be in a state of confusion as to what life is about and why they were born. These beliefs affect people's outlook and actions in this life. If we feel there's no point and we just end at death, our mind will incline to heedlessness, indulgence, or meaninglessness; if we believe we're agents of a loving deity, it will incline to interpretations of compassion and love. Views, however, subject to change, generate kamma, and even bright ones generate a self who contends with others and different views. This is what a stream-enterer knows, beyond doubt. Seeing with certainty the dukkha and the clinging in such views, they abandon them—while also having no doubt about who they "are." And they understand kamma: that those who believe there is nothing are heading to a bleak and immoral realm. Those who believe and act from a place of love will go that way. And those who don't hold a view will begin the process of liberation from birth and death.

To be brief, we could say much the same for the third fetter. It's a clinging and a dependency on customs and systems that seeks solidity. But as customs and systems vary from place to place and are at best an imposition on the flow of events, clinging to them makes us inflexible and unbalanced. The wiser option is to use a system of mind-training that will make the mind able to find stillness in the flow and surf of the waves. Then views, defenses, comparisons, and agitation don't form in those areas.

So Kondañña is one who has entered the stream of Dhamma. Seven fetters remain, but the realization that consciousness is a moment at a time and therefore flexible is where it all starts. The Buddha said if you clear the first three fetters, then what remains is comparatively small—it's like clearing a mountain of earth but still having some dirt beneath your fingernails. And a process has been set in motion that will arrive at complete liberation within seven lifetimes at most. The wheel of Dhamma has truly been set rolling.

16

HEAVEN (AND HELL) ON EARTH

When the wheel of Dhamma had been set rolling by the Blessed One, the devas of the earth raised the cry: "At Vāranāsi, in the Deer Park at Isipatana, the incomparable wheel of Dhamma has been set rolling by the Blessed One—and it can't be stopped by any samana or brahmin or deva or māra or brahma or anyone whomsoever in the world."

When they heard what the earth devas had said, the devas of the realm of the Four Great Kings cried out with one voice: "At Vāranāsi . . ." And when they heard the cry of the devas of the realm of the Four Great Kings, then the devas of the realm of the Thirty-Three cried out with one voice."

This section of the sutta describes the effect the Buddha's turning of the wheel of truth had on various celestial realms. The text is noncommittal; it simply states that various divine beings, or devas, or (to give them their more flowery name, *devatā,*) hear the teaching and start proclaiming it to each other. But to us, this may seem strange: compared with the penetrative exposition on dukkha and the human mind, this stuff about the realm of the devas seems to be of the nature of fantasy, a fifth-century-B.C. form of Walt Disney.

A point to bear in mind here is that such nonhuman beings are found in every culture of the premodern era. They were part of the worldview. In these cultures, the presence of such spirits has the effect of enshrining either a sense of reverence for the natural world, or for the world-order. The spirits keep human egotism in check by occupying a place adjacent to the human realm that can affect rainfall, fertility, disease, and other forces of Nature. Humans don't have sole say over what goes on. Instead, they have to revere, consult, and propitiate the deities. Having dropped that reference (or an effective equivalent) in our modern culture, humans have only their own wisdom and conscience to balance out their self-interest; unfortunately on a social level, so far that hasn't been enough.

But, there's still the question of whether or not these beings are real. A meditator who sees that perception and its realities depend on attention, volition, and contact might very well say, "Like everything else, it depends on how you look." The kind of attention, and the volition that supports that attention will affect what it contacts. If you want to experience the universe as a thing out there, you might use a telescope so that you can know about it. But that will only show you a telescope's view of the universe, conditioned by the ways of telescopes, and interpreted by the brain. Some of the information that comes in that way is pretty incredible: do you understand or directly perceive curved space or black holes where time slows down and stops? There was a time when we were convinced that the stars were flecks of fire set in the vault of heaven, and that God created human beings out of mud, having created the rest of the universe in five days. When looking at the world this way, one important point to ask is, "How does this affect my life?" If it makes us more aware, ethically attuned, and less driven by blindness, then however figurative or abstract it may be, we can make good use of that idea and perception.

It's also the case that to this very day, many people experience the paranormal realities of forces, energies, auras, and spirits. How they interpret these experiences varies from their being loving mother goddesses to subtle astral bodies or visitors from Lemuria. Regardless of whether or not these things are "real," what we can know is that the range of human experience has always been broader than what fits within the current interpretation of reality. However, human society is in such need of a world-order—a way of living within that reality—that it takes the set of values, beliefs, and information that's available at the time and says that this defines reality and how to be in that. This way of living is based on the belief that other views are heretical, and other realities are madness or lies. Eventually what happens is that this interpretation of reality either breaks down or adapts to encompass new dimensions of human experience or new ways that people live. For example, in this era, the dominant interpretation of reality is based on science and technology. This has been able to extend enormously in its own terms and make large contributions to human welfare (and suffering) under its principle of objective analysis. We've come to adopt as part of our current real-world viruses and radiation that are invisible to the naked eye, and we can make good use of imaginary numbers like the square root of minus one. However, this reality—which places the analyst and the analyzed at opposite ends of the telescope—doesn't encompass ethics or consciousness. So can we appreciate the scientific viewpoint, and yet also say that there's another way of seeing things that has its validity. Ethics and calming the mind are vital for human welfare. And if it helps to make this point clear, then what's the problem with a few devas? They're perhaps as "real," if not more so, than the square root of minus one.

The Buddha understood that material form exists "out there," but he concerned himself with the nature of consciousness inside himself. In this respect, Buddhist cosmology is very closely tailored to fit not the "it's out there" view of the world, but the inner path out of suffering and stress. This view of the cosmos is based on kamma, on the cause and effect of conscious volition. It includes consciousness because the reality that we dwell in is based on mind-states and mind-sets that get established as a result of our behavior. These various states equate with the hellish, earthly, or heavenly spheres of the Buddhist world-system. The use of cosmology as a map of states of consciousness, all of which are accessible to the human mind, works as a guide for conscious experience.

The cosmology presents a world-system that is much larger than the realm of our everyday senses and thoughts: which is what we begin to peek into as we engage with Dhamma practice and meditation. Through meditation we can come to know the range of our mind: how it can move to the sublime, or get captured by subliminal or irrational energies. In fact one of our aims in meditation is to widen and deepen our entry into our mind so that we come out of the ruts of our constructed reality. In the course of that exploration, a huge amount of psychological and emotional material—clinging, self-views, and unconscious craving—comes to light. And it is through clearing much of this shadow material that the very supports for consciousness—the props and dependencies that keep its mirror reflecting a "me" versus a "world of others"—start to release.

The careful and discerning easing of consciousness out of its gridlock of "I, me, my self" softens how it arises, and makes it more sensitive to realities outside of its accustomed range. And however we may choose to portray those realities, the Buddha described them in accordance with the world-order of the time, of devas, brahmas, and māras, but characteristically likened them to the many domains of consciousness. Yes, consciousness can reside, or be established, on one of a whole range of levels be they hellish or sublime, dependent on kammic input.

A Map of the Cosmos

The cosmological map is of an order of realms that ascends or descends in line with the nature of the volition that supports them. Down relates to the coarser realms and up relates to the more refined. The nature of volition that dominates a being's life determines where their consciousness dwells—and where their succeeding consciousness will arise after death. Morality plays a part, in that the lowest realms are characterized by either a lack of moral sense or of conscious evil intent. The human realm occupies a middling position, and has the greatest potential for changing volition, steering kamma, and shifting up or down the world system. This ability to step back and know the push that drives the mind is also why humans have the greatest possibility for enlightenment. And, as I mentioned, since it's less fixed in its own realm, the human mind can take on the characteristics of any of the other realms.

Above the human realm are the realms of the devatā and the brahmas— we'd call them lesser and greater divinities—while immediately below is the realm of the *asuras,* jealous titans who have a lot of power but still envy the happier deities: you might meet such beings in the political arena here in the human realm. Beneath the realm of titans is the animal realm, where volition is attuned to bodily instincts such as hunger, reproduction, and survival. If you live just on bodily appetites alone, that's the kind of mental volition that gets developed. The animal realm is anything but Disneyland: most animals spend their time in a realm of fear. They are bound to a particular habitat that they cannot improve very much, and they are at the mercy of the forces of nature and the activities of human beings who slaughter them for food or amusement.

Further down we really start to hit the pits. The realm below the animal is the realm for "hungry ghosts" of endless need and deprivation. This is the abode of the miser mentality; it's also frequented by swindlers and people who have exploited or oppressed the poor—totally selfish beings. If you're addicted to drugs or liquor, this realm is the place you're spending time in. In that "hungry ghost" realm of addiction, there's a lot of coarse selfishness, squalor, and neglect of the body, and a mind that inclines to self-pity. And if that isn't bad enough and you still can't turn your conscious trajectory around, then there's the lower "hell" realms (eight major ones). These are places of torment, where beings have a completely and grossly overridden ethical sense. Consequently here there's no ability to let go of the bad and pick up the good. You could probably make a list of tyrants who are spending an aeon or two in this sojourn, and a few who are warming up for the trip at this very moment.

So you get the idea. None of this is about divine judgment; it's just a portrayal of the laws of kamma operating in terms of the consciousness affected by clinging. In most instances there isn't the capacity or the interest to step back, review, and let go of blind volition and clinging.

Beings in lower realms are unaware of the laws of kamma and have to remain there until the effects of bad kamma have worn out. On the other hand, the realms of the devatā are happy and long-lasting, but because of that, the motivation to let go gets remote. Meanwhile up in the brahma realm, they're so refined they don't even have a physical form, so what is there to let go of? Dependent upon past good kamma, their tendency is to dwell in that until it runs out. So what characterizes all of these realms is that most of their inhabitants have not understood that their realm is dependently arisen, impermanent, and not to be clung to. From the long-life brahmas at the top of the heap on down to those doing time in hell, they haven't arrived at Kondañña's insight, "Whatever has the characteristic to arise, all that ceases." Hence all of these beings are bound up in saṃsāra. Sooner or later for the heavenly beings, their radiance dims and they start the descent, probably clinging to whatever they can as they come down. Sometimes this happens for humans at the time of death: you can read in *The Tibetan Book of the Dead* how if we've cultivated the path we might then get a glimpse of the deathless, but clinging arises that gets us grasping at radiance . . . then, grasping at that, we drop to realms of subtle and then grosser forms until we're back in a human womb . . . or somewhere less pleasant.

Just as the devas, māras, and brahmas can make appearances in the human realm, the same goes for humans traveling to other realms. The kammic potential of humans is so powerful that we can get previews of the other realms, and can assume their corresponding characteristics, just by inclining our intentions and activities within our current life span. So humans are sometimes like hell beings, sometimes like hungry ghosts, sometimes like animals, sometimes like asuras, and sometimes like the devatā. No wonder we get so confused! Perhaps it is because of this almost constant confusion that some human beings have the urge to get beyond all these realms. Humans can never become fixed in any state for too long; and thus for us there is the opportunity to counteract the drive for becoming with the understanding of impermanence. This is Kondañña's realization: that all these realms of becoming arise and pass away. The aim of the map then isn't to advocate heaven or deny it, but to point out that although it's a lot better place to abide than hell, all of it is in the same world-system of kamma and becoming. Therefore the ultimate aim is for not-abiding or nibbāna. Then there's no decline or decease, and in this very life we can surpass the glory of the devas.

Devatā

Let's look closer at the devatā, those beings who rejoiced in the Buddha's teachings, because learning about them can help our own spiritual development. Devatā are born in one of six celestial realms, in accordance with the laws of kamma. This is through having lived human lives with such virtues as kindness, honesty, harmlessness, and generosity. According to scriptural accounts, devatā are less constrained by material form, have more diaphanous bodies, and possess consciousness that is intelligent and refined. The subtlety and the skill of the Buddha's teachings appeal to the devatā, who also have a high regard for morality. However, the devatā find the direct understanding of Dhamma through contemplating impermanence, unsatisfactoriness, and not-self even more difficult than humans do. Life on their ethereal planes seems very long, so it is difficult for the devas to notice impermanence. The almost constant refined happiness does not motivate them to practice. However, they are sensitive to purity and gentleness. Whenever these qualities manifest, they experience great joy. So they all celebrate the proclamation of the Dhamma, but few gain the Dhamma eye.

The relevance of these six heavenly realms for a human aspirant is that they offer a contemplation on the "nearmisses" that we make in our search for a true world-order. In the following travelogue, we can review the levels of consciousness, their beauty and concerns, and the worldview that they are bound to. Perhaps they will offer us guidance on how to live a good life—and how to get beyond it.

The first group of devatā, the earth devas, don't have a realm of their own; they abide on the earth under the supervision of the four great kings, whom we will discuss next. Folklore of most countries mention encounters with these earth devas under many different names. They represent the pagan consciousness, which at its most elevated develops Nature mysticism. This is the level that many aboriginal people use as a basis for the world order. It attunes to forces of Nature, to rain and fertility, and to the energies of the earth. With such a worldview, the Australian indigenous people supervised their land for forty thousand years without causing the soil erosion, forest fires, and ecological problems that have been created in the past two hundred years of settlement by a modern, science-oriented people. I'm not saying that their culture was the optimal development—the medical, intellectual, and technological advances that have been made in our time have provided enormous benefits. It seems, though, like we have left an important piece of a sustainable world-order behind. There was intelligence and conscience at this level, a sensitivity that we could make use of. However, the pagan worldview also embraced animal and human sacrifice. . . . So we can get lost at this level and start a descent to the lower realms.

The earth devas live under the supervision of the four great kings, also called *lokapāla,* or "world guardians." They represent a skillful planetary consciousness. In many premodern cultures, there was an awareness that the health and order of the society was related to the health and order of the earth. If unbalanced or demonic forces broke loose in the society, they would create havoc in terms of famine, floods, or droughts. The role of the king was to be in touch and rule in accordance with the proper order or Dhamma for the society, in order to ensure that the people would prosper. In Buddhist cosmology, this is mirrored by the realm of the Four Great Kings who survey the four directions: Dhatarattha in the east, Virulhaka in the south, Virupakkha in the west, and Vessavaṇa (or Kuvera) in the north.

These four live at the foot of the central mountain of the world, Mount Sineru or Meru. This mountain is also a symbol for the upright, centered mind within the world as we ordinarily know it. This is also called the *axis mundi*—the central pole upon which our being turns. If Mount Sineru is secure from corruption and upheaval, the world system is in order. If the human mind is clear and uncorrupted by delusion, hatred, pride, and intoxication, then our world is balanced. The main job of the four great kings then is to back up the devas of the Thirty-Three (who live further up the mountain) in maintaining wise governance and in repelling the asuras. The asuras are both envious and egotistical. As is the case with egomaniacs, they couldn't share like these other devas do, and they tried to take over the whole mountain. Their conceit, pride, and love of power was tilting the *axis mundi* out of balance until the good devas overthrew them.

The other inhabitants of Mount Sineru are the devas of the Thirty-Three. This realm (called Tāvatimsa in Pāli) is variously described as inhabited by thirty-three devatā, or comprising a ruling committee of thirty-three. It is a sociable world, fantastically beautiful and pleasant. There are frequent meetings in the Great Hall, gatherings to listen to celestial concerts, and sometimes the appearance of guest deities—a visiting arahant or the Buddha himself might drop in to talk on Dhamma. This realm is the normal abode of Inda, also called Sakka (or Indra in Sanskrit), who was one of the supreme gods of the Vedas—the ancient religious texts that predate Buddhism. Just as the early Christians absorbed aspects of native religions by incorporating their pagan and primitive gods, the Buddhists transformed Inda from a thunderbolt-wielding sky warrior to a righteous monarch, lover of the Dhamma, and disciple of the Buddha. In one of the suttas (DN 21), Inda, having recognized that his time is drawing to an end, puts forth renewed spiritual zeal and attains stream-entry—one of the few devas to do so. These accounts define Inda as a righteous ruler of realms that are ethically sympathetic to the human realm and interested in its welfare.

We should also recognize that like the realms themselves, Inda bears allegorical semblance to aspects of the human mind. *Inda* is related to the word *indriya,* the term for the five spiritual faculties of faith, energy, mindfulness, concentration, and wisdom, which are discussed in chapter 6. These are the proper "rulers" over our mind.

For the four great kings and the thirty-three devatā, guidance and personal responsibility are very important. They embody an uprightness of mind that is greater than the normal moral standard. They signify a whole view on the world and on life, in which the ego is dethroned from being the moral arbiter and center of the universe. The worldview that this relates to is the early social model ruled over by a king or emperor who would preside over shrines, make appropriate sacrifices, perform rituals, and govern in accord with the will of heaven. In Buddhist cultures this ideal ruler is referred to as "the wheel-turning monarch" and he is invested with ten guiding principles, or *rājadhammas:* generosity, virtuous conduct, self-sacrifice, honesty (or integrity), gentleness, self-control, calmness, nonviolence, patient forbearance, and conformity to the principles of Dhamma. The great exemplar of this was Emperor Ashoka of India (273–232 B.C.E) who forbade the killing of animals in his court, encouraged irrigation, and who, though he himself was Buddhist, was a guardian to all religions in his realm. Other Buddhist monarchs model themselves on him, from the great Sinhalese kings who created reservoirs, canals, and irrigation schemes for their people, to the present-day king of Thailand, who has personally invented low-cost agricultural machinery and has supported many agricultural projects.

So when the ten principles are firm, in ourselves or in the world around us, Mount Sineru—the stable balance within us and in society—is secure. When these principles are decaying, the converse is true, with effects that manifest in wider contexts such as an increase in violent crime, suicide, and drug abuse:

> When people are burning up with crazy passions, overwhelmed by corrupt ambitions, entranced by wrong ideas, the rainfall dwindles. Food is hard to come by. The crops fail, are mildewed and stunted. Because of this, many people perish.
> (AN 3:56)

For these devas, being close to the human realm means that they are affected by its activities. When there's a lot of killing, stealing, lying, and greed that sets up a pretty unpleasant vibration that makes it difficult for them to function properly. So they do take time out to listen to a celestial band or two. Judging from conditions in the world today, these devatā seem to be sorely pressed to keep the asuras and demons at bay. Hence they rejoice when they become aware of the Buddha establishing an order based on ethics and conscience. What they don't always get past is the sense of identifying with the power of it all.

If you have attachment to the realm of social order, you might worship the Buddha as the epitome of everything working out in an orderly and peaceful way. The Buddha, as perceived by these devas, is called a Dhamma-rājā, the Buddha as king of the Dhamma, because right governance was their concern. However, it's the case for rulers of the human realm, as well as for these devas, that they're still bound to use force to support that order. Moreover, they never really address or come to terms with their rivals, the ruler feels divinely empowered, and—from the pharaohs on to the twentieth-century Fascist dictatorships—things can go seriously wrong. And even when the principles of the *rājādhammas* are adhered to, the kings can lose their kingdoms and their lives in miserable ways as was the case for Kings Bimbisāra and Pasenadi, the Buddha's royal supporters. That's the problem with an order that has to be held by power: it gets challenged, shaken, and loses some of its refined idealism. Its wheel gets stuck and goes no further. This is not to dismiss those aims and concerns, but to ask if there is a wider sense of Dhamma that will include and transcend the limitations of governance and planetary awareness? The devas of the higher realms present some attempts to address that question.

17

IT DOESN'T GET BETTER
THAN THIS . . . OR DOES IT?

When they heard the cry of the Thirty-Three devas, the Yāma devas cried out with one voice. . . . When they heard the cry of the
Yāma devas, the Tusitā devas cried out with one voice. . . . When
they heard the cry of the Tusitā devas . . . the Nimmānaratī devas cried out with one voice. . . . When they heard the cry of the
Nimmānaratī devas, the Paranimmitavasavattī devas cried out
with one voice. . . . When they heard the cry of the Paranimmitavasavattī devas . . . the devas of the retinue of the Brahma deities took
up the cry: "At Vāranāsi, in the Deer Park at Isipatana, the incomparable wheel of Dhamma has been set rolling by the Blessed One—
and it can't be stopped by any samana or brahmin or deva or māra
or brahma or anyone whomsoever in the world."

The message of the transmission of the Dhamma was next communicated
to the Yāma devas and from there on up to the Tusitā, the Nimmānaratī,

Paranimmita vasavattī, and Brahmakāyika realms. The direction is up and out. The beings in these realms have left solid ground altogether. All of these realms are more refined than the lower deva realms and they float above Mount Sineru. They are fittingly ethereal: the Yāma devas don't experience any unpleasant impingement, the Tusitā is the ever-smiling realm, the Nimmānaratī is the realm of delight in mental-creation—devas manifest whatever they set their minds on. The Paranimmitavasavattī realm is the place where others do the creating for you; you just sit back and enjoy the show . . . and the Brahmakāyika devas make up the retinue of the formless deities, the brahmas. Surely things can't get better than this! Who needs planet earth anyway . . . all that fuss and grime! Not to mention those troublesome humans. Well, in Buddhist cosmology this Brahmakāyika level is still only the fringe of the sublime. After this, further up in the great ascent, we have twenty ascending brahma realms—where they find happiness too gross and irritating, let alone the inconvenience of having even a diaphanous body. And the higher you go, the longer the life span. Sexless, bodiless, and serene, the brahma deities live (if you can apply such a coarse term to them) in their suffusive glow for aeons. This is where suffering stops, right?

Wrong. It's just a press on the pause button as far as Buddhas see it. And even at that level, a brahma deity can suffer the most dreadful conceit, thinking: "I am Brahma, Great Brahma, the Conqueror, the Unconquered, the All-Seeing, All-Powerful, the Lord, the Maker and Creator, the Ruler, Appointer and Orderer, Father of All That Have Been and Shall Be" (DN 11:81). Still, consciousness doesn't arise in the Brahma realms unless you have developed kindness and deep absorption. So the brahmas are benevolent and awesome, and from this galaxy of luminous beings, Brahma Sahampati came forth to encourage the Buddha to teach—so let's not speak impudently of them.

At the level that has left the earth altogether, the realms of the Yāma devas and up, the mind has entered the realms of subtle sensual form. At these levels, the realities are energy bodies and angels, attuned through sensitivity to the astral and ethereal planes. Tusitā is also a very high-minded realm, a suitable place, they say, for the consciousness of the next Buddha, Metteyya, to be taking form. According to the prophecies, his teaching will be based on spiritual love. That gives you an idea of the atmosphere in Tusitā; it's at the level of religion and devotion to the sublime. Here we are in the vision and the bliss where all that subtle and empathic consciousness is known, attuned to, and dwelt in an unbroken way for a long time: the Yāma devas experience their life span as 144 million earth years, and for the Tusitā devas it's even longer. Or at least that's the way it seems. The more refined the state of consciousness, the longer it appears to continue—time dilation is another feature of refined consciousness. States of heightened sensitivity can seem like an eternity. What is time anyway, except the registering of impingement that jolts the flow? Have you ever been so absorbed, so in flow with what you're doing, that the hours flew by? Well, for these celestials, there's nothing but flow: no jolts, no dips, no change of rhythm. Wouldn't that be great? But be careful—you forget about impermanence. And that is what happens. These devas can get stuck in the ether. And sooner or later, their luster dims, other devas ignore them, they start to feel gross . . . and down they go to another realm.

At these levels, the happiness is more refined than the delight in the musical get-togethers that happen down on Sineru: at these Yāma-Paranimmitavasavattī levels, beings are involved with rapture, devotion, and ecstasy, so external sense-realities don't touch the mind. They're certainly not stuck on functionality or materialism: unemployment, a failed harvest, or a financial crash are not issues here. They are attuned to the sense of the Divine. The same thing happens on the human plane: when we're enraptured with the teacher or devoted to a political or religious mission, hunger and hardship don't mean a thing. So the bright energy of devotion is powerful—but it can also be deluding.

The Power of Devotion

Devotion takes many forms, but in its clearest sense it's offered to ideals such as love or service or justice. Our subtle energy lifts when it has an object to resonate with, and so when coupled with meditation, devotion is a great asset. A heart sense that connects to the Buddha, Dhamma, and Sangha helps us keep the broad view: "Just as the Buddha practiced boundless patience, may the patience that I develop with my mind be for the welfare of others." It helps us keep a balance between our immediate, personal realities, and our long-term collective realities that we participate in. In the wider sphere of life, devotion manifests as the wish to offer self-less service. It's a way to meet and encompass the world. The Buddha himself, recognizing that it was proper Dhamma to serve one's teacher, rightly decided that since he had no teacher, his practice of devotion would be to serve the Dhamma. He included the world of gods, humans, and demons in his service.

Cultivation of this kind of service, maintained over years, is a standard in monastic training, especially toward the teacher when he or she is sick or dying. In the case of Ajahn Chah, who was paralyzed and unable to speak for a decade before he passed away, teams of four monks at a time, amply supported by the rest of the community, attended his every need for twenty-four hours each day. For many of the younger ones who went forth after he stopped teaching, it was the only meeting that they had with him. But the continual respectful attendance to his sick and dying body filled and strengthened their Dhamma-practice. Rightly held then, devotion gives focus to and energizes our sense of faith.

When we don't have devotion, we aren't really fully offering ourselves. But devotion could be in attending the sick, or through any means that brings up and exercises our pāramitā. It's not restricted to a refined level. Moreover if it isn't grounded, devotion can be wrongly used. When there is no calm or reflection, devotion produces rapture in the mind of the devotee, but not much else. Its energy is attractive because it resonates and holds the mind in the emotive energy that the image carries. If devotion is fettered by ignorance, its energy and conviction capture the mind. Devotion fires up religious zealots who also want to encompass the world—and it gives them the sense that doing so is within their grasp. So the religious vision gets corrupted by fundamentalists, charismatic cults, and missionaries who seek to undermine the religion and culture of other faiths—all following the will of the Divine and for the higher good, of course. In this respect, the Buddha was exemplary in his lack of predatory interest. Having met and confounded a group of ascetics in debate, his final remarks were these:

> Nigrodha, you may think: "The ascetic Gotama says this in order to get disciples." But you should not regard it like that. Let him who is your teacher remain your teacher. Or you may think: "He wants us to abandon our rules." But you should not regard it like that. Let your rules remain as they are.... Let your way of life remain as it was. . . . Let those things you consider wrong... [or] right continue to be so considered....
>
> There are, Nigrodha, unwholesome things that have not been abandoned ... fearful, productive of painful results in the future.... It is for the abandonment of these things that I teach Dhamma. If you practise accordingly ... you will attain to and dwell, in this very life, by your own insight and realisation, in the fullness of perfected wisdom.
> (DN 25:23)

What keeps the devotional mind from getting fascinated and captured is discerning wisdom, mindfulness, and concentration. A leap in faith then moves to a worthwhile object but doesn't leave the ground. We carry our discernment with us. In this way, the act of offering ourselves can take us beyond our self-view. Without devotion, we remain on the sidelines of truth; but if devotion is fettered by ignorance, it breeds attachment to special people, rituals, hobbies—even football teams.

In the next two realms—the Nimmānaratī and the Paranimmita-vasavattī—we find the devas of creation and the devas who delight in the creations of other devas. These are even more refined and long-lived than the Tusitā devas. The Nimmānaratī devas abide at almost magical levels of consciousness where the mind is so light and unburdened with temporality or form that it can create and sustain images according to its wishes. Virtual reality is permanently online. This is the realm of miracles: of turning bread into flesh, of flying through the air, walking through walls, and creating material objects. And yes, as religious healers and gurus demonstrate, miracles can happen. The Paranimmitavasavattī devas are one step further on from having to make the effort to create images of existence; they abide in the enjoyment of what others' mind-energy brings forth. This gives them a subtle power over the creators; you've probably come across this theme in sci-fi. It's blissful, of course, but by this stage of the journey, I imagine you're getting a little suspicious of bliss. It can be an indulgence, can't it? Rather like taking recreational drugs: you feel great in yourself, but you and your bliss are the center of the universe.

Here the smelly old earthly realm has been left far behind, and with it such considerations as impermanence, purpose, cause, and effect. These devas rejoice to hear that the Dhamma has been taught, but it is probably because they enjoyed the flash of light and appreciated the rejoicing from below. This is a happiness that could easily lead to indolence and decadence, and, fittingly enough, one of the two monarchs who rule over the Paranimmitavasavattī realm is Māra, the lord of delusion—whom we have met before. The other monarch is in another quarter of the realm and doesn't even know of Māra's existence. It seems to me that there's a very clear message here about the blinders that can go on at this level.

As I mentioned, we can experience aspects of these higher realms right here and now—and they arise while in meditation. It's true that these may feel blissful, but we are advised to beware of getting caught up in them. In the culture of meditation, attachment to ethereal perceptions is another aspect of becoming. The meditator gets caught in the sense of oneness or bliss and "becomes" that—takes a temporary trip to a deva realm. But it carries a risk if it causes a loss of contact with the physical or mundane realm. People forget to eat, get fascinated with energies, and get so absorbed in prayer or mantras that they can't be bothered with the details of responsible human life. If it is really strong, it can even develop into distorted perception—overwhelming rapture, visions, intimations of personal destiny, voices from the other shore, and so forth. In such cases, the teacher will usually assign such disciples simple mundane tasks that get them back in their bodies and keep them in contact with other grounded humans. It passes. Undergoing this "distorted perception" experience can really upset a person's balance and understanding. No matter how long it may seem to last, when the mystical experience ends or the ethereal body starts to droop, what happens to the so-called enlightenment? It's gone, isn't it? Then we either dismiss it or we don't see where our valid practice took a wrong turn or we hanker after getting it back. So through clinging to states, we lose touch with right view—that this very mental inclination to have a mind-state is kamma, good kamma in this case, but if clung to leads no further.

Mental kamma is a magical act. It's the ability to produce simulacra of living or nonliving entities, and to conjure up images out of principles and thought. According to the discourses, such potency can be developed to the level of psychic powers such as levitation or clairvoyance. Such powers are mentioned many times in the discourses, although by and large the Buddha forbade his bhikkhus and bhikkhunis to demonstrate them. He saw how they could be misused, likening them to a cheap striptease show. He also realized how such "magic" could distract people from what he called the real miracle: the Dhamma. At other times he would place accounts of his marvels in a pragmatic perspective. For example when his faithful attendant, Ānanda, was reciting the many marvelous and wonderful qualities of the Tathāgata, the Buddha asked him gently, and perhaps with cool humor, to remember one above all others:

> Ānanda, remember this too as a wonderful and marvellous quality of the Tathāgata: Here Ānanda, for the Tathāgata, feelings are known as they arise, as they are present, as they disappear; perceptions are known as they arise, as they are present, as they disappear; thoughts are known as they arise, as they are present, as they disappear.
> (MN 123:22)

In other words, the miraculous quality of a Tathāgata is that he's not bemused or mesmerized by the mind's dazzle. He sees the magic show as impermanent and something to wake up from because we're already in a magical creation. Just consider that this body started out as one cell: What directed it to create an eyelash cell here and a liver cell there, a bone cell here and a brain cell there? Genetic codes? Programmed embodiment energies? Whatever you call it, there's an intelligence based on the immaterial that can give form to the material. God, Logos, science? By whatever name, creation is the realm of the mages and their images of symbols and representations where the material and the immaterial can swap places. Marvelous indeed, but all of this is still bound to the world system. Creation and magic are happening all the time; what the Buddha saw as the vital issue was how to step back and not get caught in it—through staying focused on how it changes.

So let's get back to the cosmology. The Brahmakāyika realm is a realm of devotion to the higher brahma divinities. If we keep moving up—and to get this far consciousness will need to absorb into the deep concentration of jhāna—we'll get a glimpse of how it is for them. The beings in the brahma realm have no sense desire, and also have a correspondingly long life span. Despite the fundamental goodness of this realm, it is subject to delusion. The mind finds a place to hang out. There's only the inclination to stay in a state of oneness and rapture for as long as possible and avoid the more abrasive energies of the sense realms. The Brahmakāyika devas have attained this state of being through the development of absorptive meditation, but if they haven't also developed the wisdom and nonclinging of a Buddha's disciple, they eventually go into a serious tailspin:

> The measure of the life span of those devas is an aeon. The worldling [i.e. not at least a stream-enterer] remains there for the full life span, and then, after completing the life span of those devas, he goes to hell or to the animal realm, or to the sphere of hungry ghosts.
> (AN 4:123)

What goes up, must come down. So as we come to the end of our reflective journey through the deva realm, maybe it's clearer why "up" is not the way out. It must however be said that these happy realms are not to be dismissed; they are the result of good kamma, a base from which we can feel less embedded in the human realm and also feel uplifted. From there we can develop insight, if we look the right way. Because "down" isn't the way out either, nor is holding on to where we seem to be. The way out is through nonclinging. One of the complaints that people can direct toward those who incline toward a spiritual life is that it's all height, but no breadth—and sometimes no ground either. If we don't look after the planet, there won't be any trees to meditate under; if we don't have a caring and balanced social order, there will be too much impoverishment and violence to attend to Dhamma. If the emphasis is on ascent, we can forget about encompassing mundane existence, and we don't stay with that vital resonance that stirred the Buddha to bring Dhamma into the world.

The Buddha never forgot about these things. He could ascend to places that most of us, even the devas, can barely imagine. But his transcendence moved through ethics and compassion and was based on this human plane. He attended sick monks and taught others to do so. He listened to and adjudicated over monastic squabbles. During the night, apparently when various devas came to visit, he taught them. But most of his time was spent on the road, meeting people, going for alms, and giving teachings. He taught lepers and thieves, ascetics and brahmins, merchants and matriarchs and kings—whoever was ready, or interested, in terms of their own religion, concerns, or world view.

Neither lost in looking at the sense world, nor cut off and absorbed in an inner reverie, the Tathāgata is attuned to the inner and outer aspects of the world in a holistic awareness that knows it all as arising and ceasing. Not imagining transcendence to be up, let alone down, the Tathāgata sees it all as "such." Through nonconceiving, he is released.

It can be helpful to bring the Buddha's qualities to mind to uplift and inspire our practice. And we can pay homage to him. Keep in mind, though, that such a "Thus-Gone" One is not about to grant favors or give us good luck. But he can inspire something more useful, something that opens the way out of the whole world-system. It is found in the clear, calm poise of the spiritual faculties. When there is the balance of looking inward as much as looking out, even as we make offerings of flowers to images of the Buddha, the act of offering draws us back into that presence. Balance:

not up nor down, nor anywhere in-between. When faith is balanced by wisdom, and concentration by energy, and when that balance is preserved by mindfulness, our insightful knowing can penetrate the changing and unsatisfactory nature of the world-system. And in this way, such homage bears the highest fruit.

> Whatever monk, nun, male or female lay-follower dwells practising the Dhamma properly, and perfectly fulfills the Dhamma-way, he or she honours the Tathāgata, reveres and esteems him and pays him the supreme homage.
> (DN 16:5)

The Buddha didn't imagine that his sangha or his teaching would last forever. Long-lived though it may be, it will still be outlived by the Tusitā devas. But that's not the point. If the Buddha's Dhamma is well-lived for a day, that outshines the glory of the devas; and if it is lived through to the exhaustion of the outflows and the ending of suffering, we are no longer embedded in any aspect of the holistic world, and so we are able to bring the healing of wisdom and nonattachment to it. Truly, it doesn't get better than this.

18

LIGHT IN THE WORLD

So in that instant, at that very moment, the word traveled up to the realm of the high divinities. This ten-thousandfold world system trembled and shook and resounded, and a great measureless radiance, surpassing the shining glory of the devas, was made manifest in the world. Then the Blessed One uttered the pronouncement: "It is Kondañña who has seen deeply! Kondañña who has seen deeply." And so it was that the name of Venerable Kondañña became "Kondañña the deep seer."

In The Discourse That Sets Turning the Wheel of Truth, the Buddha's teachings were set rolling and produced a great light. It's a light that is said to have radiated through the ten-thousandfold world system: from the twenty brahma realms of the highest divinities all the way down through the eight hells. Even down there, according to the accounts, it was a great moment too. In those places of utter gloom, there was an illumination by which the poor wretches could see that there were other beings in the same predicament. By the standards of those places, this was a burst of light. For a moment, some sense of not being alone in the mess lessened the intensity of it. Others have been here, and are here, now. It's good to remember this.

This light has this broad focus and also is long lasting. It continues to shine today. Once again, if we translate cosmological events into events in consciousness, the light that we've seen glowing throughout the discourse is the light of wisdom:

> Bhikkhus, there are these four radiances.... The radiance of the moon; the radiance of the sun; the radiance of fire; the radiance of wisdom.... Bhikkhus, among these four, the radiance of wisdom is supreme.
> (AN 4:142)

The radiance of Dhamma-wisdom is supreme because it can bring a message that is relevant to all aspects of the world: "Having to hold on is suffering. Abandonment of that tension and stress is possible, and there's a way to do this that brings you greater peace than you've ever known." Although the devas were attuned to the sense of the Buddha's awakening and truth, at this juncture they're not presented as applying themselves to its practice. Bringing suffering to light is rarely a popular pursuit, especially with those who are having a good time. It sounds like a real killjoy. And *abandonment* is rarely a winning line—those experiencing good fortune and wealth equate it with hardship and loss of status. So although the devas were impressed with the power and depth of the teaching, and with the Buddha's own unshakable release, they're not experiencing the results of realization. However, being sensitive, they could feel the uplift and the goodness—and they rejoice in that.

At this time, the Buddha himself makes no mention of all the shining and shaking going on; more to the point, he was more concerned that the Dhamma he had taught had triggered a realization in Kondañña's mind. If this could be communicated to one person, then there was no reason why it couldn't be communicated to another. A big wheel of light—encompassing ethics, meditation, and wisdom—had started shining. This was a beginning, and it encouraged the Buddha to continue and develop his teaching. Subsequently he would refine his approach. Rather than take people immediately to the edge of the four noble truths, he'd often start with talking about values that a person had—generosity being a common enough ground. He would then lead on to reflections on morality, such as how we each don't wish to be abused, so this is a reason to not abuse others. That's simple enough. From there it was a matter of pointing out why people still do abuse each other—blinded by issues of power and possession, or mesmerized by sense-input. Then reflections on the hazards of power and attachment to sense-pleasure would follow on naturally, and would make the freedom of renunciation more apparent. These reflections would prepare a person to handle the notion that letting go might be a palatable option, and they would lay the foundation for the truth that having to hold on is suffering. In this way, the Buddha widened the span of the Dhamma-wheel. Eventually, he would even teach the devas.

Developing the Boundless Mind

So the sheer diversity of beings that can attune to the Dhamma is a feature that gives its light a wide beam. And this sense of range also works on the practitioner's mind. First it encourages us to encompass all mind-states with the same quality of seeing: that whatever we're feeling or whatever state we're in, this too is impermanent, subject to change, and is not-self. Moreover, as we contemplate our own mind and what we can notice of other people's, this encompassing insight widens to include all phenomena internal, external, near, and far. With such a wide scope, there is plenty of opportunity to develop sharing goodwill.

The Practice of Kindness

To do this in practice, you generally start with yourself, imagining a warm, bright, kindly energy sweeping and flooding through every fiber of your body. Just imagine what it's like when someone sees you in a friendly way.

(For starters, you can use how your dog feels about you.) Notice how something in you relaxes and softens. Then continue to sweep that light and warmth through one or two snags or dusty corners of your mind. Don't try to change them, but just listen without aversion and with sympathy to the sad voices and the grumbles. It's like being a nurse and looking at wounds and rashes. The feeling of warm heartedness may come in time, so if it's not there just yet, you can practice just with light. You can beam the light, and then mentally recall and begin to introduce people you know into that light.

When thinking of others in this way, just start with the easy ones—people you naturally warm to and respect, then move on to ones that bring up indifference. After that, shine light and warmth to ones that arouse difficult feelings. Try to do this while reflecting: "So with a boundless heart should one cherish all living beings." "With less defense and self-criticism may I accept myself" is the bottom line of the practice.

Spreading of goodwill can extend even further when we practice sharing our spiritual wealth—the sense of inner richness that accrues from Dhamma-practice. First of all this means acknowledging the fruits of our practice, which is good in itself. We don't often recognize that we're developing more patience or less reactivity, or that we're becoming more oriented around the quality of being and less around the drive to become. Such results are quiet but because they aren't flash-in-the-pan states, they are of great long-term value. And as we have come along the way, we may extend our health and strength to include others. We can develop this view of extending goodwill to others to take on the whole world-system from hell realms to the brahma deities, including the human realm in between—but maybe it's wiser to go slowly and be more specific: the neighbor who plays music too loud, too late; the dog that always yaps at me when I walk past its house; the local governor or politician who comes out with big words but no actions. May I include them as beings subject to kamma, and may any way I relate to them lessen the fixed position that they're in. In this way, we aspire for the welfare of any of these beings on the great wheel of becoming: "May whatever good kamma I have made be felt by them." It may seem ineffective, but when we recognize that perception is the basis for the mental action of sankhāra, and that mental action is the basis for physical action, then we realize it's not. Most hostility, especially when it's sanctioned by a government, is triggered and backed up by negative perceptions of the "others," whether they're the Spanish, Germans, or Russians. Look into contemporary history and social abuse—smearing and scapegoating are a normal part of that. Then what happens when we refuse to adopt those perceptions and instead meet the "others"? Hostility breaks down. This sharing, this meeting in the spirit, is a valid step toward that.

Another very specific use of this practice of sharing is to extend one's goodness with departed friends and relatives: "I dedicate speaking truthfully and gently in memory of my father—who did, or should have done, the same. Dad, this is for you." Or "When I give a few dollars to a homeless person, I'm doing this in memory of so-and-so." Tagging such simple daily and lived-in events to memories, losses, and aspirations helps us to come through bereavement and loneliness. And as a general overview, this huge, steady sweep of compassion and kindness broadens our vision of spiritual practice and transforms the self-oriented thinking that fosters clinging.

The breadth of the Dhamma's span is also due to its methodical approach. Many other seekers and sages of the age had very little methodology—just an unquestioning adherence to ascetic practices with a sense of moral nihilism or noncausality. There was no breadth, no relationship to social (let alone psychological) issues. The priestly approach in India kept methodology confined to the correct observance of ritual by the brahmin caste and again offered no inquiry into the mind-state of the brahmins or their devotees. Other wanderers may have been following inquiry into higher Self and Brahman (a Supreme Being) as set forth in the Upanishads, but none used the same kind of logic and thoroughness that epitomizes the Buddha's approach.

The Buddha's method was a breakthrough in that it was based on empirical principles: if this is what you want, this is what to do, and this is how to check the results for yourself. He introduced a "scientific" method to a realm that is normally understood to be mystical, beyond reason, and ineffable. We may be rather blasé or even negative about science because much of mainstream, contemporary science leaves out ethics and consciousness, but its methodology is sound. The scientific principle is that the same set of inquiries or methods can be made in a number of instances to a range of subjects, and the results will be predictable and consistent. This is the foundation for the "modern" age, a development of consciousness that bears the mark of see-for-yourself wisdom (rather than belief or indoctrination). As the Buddha put it:

> By practising as you are instructed you will, by realizing it yourselves here and now through direct knowledge, enter upon and abide in that supreme goal of the Holy Life.
> (M 1)

The Buddha's Dhamma centers around the principle of kamma: you do this, you get that result. It places each individual as the responsible center of their life. How you do things affects how you are and how you will be; you have a choice, you're not the victim of fate or subject to the will of impassive deities. This understanding, which still hasn't been taken on by many human beings, is already a release from the shadows and from somebody "up there" (who has His own ideas about how things are going to be). Even appreciating what kamma is brings personal results. Furthermore, there is a great clarity and focus that arises when we understand how to apply ourselves to the four noble truths. Just knowing that all we have to do is to abandon the blindness and the biases that bring us bondage and suffering is a great light to the mind. Even if we haven't yet fully accomplished the results, to see no contradiction between the urge for well-being, for truth, and for release is a wonderful guiding light. And finally, that this can be done by anyone at all is a sign that we are not just inevitably bound to kamma, that there is a way out. So the Dhamma offers empowerment. As the Buddha explained, it's through developing our innate capacity for wisdom and nonattachment to the level of firm and pure insight.

The span of the Dhamma is wide also because it offers an integration of what we might call mundane and spiritual cultivation, so that there is no cutoff between speaking, acting, and meditating. The eightfold path proceeds from this integrationist paradigm, and it was a theme that the

Buddha continued to work on throughout his life. From his viewpoint, life was a Dhamma-practice; and he put considerable attention into creating social structures that would keep the Dhamma livable and directly experiential. For instance, most people lose sight of wisdom and nonattachment through the influences of the social mainstream. So the Buddha saw the creation of a "Fourfold Assembly" of bhikkhus, bhikkhunis, laymen, and laywomen as something that would create its own mainstream, a Dhamma-stream that could lead to nibbāna. In his old age, he saw the actualization of this Dhamma-society as an achievement that would signify that his life's work was complete. This was confirmed by the Buddha's final dialogue with Māra in his last year, when Māra reminds him:

> The Blessed Lord has said this: "I will not take final Nibbāna till I have monks, . . . nuns, . . . laymen-followers, . . . laywomen-followers who are accomplished, trained, skilled, knowers of the Dhamma . . . and walking in the path of the Dhamma . . . able to refute false teachings that have arisen . . . I will not take final Nibbāna till this holy life has been successfully established . . . well-proclaimed among mankind everywhere." And all this has come about. May the Blessed Lord now attain final Nibbāna. (DN 16:3)

Acknowledging this to be the case, the Buddha relinquished the will to live. After his demise, he declared, his teachings would be the guide.

To create a microsociety, a culture that crossed over the boundaries of class and gender, householder and recluse, might seem to be a lot of work. But it draws its strength from the eightfold path, and from people's eagerness to commit to that, because it touches into core values such as mutual respect, generosity, honesty, and nonviolence. As long as people acknowledge these as values that impart real benefit and are verifiable through introspection, then materialism, ego-needs, and social pressures diminish.

Because of that mundane release from stress and mistrust, people by themselves feel the incentive to follow the wheel further. And that always means placing it on the ground of their lives. Values become ideologies and mere customs unless they are tested and fine-tuned by each individual rather than through a slavish obedience to a dogma, a leader, or an upper class. Hence it requires an assembly in which each aspect is both autonomous and co-operating toward the greater good. This is typified by the Fourfold Assembly: the laity holds the material resources and the power, and the samanas look in-to and explain the details of the teachings. Nowadays the distinctions are more blurred, with a huge growth in lay meditation practice, and a similar growth in the material side of samana life that has become increasingly geared to mon-asteries and society. And here there are advantages and disadvantages.

Over the years the Buddha gave more detailed teachings on conduct to both those who had gone forth and to householders. He also set up the relationship between the two that continues to sustain the sense, if not al-ways the practice, of the Assembly to this day. Now the gone-forth people are often referred to as monastics, following the designations of a Chris-tian culture. But originally these samanas were not bound to monasteries, in fact they generally kept on the move in order to avoid the corrupting ef-fects of acquisitions and intermonastic rivalry. They were bound to a train-ing through many rulings that the Buddha made. These include complete harmlessness and nonabuse through body or speech, complete abstinence from sexual activity, not acquiring or using money, and not storing food. They could keep just three robes, a bowl, a razor, and minor requisites like medicine. All offerings were to be shared among their fellow samanas. There was to be no begging or pressuring householders for donations of any kind. Regular fortnightly meetings of all the samanas in the area were held in order to recite the training rules and settle any differences. Com-munity agreement was the standard for decision making.

The Buddha also established an order for women (the bhikkhuni sangha) with the same guidelines. And as a mark of the Buddha's foresight and thoroughness, he laid down a set of standards whereby the sangha of bhikkhus and bhikkhunis could adapt the training to suit new circum-stances as time went by, provided that they kept to the same spirit of the way. All this was called Vinaya, and the Buddha specifically laid down its guidelines so that after his death, his teaching would survive as a lived prac-tice. In fact, he generally referred to his teaching as "Dhamma-Vinaya." In this spirit, he also provided guidelines for householders on livelihood, supportive friendship, family roles and responsibilities, and intelligent relationships with the samana community.

The Buddha didn't work this out on paper, or in advance, but through the empirical method of looking for a sustainable common good and using a trusted method. That is, to cause people's innate goodness to come forth and see what supported or hindered that. How it all works is very down-to-earth. The principle of living on alms-food sets up a situation whereby the bhikkhu or bhikkhuni is encouraged to make themselves worthy of the generosity of others. For the householders who provide the alms-food, the alms round helps to give the day a structure that reflects on spiritual themes and keeps them in touch with renunciation—which isn't always apparent in the secular world. From their side of the relationship, the connection and contact would encourage the samanas to give teachings or advice to the householders. And in this way, a minisociety was created on a day-to-day basis.

In terms of the wider society, one of the Buddha's most political utterances was about proper governance. He seems to have admired the way that the people of the Vajjian confederacy governed their state. It was an early form of democracy, in which all the nobility met to decide on matters of state, just as was done in Greek democracy. When asked by the envoy of an aggressive monarch how to overthrow the Vajjians, the Buddha politely replied that as long as the Vajjians kept to their principles, that would be impossible. The principles were to meet in harmony, conduct their business in harmony, and leave in harmony, to stay within the bounds of their authorized constitution, to respect and give ear to their seasoned elders, to allow women choice in terms of relationships, to respect their shrines, and to look after enlightened beings who came their way (DN 16:1). In the context of fifth-century-B.C.E. India, where rule by the king's sword was the norm, this is pretty amazing stuff. But whatever you think of the seven points, it's significant that the Buddha even made them, and that he clearly gave attention to matters of social and political organization. After he had made this pronouncement to the envoy, he later made a similar announcement to the assembly of bhikkhus, modifying the points and expanding them into a table of forty-one points, integrating the social, individual, and relational aspects of their lives. Here are a few points:

As long as the monks hold regular and frequent assemblies . . . as long as they meet in harmony, break up in harmony, and carry on their business in harmony . . . as long as they preserve their personal mindfulness, so that in the future, the good among their companions will come to them, and those who have already come will feel at ease with them . . . they may be expected to prosper and not decline.

As long as monks continue with faith, with modesty, with fear of wrong-doing, with learning, with aroused vigour, with established mindfulness, with wisdom. . . .

As long as monks develop the enlightenment factors of mindfulness, of investigation of phenomena, of energy, of delight, of tranquillity, of concentration, of equanimity. . . .

As long as monks both in public and in private show loving-kindness to their fellows in acts of body, speech, and thought, . . . share . . . whatever they receive as a rightful gift, including the contents of their alms bowls, . . . they may be expected to prosper and not decline.

(DN 16:1)

Today we might disagree with aspects of the social norm of the time of the Buddha: that it is a nonparity set up for example, with different roles for men and women, but the point to bear in mind is that the Buddha always operated within the cultural worldview of his age, and tweaked it where he could toward offering the occasions for skillful kamma and liberation. He might very well have set things up differently today. However, the fact that he thought and worked in terms of breadth and integration is a bright light of the Dhamma. Its spirit has allowed Buddhism to adapt to cultures as different as Korea and India, and even the United States. Furthermore it is through this attitude and through the means of the Fourfold Assembly that effective social change can come about. There is always a responsibility to determine how much dukkha is simply the "way it is" right now, and how much is something we can move toward changing in the society around us. Poor health facilities, diminution of human rights and dignity, power mongering, and destruction of the environment are not in themselves "natural" or an inevitable aspect of the human condition. It is the responsibility of the Assembly to turn against this suffering, since it is based on greed, hatred, and delusion.

So through the rise and fall of empires and nations, the wheel has been rolling. Along the dusty desert tracks of Central Asia, through the humid forest of Southeast Asia and down the highways of the United States it has rolled on. Inspiring kings, merchants, and scholars, the Buddha's teachings, philosophies, and art have steered world-culture. Transmitted by bhikkhus, bhikkhunis, and twentieth-century wanderers who learned to teach through their own experience, that wheel has showed no signs of slowing down. Discussed by sociologists, incorporated by therapists, and probed by neuroscientists, its span hasn't diminished. In this steady light, a huge flowering of scrolls, woodblocks, books, tapes, CDs, and web sites has blossomed. Not to mention social work: Buddhist prison chaplains, Buddhist hospice workers, Buddhist AIDS foundations abound.

But along with height and breadth is the need for depth. We might very well ask: "How much does the Dhamma's breadth weigh against its penetrative depth? Is it in danger of becoming diluted—of Buddha becoming a fashion icon, a figure to put in shop windows and on greeting cards, of Dhamma transmitted as maxims scrolled onto tea bags? Where among all this is there the realization of release from suffering? Well, it's up to each of us to approach it from where we are. So as we get to the end of the discourse, and attune again to where we are . . . in a bedroom or on a plane, aware of sounds around us, with our attention shifting and mind-states changing, feeling ourselves come into a different focus—is that possibility here? Can we sense the ephemeral nature of our world right now? If not, where else? Where else does our individual world-system of rogues and heroes, of the beloved and the rejected and the undetermined shake and resound?

At the conclusion of this commentary, let's return to what the Buddha himself was most pleased with at that moment. It was that his Dhamma had become a shared realization. A way to the truth that he felt would be difficult for people to understand had been communicated; through a verbal means, awakening is possible. There is a systematic way out of suffering, and it can be developed. Embarking on that way is up to each of us as individuals. In the light of the Buddha's last words: "All structures (sankhāra) break up; be diligent in your practice."

CREDITS

All translations are by the author except for the following, which are reprinted with permission: